Saved, Delivered, & Healed

Saved, Delivered, & Healed

Introducing a Pentecostal Theology of Salvation

TONY RICHIE

Foreword by French L. Arrington

CASCADE *Books* • Eugene, Oregon

SAVED, DELIVERED, & HEALED
Introducing a Pentecostal Theology of Salvation

Copyright © 2022 Tony Richie. All rights reserved. Except for brief quotations in critical publications or reviews, no part of this book may be reproduced in any manner without prior written permission from the publisher. Write: Permissions, Wipf and Stock Publishers, 199 W. 8th Ave., Suite 3, Eugene, OR 97401.

Cascade Books
An Imprint of Wipf and Stock Publishers
199 W. 8th Ave., Suite 3
Eugene, OR 97401

www.wipfandstock.com

PAPERBACK ISBN: 978-1-6667-3143-9
HARDCOVER ISBN: 978-1-6667-2392-2
EBOOK ISBN: 978-1-6667-2393-9

Cataloguing-in-Publication data:

Names: Richie, Tony, author.

Title: Saved, delivered, & healed : introducing a Pentecostal theology of salvation / Tony Richie.

Description: Eugene, OR: Cascade Books, 2022 | Includes bibliographical references and index.

Identifiers: ISBN 978-1-6667-3143-9 (paperback) | ISBN 978-1-6667-2392-2 (hardcover) | ISBN 978-1-6667-2393-9 (ebook)

Subjects: LCSH: Salvation, Christianity. | Holy Spirit. | Salvation—Christianity—History of doctrines. | Pentecostalism.

Classification: BT121.3 R50 2022 (paperback) | BT121.3 (ebook)

08/29/22

Unless otherwise noted, scriptural references are from the New King James Version (NKJV) of the Bible. Nashville: Thomas Nelson, 1982.

Dedication
to
Andrew Richie
&
Frank Romines
~ Your influence lives still ~

Oh, when the saints go marching in
Oh, when the saints go marching in
Oh Lord I want to be in that number
When the saints go marching in.

—From "When the Saints Go Marching In," a folk spiritual attributed, at least in part, by some historians to Emma Cotton (1877–1952), Azusa Street Mission pioneer, preacher, church planter, and songwriter.

Contents

Foreword by French L. Arrington   ix

Acknowledgments   xiii

Introduction   1

1   Soteriological Assumptions (Basic Ideas about Salvation)   12

2   Soteriological Foundation (Place of Grace in Salvation)   40

3   Paradigmatic Soteriology (Models of Salvation)   61

4   Soteriological Ethos (Salvation Identity)   78

5   Oppositional Soteriology (Spiritual Warfare in Salvation)   104

6   Eschatological Soteriology (Salvation's Eye on Eternity)   129

7   Corporeal Soteriology (Physical Healing in Salvation)   147

8   Pneumatic Soteriology (Spirit Baptism in Salvation)   163

Bibliography   191

Name and Subject Index   205

Scripture Index   209

Foreword

In this book, Dr. Tony Richie presents foundational biblical truths in accessible, understandable terms. He offers a credible dynamic Pentecostal view of salvation, explaining to his readers the concepts of being *saved, delivered*, and *healed*.

Dr. Richie's book celebrates the here and now blessings of salvation, as well as the promise of heaven someday. In doing so, *Saved, Delivered, & Healed* holds a high view of the Scriptures and their authority, while presenting the shape of Pentecostal theology with a free moving of the Holy Spirit in the context of order in worship.

Dr. Richie in his writing strives to connect with both pastors and laypeople. Through his deep understanding of the Bible and his own personal experience with his Lord, he communicates truths of the Scriptures by:

- presenting straightforward interpretation of the Scriptures
- emphasizing the Pentecostal view of salvation
- accenting a good balance between biblical truths and living the Christian life, underscoring the importance of Wesleyan holiness
- mining incredibly rich truths from the Scriptures that enhance the serving of God and God's people
- stressing that faith is a lived faith in relation to God, the faith community, family, and humankind.

Dr. Richie has been a Pentecostal pastor, a seminary professor, and a strong advocate of Pentecostal spirituality as he has walked in many of the spiritual paths of his Savior Jesus Christ. He understands that the Pentecostal view of salvation embraces living biblical teachings in all of life—including the experiences of faith, repentance, justification, adoption, regeneration, assurance, resurrection, service, and ultimate transformation. In his Pentecostal view of salvation, Tony Richie recognizes that the Holy Spirit is involved in the saving process from beginning to end, and that the entire process rests on divine grace. He affirms that the Pentecostal doctrines of the *Holy Spirit* and *salvation* are not firmly separated from one another. Rather, in the Scriptures, these doctrines are woven together, and the ways we experience the Holy Spirit's work in our salvation and life are often more fluid than we expect.

This book provides us with a great discussion of *divine grace*—"*totally free—not a reward or payment for service or anything we can do.*" It is what God is and what God does. *Grace* is one of those great umbrella terms, including both the work of the Holy Spirit in salvation and the charismatic gifts of the Holy Spirit. Here, the focus of the work of the Holy Spirit and divine grace is on the end-time, when redeemed people will be completely conformed to the image of Jesus Christ, and they will enter into glory. In view of this final completion of salvation, "*Grace comes down to God's ultimate purpose in Jesus Christ and of saving lost humanity and restoring a broken creation.*" Through Jesus our Lord, our salvation will be complete, all darkness will end, and all things will be made new.

This day of final salvation still lies in the future. Until that day, through the ministry of the Holy Spirit to us and through us, we can bring God's grace and the light of Jesus Christ to a world in need. Shining God's grace and light in the world today means that believers will be engaged in spiritual warfare with their adversary the devil. Prayer is the key to victory along with two particular weapons: "*the sword of the Spirit*" and "*praying . . . in the Spirit*"—whenever we have an encounter with the adversary (Eph 6:17–18). Victory over the devil and over worldliness is a way of getting ready for the rapture of the church and for life in eternity. Of critical importance to Pentecostal theology is the emphasis on the imminent return of Jesus Christ, the ministry of the Holy Spirit, and the preparation for the salvation of the whole person. The healing of humanity, both spiritual and physical, has been provided in the atonement of Christ. This wholistic understanding of salvation sums up the purpose of Christ coming into the world and of the outpouring of the Spirit on the Day of Pentecost, and it sums up what Christian salvation is.

The last chapter of this book focuses on the baptism in the Holy Spirit. As a model for the Christian life and service, classical Pentecostals appeal to the book of Acts. This experience is promised to every believer as distinct and subsequent to conversion. Furthermore, it empowers the believer to be a Christian witness of Christ and to do mighty works—and is accompanied by speaking in tongues as the initial evidence of the experience. This interpretation differs from the viewpoints of other branches of the Christian faith. Over the years, these doctrinal differences have generated much debate.

Dr. Richie shows his knowledge and theological skills in sifting through much of the contemporary debate. After he has carefully analyzed various theological positions of scholars, Dr. Richie concludes, "I describe the Spirit baptism as distinct from and subsequent to conversion, but not as distinct from and subsequent to salvation." Therefore, the way that both salvation and baptism in the Spirit are related is that both are received through faith that is manifest in prayer, obedience, and yielding. Pentecostals should endeavor to present Spirit baptism overall within the scope of salvation. After all, not only salvation, but all that happened on the day of Pentecost, flows from the exalted Christ (Acts 2:33).

What more can be said? The author has said it the best way: "There is perfect unity and harmony between conversion experience and a distinct, subsequent experience of Spirit baptism."

This book is well worth your investment in time and attention.

FRENCH L. ARRINGTON, PHD, DD
Professor of NT Greek and Exegesis
and Chair of the Niko Njotorahardjo
Restoration of the Tabernacle of David
Pentecostal Theological Seminary

Acknowledgments

I am especially appreciative for those who sacrificed their time and energy to share their expertise in all or part of this present work. My old teacher, mentor, colleague at the Pentecostal Theological Seminary (PTS), and dear friend, French Arrington, read the entire manuscript and wrote the foreword. His encouragement and insight have been invaluable for this work (not to mention that his own work serves as a significant resource throughout!). The friendship and support in life and ministry of French and Joyce have enriched Sue's and my life immeasurably.

Josh P. S. Samuel (McMaster Divinity College) helped immensely with the early chapters on redemption experiences and the place of grace. Another PTS colleague and friend, Daniel Álvarez, helped refine the chapter on Pentecostals' distinctive salvation ethos. Dale Coulter, our newest colleague at PTS and a longtime friend, shared invaluable insights regarding the chapter on salvation and healing. My friend and kindred spirit from Down Under, Jacqui Grey (Alphacrucis College), helped make the chapter on salvation models much better with her keen insights into biblical theology and its implications. My double sister (natural and spiritual), Sharon Ann Richie Grooms, a longtime pastor (Open Arms Mission) and a PTS graduate herself, greatly helped with the chapter on spiritual warfare, one that necessitates a special integration of the gifts of a pastor and a seminarian. Engaging conversations with Daniel Tomberlin, another PTS colleague and dear friend with whom I shared in pastoral ministry and ecumenical work, literally inspired the chapter on Spirit baptism and salvation; and his input on the earlier manuscript form of that chapter and the one on salvation and eschatology were invaluable.

For his gracious interaction with me concerning my appropriation of his work regarding pneumatology and soteriology, I am indebted to Steve Studebaker (McMaster Divinity College). Over the years, Steve and I have collaborated many times on different projects. I have always found him to be a consummate scholar and a true Christian gentleman. His expertise and input contributed significantly to the final shape of the chapter on Spirit baptism and salvation.

I have collaborated frequently, and happily, with Wipf and Stock and their staff, and am ever grateful for their assistance and guidance. I am particularly indebted to Karen Luke Martin, a dear friend whose expertise as a retired high school English teacher has been so helpful in producing this manuscript. Actually, it is probably next to impossible for me to properly acknowledge all those who have contributed to this work in some significant way. Over the years—long before even the conception of this specific work—so many conversations regarding a myriad of related/interrelated subjects have gone into my own development and formation, on both conscious and unconscious levels. But I am no less sincerely grateful to all who have taken the time to invest in me as a Christian theologian. Sadly, I must admit that there are undoubtedly numerous shortcomings of this work, which I may only attribute to myself.

My wife and family are always supportive of my work. I am sure my odd hours and activities are often a puzzle and sometimes a hurdle. Nevertheless, my wife, Sue, and our children, Josh, Kimberly, Kathy, and Shannon, and their wonderful spouses and God's gift of grandchildren, are priceless treasures to me. Recently someone asked my wife if she read my writings. Sue quickly quipped, "Why would I have to read them when I hear them?" It certainly is true that while I pray through my writing with the Lord, I also talk through it with my wife. Readers will note that this book is dedicated to Frank Romines (1930–1986) and Andrew Richie (1934–2020). My father Andrew passed into the presence of the Lord just as I was finishing this book. He has consistently been the single most influential person on my ministerial life. Sue's father, Frank ,passed into the presence of the Lord long before I met Sue, but his immeasurable influence on her has touched my life as well. We thank our heavenly Father for our earthly fathers. Without them we would neither *be*, nor be who we *are*.

Introduction

In a sense, I consider this book the most important writing I have ever done. Perhaps I should explain why after the humbling privilege of writing or contributing to dozens of books and hundreds of articles and essays, I would say this volume is of supreme significance. It is because it is about *salvation*. For lost souls, nothing could be more paramount. For me, salvation is the unparalleled priority. Is it so for the reader? I hope and pray that that is the case. Nevertheless, I will share why it is for me.

Commenting on 1 Timothy 2:6, French Arrington accurately says, "The stress must fall on the cost of man's redemption. To be the Savior of mankind cost Jesus everything."[1] Accordingly, we deduce the inestimable valuation God places on salvation. Would God's Son give everything unless our salvation meant as much? Of course not. Salvation's cost clearly indicates that it means everything to Christ. I submit that if salvation cost the Savior everything, then salvation, to us, should be worth everything.

I was raised in a Christian home by fine Christian parents. I come from a family of multigenerational Pentecostals. My father was an evangelist, church planter, and pastor for more than sixty years. Growing up, I considered myself a Christian. But I was not *saved*. I did not really understand what "saved" meant. I thought I did. But I did not. Sadly, I discovered my deficiency in a difficult fashion.

As an adult I became a stereotypical "prodigal son" (Luke 15:11–32). It was a hard road. When I did decide to "go home" I found that I did not know the way. Family and friends tried to guide me, but I just did not follow well. It made no sense to me that all I had to do was tell God "I'm sorry" and

---

1. Arrington, *Maintaining the Foundations*, 62.

then, somehow, everything would be forever okay. Although I did not quite understand it myself, I knew I "owed" God more than an "apology."

When I read the Bible, I encountered a foreign language. I am not talking about Greek and Hebrew. I hit that hurdle later. Rather, Scripture itself contained concepts and terms that were strange and so unfamiliar. Certainly, I had heard these terms growing up in church, but their fuller significance eluded me. Justification is a prime example. What does "justification" mean in Paul's letter to the Roman believers? I found its correlate, "imputation," to be mind-boggling. How justification, faith, grace, and works were related to each other in Galatians, not to mention in James's epistle, and more importantly, how they impacted my personal salvation, became a torturous conundrum. I struggled to attain not only understanding but, as I would later know to call it, personal assurance of my salvation.

It was too much for me. I backslid.

But God never gave up on me. The praise and worship team where until recently I served as pastor frequently sang "Rescue Story," which has a repetitive phrase in the chorus that juxtaposes "You never gave up on me" with "You are my testimony."[2] Indeed, the words of that song encapsulate my testimony. The Lord continued to deal with me, to strive with me, to draw me with cords of love to the cross of Christ. And I finally got *saved*! I did not just get religion. I did not merely become "spiritual," as is popularly said. I really got saved. Somehow John 20:31 took on a special penetrative power for me. I believed on Jesus the Messiah, the Son of God, and I received eternal life through his name. I have never been the same since. Not for one instant, not even for a nanosecond, have I ever doubted, from that day to this, that I am really and truly saved.

Since then, I have spent forty years plumbing the depths of that salvation experience and its implications for the here and now and for the hereafter, too. I suppose I have learned a great deal about the Christian doctrine or theology of salvation (soteriology). Still, I do not claim to fully comprehend all the treasures residing in that richest of words: *salvation*. However, unlike U2's hit song about unsatisfied spiritual yearning, "I Still Haven't Found What I'm Looking For," I do have a deep sense of satisfaction, of spiritual fulfillment, which abides with me to this day.[3] No, I cannot boast that I have

---

2. For the story behind this exceptionally moving song, see Carpenter, "Zach Williams." I served as lead pastor at New Harvest from 1998 to 2020. Thanks to Dawn Lynn-Breen for introducing me to this song and to its background.

3. On this haunting "gospel song with a restless spirit" see Blair, "Restless Search for Meaning." Interestingly, Brown, *Spirit of Protestantism*, suggests "common" songs and tunes can be "a notable way of destroying the barrier between the sacred and the secular" and for conveying profound truth (137).

"arrived"; but Christ Jesus has taken hold of my life, and I am no longer the same (Phil 3:12). I do know that salvation is all-important. I am persuaded it is of the utmost significance for every human being.[4] I know it is for me. That is why I consider this book the most important writing I have ever done.

Beyond my personal experience is the larger importance of the doctrine of salvation for Christian theology as a whole and for Pentecostal theology in particular. Christian theologian Justin Holcomb says, "The role of soteriology [the doctrine of salvation] is to show how and why Jesus is significant."[5] Although coming from the standpoint of Christology (the doctrine of Christ), this statement nevertheless expresses the paramount significance of salvation for the Christian understanding of Jesus Christ—which is, of course, what Christianity is all about. Therefore, theologically speaking, the importance of the doctrine of salvation can hardly be overstated. The doctrines of Christ and of salvation are tied together as the definitive teachings of the Christian religion.[6]

Although probably not as popular now as it once was, for a time the motto "What would Jesus do?" (abbreviated simply as "WWJD") seemed to be everywhere, at least in the United States. However, as a prominent British theologian Alister McGrath rightly points out, a proper discussion of the doctrine of salvation, after addressing who Jesus Christ is or his identity as Son of God, Savior, and Lord, then will ask, "What did Jesus do?" or even "What *does* Jesus do?"[7] This means that the identity of Jesus Christ and his achievement in accomplishing salvation are not only related but inseparable. It also means that the historic events of his sinless life, atoning death, bodily resurrection, and ascension to glory continue to be active and operative, that is effective or efficacious, in human lives today wherever trusting faith is placed in his name. Again, the person and work of Christ and of the salvation which is in Christ are at the heart of what it means to be a *Christian*.

Wolfgang Vondey notes that the doctrine of salvation dominates the Pentecostal narrative of theology, both by its primary position in Pentecostal

---

4. As Wright, *Justification*, 23–25, passionately argues, we humans are not the center of the universe and everything is not about us, nor even our salvation. Yet God's wise and righteous purpose for setting things right in the cosmos would not mean much *for me* if I am not saved, would it? I do not think it at all inconsistent to admit that everything is not *about me* and yet to affirm that *for me* (and *for you*!) salvation is of ultimate importance.

5. Holcomb, ed., *Theologies of Salvation*, 1.

6. Yet modern social, political, and philosophical ideas are influencing many contemporary theologians away from the historic character of salvation. See Reeves, "Theologies of Salvation," 259.

7. McGrath, *Christian Theology*, 326. Italics are original.

theology and in its distribution throughout the task of doing Pentecostal theology.[8] In other words, for Pentecostals "salvation marks the beginning and overall direction of their theology."[9] Vondey drives home the point further: "all Pentecostal theological discourse is fundamentally soteriological."[10] I suggest that it is impossible to understand Pentecostal theology as a whole apart from a clear articulation of its theology of salvation (soteriology). Putting it another way, perhaps the best introduction to Pentecostal theology is an in-depth study of its doctrine of salvation. So, as far as Pentecostals are concerned, the subject of salvation is of greatest importance, not only for personal salvation but for theological understanding itself. If that assertion is correct, then the present text may serve to introduce not only a specifically Pentecostal doctrine of salvation but, more generally, a core understanding of Pentecostal theology itself.

I chose the title of this text carefully. *Saved, Delivered, & Healed: Introducing a Pentecostal Theology of Salvation* is not merely descriptive; it is prescriptive. Chapter 8 of my previous work, *Essentials of Pentecostal Theology*, made, I felt, something of a start on this topic; but it clearly calls for further development.[11] Thus, I offer the present work as a follow-up with more specificity. The subtitle *Introducing a Pentecostal Theology of Salvation* fixes my focus. The introductory nature does not mean it will draw back from in-depth theological engagement where necessary; rather, it informs that this text will make an extra effort to present profound theological truth in accessible, understandable terms that do not assume readers are trained theologians. I do not give a history of salvation for all of the religions of the world, nor do I attempt a presentation on what all Christians believe about salvation. I focus on my faith community, my church family, Pentecostals. Yet even for my own tribe, as they say, I do not claim to be exhaustive or definitive.

What do I claim, then? My purpose is to identify a quite distinctive and incredibly dynamic view of salvation as being saved, delivered, and healed. I will not now unpack the implications of that statement. After all, that is what the rest of this book is about. But I will say that those three words in the mouth of a Pentecostal can take on a dramatic tone describing—and accessing—salvation in a manner with which with no other Christian

---

8. Vondey, "Soteriology at the Altar," 1. True enough, as noted by Ryan M. Reeves, "Theology of Salvation," 251: "Christian theology is *salvation theology*" (original italics). Nevertheless, Vondey correctly draws attention to a distinctive Pentecostal focus on salvation.

9. Vondey, "Soteriology at the Altar," 7.

10. Vondey, "Soteriology at the Altar," 12.

11. Richie, *Essentials*, cp. 148–52, 158–62.

tradition compares. Discovering what that means and how it may apply has been central to my life's journey and is the driving force behind the writing of this little work of theology.

However, I might here recruit Jeremiah 17:14 to at least introduce this topic in the prophet's own poignant speech. In his words:

> Heal me, O Lord, and I shall be
> healed;
> Save me, and I shall be saved,
> For You *are* my praise.

What a glorious passage! Surely, we may join Jeremiah in praise for God's saving power. And this wondrous salvation apparently includes deliverance and healing in this age as well as for the age to come.

Admittedly, precise equivalence does not exist between the prophet's employment of salvation language and that of certain portions of the New Testament (NT).[12] For example, quite obviously, Jeremiah is not explicating the doctrine of justification by faith. The subsequent context (vv. 14–18) indicates that he is appealing to the Lord for deliverance from the immediate threats of earthly opponents. In a word, Jeremiah is not concerned about "going to heaven" someday. He needs God's help here and now. Such earthly orientation is consistent with ancient Israelite belief in the nature of divine salvation as inclusive of victory over tangible enemies encountered in this journey of life (Exod 14:13). Of course, it is quite understandable for anyone to be keenly concerned regarding a "clear and present danger." Indeed, it is likely a keen concern for many.[13]

However, verse 14 flows smoothly out of the preceding (especially vv. 12–13), where faithful relationship with the Lord and spiritual life versus earthly temporality are the setting for prophetic declarations.[14] These verses appear to point beyond the prophet's immediate needs. So then, is salvation earthly or heavenly? Is it physical/material or spiritual? Is it temporal or eternal? I am getting ahead of myself, but I might as well ask it anyway: is salvation juridical or participatory? Is it forensic or transformational? And so on. As my colleague Steve Land is fond of answering when confronted with these types of questions, "Yes!"[15]

12. Huey, *Jeremiah, Lamentations*, 176.

13. Note that a popular political thriller novel *Clear and Present Danger*, by Tom Clancy, debuted at number one on the *New York Times* Best Seller list. A hit film adaptation featuring Harrison Ford was released on August 3, 1994.

14. Jamieson et al., *Commentary*, 523–24.

15. Steven Jack Land has taught theology at Pentecostal Theological Seminary for years, as well as formerly serving as dean and president.

I suggest that salvation is complex without necessarily being complicated. In fact, we have probably overcomplicated it. Yet, it has multiple layers. Or in other words, salvation is multifaceted.[16] It is about preparation for the afterlife, of course. But not only so. It is also about navigation of the challenging circumstances of the present age and its world order. It is about one's soul or spiritual well-being. However, it is also about emotional and physical wholeness and well-being, and even includes financial and vocational provisions. All of this and more is *salvation*. Pentecostal soteriology flows out of a holistic worldview that does not fragment divine creation or segregate human existence. Therefore, I invite readers to join me in mapping out the spiritual and intellectual odyssey of the salvation that brings us home to the heavenly Father, no matter where life's journey takes us or how it impacts us (Luke 15:11–32).[17]

Now for a few words on authorial methodology, which I hope will be helpful for readers; and then we can dive into the topic itself. I quite enjoy Paul van der Laan's apt description of doing Pentecostal theology as "catching a butterfly."[18] Pentecostal theology is living and moving. It is beautiful and delicate. To catch it and hold it too tightly risks crushing it and killing it. Dead theology is no longer Pentecostal theology. Pentecostal theology is alive. Perhaps not surprisingly, a Pentecostal theology that is inherently *alive* inevitably has a great deal to do with *life*. One may not accurately describe Pentecostal theology as all about the "by and by" or as having a "pie in the sky" predilection. It is concerned with living both in the here and in the hereafter.

I invite the reader to think of this volume as a kind of grassroots Pentecostal theology.[19] In many ways, Pentecostalism is an expression of popular

---

16. Stronstad, *Charismatic Theology of St. Luke*, argues that the NT emphasizes three dimensions of the Christian life—salvation, sanctification, service—and that the charismatic understanding of Spirit baptism applies to the third, 14, 98. I do not disagree. I am also sympathetic to Yong's argument for an expansive soteriological multidimensionality, *Spirit Poured Out,* 91–98. However, what I wish to plumb more fully is salvific superabundance, in and of itself.

17. The confessional and/or testimonial qualities of the present work, along with its pastoral elements, seek to serve as a kind of aeolian cross-pollination with biblical exposition and theological elucidation in which the reciprocity becomes mutually productive via the moving of the Holy Spirit (á la John 3:8).

18. Van der Laan, "Catching a Butterfly." I cannot help but observe, however, that life is surprisingly resilient after all.

19. Therefore, I feel free to discreetly utilize a wider range of resources than usual in theology texts, including not only biblical, historical, and theological works but also popular and general church-level materials as well.

religion.[20] It does not focus on the abstract, conceptual, dogmatic side of religion so much as on the lived faith of people—their relationship with God, their felt needs, and their faith community and family. It tends to be holistic and practical with an integration of everyday life and spirituality. One might even call it "real-life theology" or simply "real theology" vis-à-vis highly speculative systems, which—rightly or wrongly—often appear to have tenuous connections to the life and faith of the people.[21] Accordingly, the present volume strives to stay in touch with the pastor in the pulpit and the people in the pews. Yet, it is no less a theology book intended for use in school classrooms as well as in church sanctuaries. Therefore, it aims at a valid level of academic credibility and intellectual coherence.

Fortunately, Pentecostalism is a full reservoir of vibrant theology that can both refresh the soul and stimulate the mind. As I have discovered to my delight, "this 'old time religion' has incredibly fresh and rich implications."[22] Accordingly, this volume will not shy away from doing rigorous theology. The dividends are too great to dismiss. For that reason, I hope theologians and their students alike will benefit from reading this volume. But I will do a bit of "interpreting" of our theological "tongues" for nonprofessional theologians. Accordingly, the present volume has an introductory character, even as it occasionally seeks to challenge or stretch.

A chaplain friend once told me regarding a previous work of mine that she enjoyed the book but had to keep a dictionary on hand while reading. I responded that I thought that only fair, since I had to keep a dictionary on hand as I wrote it. She thought that was funny, and we had a good laugh together. The truth is that any field of study has some specialized terminology that can tend to be dense or obscure. Believe it or not, that technical terminology is often necessary for the kind of precision—exact accuracy—that the specialists are striving to achieve. It also however, can be a hindrance to nonspecialists (read nonprofessionals).

Accordingly, in the present work I rely on esoteric jargon as little as possible. When necessary, I clarify technical information in more understandable language, especially when introducing new terms into the text. A look at the Table of Contents in this volume should demonstrate my bifocal approach. Specialists/professionals may tire of the extra verbiage and,

20. Parker, "Popular Religion."

21. My aim is not to come across as denigrating advanced theological endeavors—quite the contrary; rather, I only describe the focus of many people in the Pentecostal movement—and my personal sense of what they expect from their theologians. In any case, I endeavor to mine the riches of theology in a relatively accessible mode.

22. Richie, *Essentials*, 1.

perhaps, be put off by my conversational manner.[23] Laypeople may wonder why the technical terminology is needed at all.[24] But this is my way of bridging the distance between church and academy. I hope it is helpful. If not, I plead for the reader's patient indulgence.

Readers may consider my exegetical use of biblical languages (Hebrew and Greek), and occasionally of theological language (Latin), an exception to my commitment to accessible language. Rather, these are essential to my design. First, I carefully transliterate and define all these terms. It is entirely possible not to know anything about these languages and still follow my meaning. Second, I try to keep their use to a minimum, only employing them when I think it will be helpful to the *reader*. Third, even here, I often place this material in a footnote in order to resource those interested without distracting others. In any case, I am confident that my occasional use of languages will not make the present text overly dense.

I wish to emphasize how hermeneutics (biblical interpretation) impacts the approach of the present work.[25] Traditional Pentecostal interpretation of Scripture is driven by a rather straightforward, literal approach to the Bible. As a Pentecostal, I hold to a high view of Scripture's inspiration and authority coupled with the value of spiritual discernment and spiritual experience. Along with the Holy Spirit's inspiration of the biblical text itself, Pentecostal communities embrace the Spirit's illumination, or continuing guidance, in interpreting the truths of the Bible. I wholeheartedly affirm a high view of Scripture as divine revelation and, consequently, its preeminent importance for the task of doing theology.

Attentive readers will notice that I adhere to a generally literal, straightforward interpretation of Scripture. I avoid the hermeneutical acrobatics, as I sometimes call it, of interpreters who appear to be trying to prove a point at the expense of the plain truth of God's Word. Of course, a straightforward reading of Holy Scripture still allows for consideration of various types of literary genres that greatly enrich the biblical canon (e.g., historical narrative, poetry, prose, wisdom literature, didactic, apocalyptic).

---

23. For what it is worth, I consider the task of theology to be inclusive of a kind of formal "conversational" process in which believers talk together about their faith in God and its implications. So much of my own theology has been immeasurably enriched by innumerable conversations, both in person and in print, with other theology lovers.

24. However, I tend to use footnotes for asides that may be of interest to some readers. I have been told by readers who are interested in such discussions that they enjoy the footnotes as a kind of bilateral conversation.

25. Cp. Richie, *Essentials*, 2–3.

As a systematic theologian, I utilize the theological interpretation of Scripture.[26] To name just one precedent in Scripture itself for this approach, recall Paul's rich theological interpretation in Romans 5:12–21 of the Adamic history and motif with its wealth of implications for developing the doctrines of Christ (Christology), sin (hamartiology), salvation (soteriology), and humanity (anthropology). For me, interpreting Scripture theologically means identifying its theological message and applying it consistently in terms of the faith and values of a Pentecostal believer with consideration of Christian history and thought. Theological interpretation of Scripture is in rather stark contrast to a historical-critical analysis of the Bible as a piece of literature apart from, or at least without primary consideration of, its distinctive nature and unique message. For present purposes, I merely wish to signal readers that my work focuses on the message of the Bible regarding our topic, that is, on salvation with its doctrinal implications.

Before moving forward, I confess a sense of camaraderie when reading Robert McAfee Brown's "Foreword" to one of his own works on Protestant theology. His honest admission that his faith convictions have been received as gifts from others resonates well within my own heart.[27] The present text has an Acknowledgments section that identifies some specific people who have especially influenced its work. However, there is no way to enumerate all the persons who have poured into my life. Most of all, I am grateful for those whose commitment to and embodiment of Christian truth has impacted my life and my theology immeasurably.

Further, Brown's humility sets a standard for me. The following is worth quoting in full:

> No Protestant theologian has a right to be too impressed with his own theologizing. There is something comic, if not downright absurd, about the claim that a human creature can penetrate the veil of holiness surrounding the transcendent God, or describe with accuracy the events that took place when God penetrated that veil himself in the incarnation of his Son.[28]

When reading these words, I am moved to exclaim in wonder with poor Thomas, "My Lord and my God!" (John 20:28).

Finally, Brown's "Rule One" for every theologian exhibits classic wisdom: "Do not take yourself too seriously." It is, of course, set straight by his

---

26. For more on this approach, see Leulseged, *Pneumatic Hermeneutics*.

27. Brown, *Spirit of Protestantism*, x. By the way, as is obvious already, this work on Pentecostal theology focuses on Pentecostal resources but also recruits and engages theologians from other contexts.

28. Brown, *Spirit of Protestantism*, x.

immediate qualification: "This is very different from saying 'Do not take your faith seriously.'"[29] I certainly do take the Christian faith seriously. My efforts to explicate, as I said, perhaps the most important aspect of that faith, is serious business to me. Certainly, I am not unaware of my own limitations. I do not doubt that there will be much for colleagues and peers to discuss, clarify, or even call for correction.[30] I anticipate that important process with what I hope are attitudes of openness and honesty. Perhaps I will be forgiven if I also express an appeal for clemency.

Accordingly, the following chapters are written with much prayer and more than a little fear and trembling. Here, at least, I find myself in complete agreement with the celebrated Swiss theologian Karl Barth (1886–1968):

> The first and most basic act of theological work is *prayer* . . . But theological work does not merely begin with prayer and is not merely accompanied by it; in its totality it is peculiar and characteristic of theology that it can be performed only in the act of prayer.[31]

Amen!

Now then, a short summary of what is to come, and we can get to the task before us. Chapter 1, "Soteriological Assumptions (Basic Ideas about Salvation)," briefly explains elemental terms and concepts describing Christian salvation in terms of conversion experience. I confess that I continue to be amazed at the fresh ideas discoverable in these old truths. Chapter 2, "Soteriological Foundation (Place of Grace in Salvation)," examines the indispensable distinctive of divine grace in the whole of salvation. For me, it helps us understand why "amazing grace" is so *amazing*. Chapter 3, "Paradigmatic Soteriology (Models of Salvation)," explores the templates through which Pentecostals view soteriology. It begins to move into the truly distinctive nature of Pentecostals' doctrine of salvation, while chapter

---

29. Brown, *Spirit of Protestantism*, x.

30. This seems like a good place to mention the observations of Frank A. James III, "Theologies of Salvation in the Reformation and Counter-Reformation," that "Theology can be a dangerous occupation" and "Among the theological loci, soteriology (the study of salvation) is among the most dangerous of all" (181). Why does James warn us thusly? "To take a stance on the meaning of salvation is especially serious business because it touches the most vital religious nerve—where one spends eternity. To err on this topic may very well entail condemnation to eternal hellfire and damnation" (181). While I certainly understand what he is saying, I prefer to think of it the other way around. For me, probing the depths of the doctrine of salvation offers opportunities for discovering and receiving ever deeper riches in God's gracious gift of eternal life and salvation. But the point is well taken.

31. Barth, *Evangelical Theology*, 160.

4, "Soteriological Ethos (Salvation Identity)," examines how our perspective on salvation makes a difference in who Pentecostals are and what we do.

Chapter 5, "Oppositional Soteriology (Spiritual Warfare in Salvation)," invites readers into a worldview in which the divine and the diabolical contend for the souls and lives of believers. Although understandably controversial, there are some eureka insights here for the brave of heart. Chapter 6, "Eschatological Soteriology (Salvation's Eye on Eternity)," insists that salvation is teleological (goal-oriented) in nature and thus directs toward the future and God's destiny for creation and creatures. It both challenges some current directions in Pentecostal academia and offers a definitive alternative, while chapter 7, "Corporeal Soteriology (Physical Healing in Salvation)," announces a view of salvation that goes beyond an ethereal afterlife to enthusiastically embrace the needs of embodied human beings. Finally, chapter 8, "Pneumatic Soteriology (Spirit Baptism in Salvation)," elucidates where and how a primary emphasis in Pentecostal spirituality and theology on baptism with/in the Holy Spirit fits and functions within the contours of its soteriology. This last chapter is perhaps the most demanding but, for me, also quite rewarding.

Although without any claim to similar inspiration, I nevertheless sense a strong camaraderie with the words of the ancient psalmist, "My heart is overflowing with a good theme; I recite my composition concerning the King; My tongue *is* the pen of a ready writer" (45:1). Lord, grant me understanding, please. Help me to communicate truth clearly. Help me in conduct to demonstrate it consistently. May your Spirit use this humble offering to lift up Jesus and to be of service to your people! Amen.

1

Soteriological Assumptions

(Basic Ideas about Salvation)

There is nothing ordinary about anything Pentecostal. From almost any angle of observation, Pentecostalism is an extraordinary movement. Not surprisingly, Pentecostal theology of salvation is special. However, before zeroing in on a few standout features of Pentecostal views on salvation in subsequent chapters, it is helpful to identify certain shared assumptions about the nature of salvation. By "shared assumptions" I mean that which is generally accepted as true or certain among many Pentecostals but also enjoined in the heritage of the broader Christian tradition.[1] A disclaimer is likely in order. Although the term *assumption* can sometimes be used to describe that which is *affirmed as true without any proof or foundation*, I do not, here, use it so. Certainly, Pentecostals do not think of these beliefs as unfounded assertions. Rather, a process of engagement with the overall

---

1. My background reflects my southern United States culture and includes the classical version of the Pentecostal movement with roots in the American Holiness Movement of the late nineteenth-early twentieth centuries and the subsequent global revival associated with it. Nevertheless, I have been enriched by engagement with international and interdenominational Pentecostals to an extent that I am challenged to guard against parochialism or myopic naïveté. Still, when I make statements like "many" or "most" Pentecostals believe or do this or that, the reader should understand that the writer is drawing on more than six decades of experience with the inner workings of the movement. I do not claim to offer infallible analysis, but I do represent an informed perspective regarding a particular viewpoint.

witness of Scripture and of the associative history of Christian thought have led to certain suppositions being *tested and tried over time and found to be reliable* interpretations of salvific experience. It is in this latter sense that I speak of "shared assumptions."

In other words, we may regard these soteriological assumptions as statements or affirmations that have been assessed (judged) to be valid (true) by prior testimony (of the historical church) and, subsequently, confirmed and demonstrated to be deserving of acceptance (by the present generation). First Timothy 1:15 exemplifies the point, albeit in an incomparable inspired manner: "This *is* a faithful saying and worthy of all acceptance, that Christ Jesus came into the world to save sinners, of whom I am chief" (cp. 1 Tim 3:1; 4:9; 2 Tim 2:11; Titus 3:8). For our purposes, these assumptions can be described as basic ideas about salvation, which Pentecostals tend to hold in common with one another and with many other Christians.[2] These basic ideas will serve as a fundamental starting point for describing the concept of salvation as held among Pentecostal believers.

GENERAL THEOLOGICAL ORIENTATION

Johnny Appleseed was a popular North American frontier folk hero who went walking about the countryside scattering apple seeds. Actually, this version of his life is mostly legend, since John Chapman (his real name) carefully planted and cultivated apple tree nurseries.[3] Nevertheless, his story helps explain the presence of apple trees today throughout much of Illinois, Indiana, Ohio, Pennsylvania, and the northern parts of West Virginia, as well as Ontario. Several years ago, while preaching a series of services in Michigan City, Indiana at the Full Gospel Church, Pastor Dennis Pickens took me to a nearby orchard to gather apples—an annual event for his family. I recall thinking at the time that I probably owed more than a little to Johnny Appleseed for every bite I enjoyed of those indescribably delicious apples.

The development of Christian doctrine is, to some degree, like the Johnny Appleseed story. While Pentecostal theology is firmly rooted in biblical teaching, the way we think and speak today about our most dearly

---

2. A major exception to Pentecostal consensus would be Oneness Pentecostals. Rejection of the Trinity influences significant aspects of their soteriology as well. This volume focuses on the soteriology of Trinitarian Pentecostals (which encompasses about 75 percent of Pentecostals). However, Reed, *"In Jesus' Name,"* tends to be optimistic about how close Oneness Pentecostals are to traditional Pentecostals.

3. See Kerrigan, *Johnny Appleseed and the American Orchard*.

beloved truths did not just spring up haphazardly. Haphazard handling of doctrinal truth can—and has and does—end up in heresy (false doctrine).[4] Sound doctrine or good theology is the result of painstaking historical and intellectual processes. For the purposes of this text, it is not necessary to dive deeply into those waters; but it will be helpful to wade around a bit on the shallow side of the stream. Accordingly, let's take a quick look at Pentecostals' general theological orientation relative to the Christian doctrine of salvation.

When it comes to conversion, Pentecostals usually affirm traditional Protestant/evangelical conceptions of such matters as faith, repentance, justification (forgiveness, pardon), adoption, regeneration (new birth), and assurance (of forgiveness of sins and of the gift of eternal life)—although clearly from a Wesleyan-Arminian rather than from a Calvinist/Reformed perspective.[5] Please note that I am moving specifically to address conversion—how one becomes a Christian or "gets saved." This move is not because I consider, or that I suppose other Pentecostals consider, salvation to be exclusively limited to conversion. Subsequent chapters will clearly indicate otherwise. Rather, conversion is where Pentecostals enjoy the closest connections with other Christian traditions. Even more importantly, conversion is the critical beginning of salvation experience. As such, it is not only essential for becoming a Christian, but it is foundational for innumerable benefits of salvation that follow upon it.

Protestant and Evangelical

Furthermore, note that the specific historical-theological trajectory for our discussion of Christian conversion and salvation is Protestant and evangelical. The sixteenth-century Protestant Reformation, as led by then Roman Catholic monk and theologian Martin Luther, sought to reform the church of his day. His biblical studies (especially of Paul's Letter to the Romans) and theological studies (especially the writings of Augustine) convinced him that the church had drifted into corruption. Luther called loudly for reform. He was especially concerned that the church had developed a rival system of granting salvation,

---

4. Perhaps much of what the so-called "prosperity gospel" teaches (refocusing the gospel on physical health and material wealth) could fit into this category. Another example could be the rampant speculations on end time prophecies (untethered from either Scripture or sound reason) that have plagued certain movements.

5. Sims, *Our Pentecostal Heritage*, 63, 68. As Black, *Apostolic Theology*, 715–31, exemplifies, Pentecostal groups attempting to acclimate to Calvinist themes such as perseverance of the saints and unconditional election do exist; but they are rare and, in my assessment, wrestle with theological inconsistencies.

thereby effectively making the church the dispenser of salvation and departing from the NT teaching of salvation by faith in Jesus Christ.[6]

Luther and other Protestant Reformers emphasized themes such as *sola scriptura* (scripture alone), *sola gratia* (grace alone), and *sola fide* (faith alone). Latin was the theological language of Luther's day, so these technical terms serve to summarily articulate that Scripture alone (rather than church tradition) has authority to determine Christian doctrine, that salvation is accomplished by grace alone and received only by faith in Jesus Christ (rather than by human merit or ecclesial indulgences). Some resisted Luther's efforts; others embraced them. Long story short, there was a split between opposing factions. The group that followed Luther's reform efforts became known as "Protestants," because they *protested* theological aberrations, primarily regarding salvation, and sought to bring about radical reform, although there were other issues, in the established Roman Catholic Church.

Even among Protestant churches there are additional subtleties. In the eighteenth century, British evangelists like the Wesley brothers (John and Charles) and George Whitefield, along with Americans like Jonathan Edwards, became increasingly convinced that the church of their day desperately needed new life and energy, or "revival." They affirmed definitive, and sometimes (but not always) dramatic conversion to Christ as an essential component of receiving the gospel or evangel, and even though the term had been variously used throughout Christian history, followers arising up around these revival movements eventually became known as "evangelicals."[7] More recent evangelical figures have included Americans such as theologian Carl F. H. Henry and world-renowned evangelist Billy Graham. Evangelicals are committed to a cruciform vision of Christianity. "Cruciform" signifies determinative shaping of Christian faith and practice by the doctrine of Christ's death on the cross.[8] Evangelicals are committed to the centrality of Jesus' atoning death for salvation and its significance for all of Christian faith and life.

Major Pentecostal denominations, such as the Church of God, Assemblies of God, Church of God in Christ, International Pentecostal Holiness Church, Pentecostal Church of God, and the Foursquare Church, identify as evangelical Protestants.[9] Pentecostal theology affirms the basic principles of

---

6. Cp. Trueman, "Martin Luther."

7. From *euangelion* in the Greek NT, meaning "good news" or "glad tidings."

8. Conn, "Crisis of the Cross," describes the cross of Christ as the dividing line for all humanity. For more on evangelicals' views on conversion and other matters, see the National Association of Evangelicals website at https://www.nae.net/what-is-an-evangelical/.

9. In the interest of full disclosure, my own church membership and ministerial

sola scriptura, sola gratia, and *sola fide.* Clearly, these Protestant principles directly impact one's theology of salvation. Identification as evangelical Protestants means that Pentecostal soteriology tends to emphasize the importance of definitive, perhaps sometimes dramatic, conversion experiences, and that Pentecostals interpret these experiences in light of the centrality of Christ's atoning death for the sins of the world.

To be sure, aspects of some versions of evangelical Protestant theology have long troubled Pentecostals. A most emphatic divergence involves the ongoing agency of the Holy Spirit. *Cessationism,* or the view that the miraculous gifts of the Holy Spirit prominent in the NT no longer operate in the churches (have ceased), has been a serious fault in the thought of much of Protestantism, including evangelicalism.[10] Based on a straightforward approach to the Bible, Pentecostals are *continuationists,* affirming that NT spiritual gifts continue to be active today wherever believers yield in humble obedience to the Holy Spirit's gracious working. Pentecostals find it disingenuous that those who insist on *sola scriptura* appear to resist the Bible's teaching on the *charismata* (gifts of grace), another name for spiritual gifts or gifts of the Holy Spirit (cp. 1 Cor 12:1–11).

Consequently, while Pentecostals avidly affirm evangelical Protestantism, they find it incomplete on its own, which is why Pentecostals continue to celebrate and participate in the contemporary global Pentecostal revival. This revival movement arose spontaneously and somewhat sporadically around the world during the late nineteenth and early twentieth centuries, but found its international catalyst in the Azusa Revival that began in Los Angeles in 1906, under the dynamic leadership of African American pastor William J. Seymour. Like Seymour and his Azusa Street Mission, Pentecostals are Protestant and evangelical. Again, like Seymour and the Azusa Street Mission, Pentecostals are, well, distinctively *Pentecostal.* Among other things, being Pentecostal includes avidly affirming that the day of Pentecost outpouring of the Holy Spirit continues to be available, desirable, and indispensable for Christians today (Acts 2).

Wesleyan-Arminian Perspective

Finally, note that my discussion of a Pentecostal doctrine of salvation arises out of a Wesleyan-Arminian perspective vis-à-vis a Calvinist/Reformed perspective. Along with Luther, John Calvin was one of the great Protestant

---

credentials are with the Church of God, with international offices in Cleveland, TN. See http://www.churchofgod.org/ for more information.

10. E.g., see Schreiner, "Miraculous Gifts and the Question of Cessationism."

Reformers. While Luther's theology tended to be intuitive and occasional, Calvin was the ultimate logician and systematician. Calvin's intense interest in divine sovereignty led him to establish a soteriological system that meticulously sought to exclude any and all human involvement—even to the extent of denying human responsiveness to divine initiative and action. Calvin's theology, often called "Reformed" theology, or more popularly simply "Calvinism," is famously summed up in the acronym TULIP:

- T *total depravity*: sin has so destroyed human nature that it is entirely and completely incapacitated; it cannot even respond to God's offer of salvation in Jesus Christ.
- U *unconditional election*: before anyone is ever born, God chooses whether they will be lost/damned (reprobate) or converted/saved (known also as the doctrine of double predestination).
- L *limited atonement*: since the death of Christ must be efficacious, that is, cannot not be effective, then he only died for those whom God foreknew would be saved.
- I *irresistible grace*: since God chose who will receive salvation or be consigned to reprobation and damnation, then it is impossible for anyone God has so chosen not to experience saving grace.
- P *perseverance of the saints*: it is not possible for any of the elect to be finally lost or apostate (popularly known as "once saved, always saved").[11]

Although Calvinism is a complicated system with many variations, ultimately it presents a deterministic portrayal of God and human salvation that Pentecostals reject.[12]

---

11. Arrington, "Once Saved, Always Saved?," describes unconditional eternal security, as it is also called, as a dangerous doctrine that undermines godly living, gives false assurance, contradicts scriptural teaching, and diminishes the importance of discipleship.

12. As noted previously, Black, *Apostolic Theology*, 715–31, exemplifies a rare Pentecostal group attempting to acclimate to Calvinist themes such as perseverance of the saints and unconditional election. However, admittedly I have in recent years encountered an increasing number of intelligent and articulate, often younger Pentecostals, enamored with Calvinist/Reformed theology. This phenomenon, however, I chalk up to one or more of three factors: (1) in an age of exhausting uncertainty, Calvinism is attractive to those seeking exhaustive certainty, (2) failure to be rooted and grounded in Pentecostal theology during formative stages of spiritual and intellectual development, and/or, (3) exposure to and disenchantment with a fundamentalist form of Pentecostalism that is unpalatable to any thinking believer. On another note, some, like James K. A. Smith, who holds to both the Reformed and Pentecostal traditions, having come into the latter subsequent to and conjointly with the former, comprise a different sort of group that has opened up to Pentecostal experience from within a different tradition.

James Arminius was a sixteenth-century Dutch theologian and pastor trained extensively in Calvinist theology. However, he came to suspect and eventually to reject key Calvinist positions as inconsistent with the overall witness of Holy Scripture. Arminius argued for a return to the pre-Calvinist and pre-Augustinian views of the early church concerning divine foreknowledge and human liberty or free will as more consistent with the Scriptures' allowance for universal or general redemption.[13] In other words, he believed salvation in Christ is freely offered to all who may then freely accept it or reject it. Although Arminius was severely opposed by Calvinists, many Christians were persuaded that he was correct. Those who agreed with Arminius against Calvinism became known as Arminians.

In the eighteenth century, in spite of intense pressures to the contrary, and including disputes with close friend and fellow revivalist George Whitefield, John Wesley agreed with Arminius. Wesley argued that, although sin indeed *incapacitates* humans, God's grace *recapacitates* lost and sinful humans, so that they might respond, either positively or negatively, to God's gracious offer of salvation by faith in Jesus Christ. God's "prevenient grace," or grace that precedes or goes before conversion, enables humans to accept salvation if they will respond positively. In other words, no one is doomed to be damned without a chance for a choice. Wesley did not think that the God of the Bible is the kind of God that damns people without any hope for help. Significantly, Wesley was less rationalistic than Arminius tended to be, and certainly than some of his followers turned out to be; Wesley and Wesleyans tend to be more fervent (fiery!), too. But Wesley was, if possible, even more adamantly opposed to Calvinism. Wesley felt Calvinist theology distorts one's view of the God of holy love encountered in Scripture and known in personal piety. Calvinism turns God into a capricious monster. Those who agree with Wesley's application of Arminian theology are known as Wesleyan-Arminians.[14] Classical Pentecostalism has been staunchly Wesleyan-Arminian since its inception.

Accordingly, we describe the general theological orientation of Pentecostals as evangelical Protestant and Wesleyan-Arminian. However, it is important to note that Pentecostal theology does not depend on the currents

---

See Smith, "Teaching a Calvinist to Dance."

13. Calvin drew heavily from Augustine (354–430 AD), who so connected grace and predestination as to make the latter essential for the former. Calvin went beyond Augustine, however, on so-called "double predestination" (teaching that God foreordains *both* some to salvation *and* others to damnation). Contrariwise, Pentecostal theology interprets soteriological aspects of predestination in terms of the corporate election of Israel and the church (Rom 9–11).

14. Cp. Brian, "Arminianism, Calvinism, and Their Influence on John Wesley."

of history—not even of Christian history—for its essence or ethos. Pentecostals are Protestant because they believe Jesus and Jesus alone is Savior and Lord due to their understanding of biblical truth (e.g. John 14:6; Acts 4:12). Pentecostals are evangelical because of their commitment to the biblical truth that the gospel is the power of God for salvation (e.g., Rom 1:16). Pentecostals are Wesleyan-Arminian because of commitment to the biblical declaration that "Whoever desires" may "take the water of life freely" (Rev 22:17). In short, Pentecostals' high view of scriptural inspiration and authority is determinative for the shape of Pentecostal theology.

Nevertheless, some understanding of the historical-theological background for Pentecostal belief is immensely helpful for probing and developing a consistent, coherent Pentecostal theology of salvation. Pentecostal theology and spirituality set a context that particularly values the *relational* and the *dynamic* aspects of the Christian life. Although many might not agree (!), in my opinion, Calvinist monergism is not nearly as conducive to these values as Wesleyan-Arminian synergism. Monergism is a one-sided view that denies human cooperation with God, even grace-enabled responsive cooperation, and thus is not primarily relational and certainly does not encourage dynamism. Wesleyan-Arminian synergism affirms divine sovereignty without eliminating human responsive cooperation with God's enabling grace.[15] Arguably, Wesleyan-Arminian theology is, therefore, much more conducive to encouraging relational and dynamic aspects of Christian life rightly so highly prized by Pentecostals. They are a good fit. Contrariwise, Reformed theology, like David trying to wear Saul's armor (1 Sam 17:38–40), does not fit so well. It encumbers Pentecostal spirituality and vitality. In a word, the Calvinist/Reformed system restricts Pentecostals in such a way that free movement or action becomes at best difficult. This is a particularly serious factor, since the liberty of the Spirit is a core value for Pentecostals (cp. 2 Cor 3:17).

Arguably, the conducive qualities of the Wesleyan-Arminian synergism for Pentecostal theology and spirituality are not merely preferential opinions. The dynamic catalyst for the rise of contemporary Pentecostalism was, as stated above, the Azusa Street Mission revival led by William J. Seymour. Pastor Seymour and Azusa were from an American Holiness background. The American Holiness Movement was (and is) Wesleyan-Arminian. I suppose one may assume that the meteoric rise of the Pentecostal revival among Wesleyan-Arminian-Holiness (or for short, Wesleyan Holiness) churches was an accident of history. I cannot agree. I argue that

---

15. Wright, *Justification,* describes synergism as the Spirit working with us and in us to free us from slavery to sin (Phil 2:13), 188–89.

Wesleyan Holiness spirituality and theology are conducive to Pentecostalism. By this, I suggest that Wesleyan Holiness belief and practice encourage an environment of fervent spirituality and seeking that increases opportunities for experiencing the Holy Spirit in ways that Pentecostals appreciate as a restoration of biblical spirituality.

If I am correct, of course it would not suggest that only Wesleyan Holiness devotees are able to receive experiences of the Holy Spirit that resonate with the day of Pentecost. Not at all! Thankfully, the Holy Spirit has clearly demonstrated in today's diverse renewal movements that the moving of the Spirit cannot be monopolized by any denomination or sectarian movement. However, it may well suggest, and I think it does, that a Wesleyan-Arminian-Holiness mindset (perhaps I should add, and heart-set) is especially favorable for promoting and stimulating—and sustaining—an environment suitable for spiritual experience in a Pentecostal mode.[16]

In any case, and to reiterate, this section describes the general theological orientation of Pentecostal theology as evangelical Protestant and Wesleyan-Arminian. This identity directly influences the manner in which Pentecostals interpret and apply their understanding of biblical teaching on the Christian doctrine of salvation. The remainder of this volume will not emphasize these historical features of Pentecostal identity (or their doctrinal differences). Its purpose is not to present apologetics or polemics either for or against various theological schools of thought. However, it is important to have this orientation and its implications firmly in mind for purposes of acquiring clarity regarding the theological task as Pentecostals approach it.

SPECIFIC SALVATION EXPERIENCES

In the so-called Bible Belt of the United States (I live in Tennessee), when someone says "I got saved!" there is a cultural understanding in place about what that means.[17] However, I have been places where such a statement was confronted with confusion. "Saved from what?" has sometimes been the response. And that is a great question. It really is impossible to understand *salvation* without understanding something about *sin*. Sin and its consequences are what we are "saved from."

---

16. Anecdotally, I have observed that congregations led by long-term pastors influenced by Reformed theology become unrecognizable as overtly Pentecostal.

17. "Bible Belt" is an informal but common designation for a larger section of the southern United States, because of the prominent influence of evangelical Protestantism and higher-than-national-average church attendance.

When we were boys, my little brother liked to trade. Tim was always swapping something—baseball cards, comic books, marbles, and pocket knives were some of his favorite trade items. He would trade for anything. Somehow, he gained a wristwatch; although I did not trade much, I ended up with it. It did not have a band, so I bought a new one for a few dollars saved from my weekly allowance. It was a wide leather band in style at the time. I sure was proud of that watch. It looked great, but it did not keep good time. I really liked that watch, so it took me a while to accept that a watch that does not keep correct time is not worth much. I think I eventually just threw it away.

For me, that old wristwatch illustrates something about the nature of sin.[18] Human beings have a lot of potential, but there is something not quite right. Sometimes, it is really wrong. We are all broken. The word I am looking for is *fallen*. Genesis 1–3 tells the story of how this tragedy happened. A good and loving God created human beings in his own image. We were created to live forever in fellowship with our Creator. We were created without sin. Tragically, we doubted God's word and rebelled against God's will. We fell from our lofty position, becoming broken, distorted, twisted. We became lost.[19]

Only God did not throw us away. God loved us enough to send his Son to save us (John 3:16). We could not save ourselves. We were helpless and, on our own, hopeless. So, Jesus came "to seek and to save that which was lost" (Luke 19:10). As Paul told the church in Rome, "For the wages of sin *is* death, but the gift of God *is* eternal life in Christ Jesus our Lord" (Rom 6:23). Human beings deserve—we have literally earned—the sentence of spiritual and physical death, eternal judgment. God, however, freely gives sinners eternal life in Jesus Christ our Lord. We are saved from death and judgment. We are saved for life and for eternity. We are saved from sin and death; that is what we are saved *from*. We are saved unto eternal life; that is what we are saved *for*. That is salvation.[20]

---

18. Although for purposes of brevity and focus we will not delve into it further, an astute insight of McGrath's *Born to Wonder* (120) into the theology of sin "as a relational notion, expressed in dysfunctional relationships with other people, the environment, and God" is worth noting. I would add that relationship of the self with God is the ground of all others.

19. The primary Greek word for sin, *hamartia*, means "to miss the mark" and thus "to err." Because of sin, humans become other than what God created us to be. You might say we are "off target." In ancient Greek tragedy, *hamartia* signified a fatal flaw that led to the downfall of a tragic hero or heroine.

20. As Thomas H. McCall, "John Wesley," observes, the remarkable eighteenth-century revivalist and theologian John Wesley taught that "We are saved *for nothing* less than communion with the Triune God, and thus we are saved *from* the sin that

A Doctrinal Complex

According to Christian anthropology (doctrine of human beings), a faithful Creator made the world and its inhabitants, including humans. He pronounced that they were good. Human abuse of free will resulted in a breach in their relationship with the Creator God and marred human nature. Thereby, humans became sinners. Humanity, while capable of good, is bent toward evil. Sin or evil—immorality, impiety, wickedness—is the root cause of universal suffering in all its myriad forms. Theodicy is the doctrine of the origin and nature of evil and suffering. Sin is grounds for eternal damnation at the final judgment (relating to eschatology). Soteriology at its simplest is about how God's creation and his creatures, especially humans, are set right again through Jesus Christ after the fall of humanity into sin and its tragic consequences.

Accordingly, Christian salvation is not an isolated truth; it is an intricate part of a set of doctrines about the nature of God, of creation, of humanity, of sin and suffering, and of the last things. It is not necessary for us to delve deeper here into these specific doctrines or their implications. I do deem it necessary to bear in mind that they constitute the theological canvas upon which we paint the portrait of salvation. Now, let us turn to some very important soteriological specifics.

Faith

As already stated, when it comes to conversion, Pentecostals specifically affirm faith, repentance, justification (forgiveness, pardon), adoption, regeneration (new birth), and assurance (of forgiveness of sins and the gift of eternal life).[21] Let's work through this list one by one. Faith involves intellectual assent to the truths of the gospel but goes beyond it to include trust in Jesus Christ as Lord and Savior.[22] Faith, in this sense, encompasses both mind and heart. In other words, it is both cognitive and affective. Critically, saving faith does not stop with general affirmation of theism rather than atheism, or even that a man named Jesus of Nazareth really existed and is the founder of Christianity. Saving faith goes further. It believes that Jesus

---

would separate us from God's holy love," 262. Italics are original.

21. Gause, *Living in the Spirit*, xxx.

22. Interestingly, the NT word for faith, *pistis*, means not only that which can be believed but also describes faithfulness or fidelity as well as trust or trustworthiness. Faith as inclusive of faithfulness flies in the face of any sort of "easy believe-ism."

is the Son of God, that he died for the sins of the world, and that he rose bodily from the dead.

Furthermore, faith is personal.[23] Again, it does not stop with confessing that Jesus is the Savior of the world; it confesses that Jesus is *my* Savior, *my* Lord. Personal faith believes Jesus loved *me* and gave himself for *me* (Gal 2:20). Accordingly, faith includes both objective and subjective elements. While it affirms the objective truth of the gospel of Jesus Christ, and it regards the gospel of Jesus Christ as absolute truth, it also subjectively accepts the implications of the gospel's truth in personal experience by accepting and applying the gospel to one's own life. At the risk of oversimplification, faith includes intellectual *assent*, emotional *affirmation*, and volitional *acceptance* of Jesus Christ as Lord and Savior.

Personal faith is not equivalent to *privatized* faith. In other words, to say that faith is personal is not to say that it should be confined in a closet (out of sight or sound). Contrariwise, Jesus insistently calls for his disciples to publicly confess their faith in him (Mark 8:27–33; John 6:67–71). He further identifies faith's public confession of the Son of Man as an identifying mark of a true disciple, which will be reciprocated by him in the coming eschaton/consummation of history (Luke 12:28–29). Paul makes faith's confession integral to the salvation experience (Rom 10:9–10). While Luke lifts up the importance of baptismal confession (Acts 8:37), Paul links Christian confession to following Christ's example in all of life, in both word and deed, and in every situation (1 Tim 6:11–16).

Faith is not mute. As popular as it may be in some circles to offer the feeble, insipid explanation that "faith is a private matter," in an effort to excuse an inexcusable cowardly refusal to publicly declare one's self for Jesus Christ, it exposes an attitude that is completely foreign to anything even remotely resembling a biblical notion of faith. Indeed, arguably, a living, vital faith simply must speak out of the essence of its heart (Ps 116:10; 2 Cor 4:13). A Christian's faith is intensely personal, but unashamedly *public*. Confine faith in a private closet? Faith cannot be contained! It breaks out and boldly proclaims Jesus to all who will hear.

It is especially suitable that faith is vital to the way we come to God. Recall the Edenic tragedy. Note that the serpent *defied* God's word; then Eve *doubted* God's word; and, finally, both Eve and Adam *disobeyed* God's word (Gen 3:1–7). If fallen humankind is to return to God, that process must be reversed. Of course, the serpent still defies God's word; but if we will believe God's word and obey it, then we can be restored to fellowship with God. No wonder Paul stresses "the obedience that comes from faith" (Rom 16:26; cp.

---

23. Cp. Bloesch, *Essentials of Evangelical Theology*, 242–47.

1:5). Just as unfaithfulness to God's word led to the fall, so faithfulness to God's word leads to the rising again. When Adam and Eve failed to believe God's promise of death regarding Eden's tree, they died (Gen 2:15–17). Everyone who doubts God's word and disobeys God's will follows that path to death. Yet whoever believes God's promise of life regarding Calvary's tree— the cross—obeys unto eternal life (1 Pet 2:24). The ultimate issue between humanity and God is whether humans will believe and trust their Creator. Faith in Jesus Christ is ultimately an affirmation of God's absolute faithfulness. It is quite appropriate that receiving salvation therefore begins with that step of faith.

Repentance

Jesus famously preached his first recorded sermon on repentance in Mark 1:14–15.[24] Mark does not appear to mean merely that repentance was the topic of a specific sermon one Sabbath day at the local synagogue—although it well might have been; rather, Mark offers a thematic summary of Jesus' preaching ministry. Thus, the message of repentance was at the core of Jesus' ministry. Jesus placed repentance in the context of the eschatological urgency of God's coming reign and connected it to the imperative of believing the gospel. Repentance, therefore, involves crisis preparation with a future orientation. The crisis of God's coming reign involves accountability for one's conduct in the present age. The righteous God will set all things right, judging that which is wrong and rewarding that which is right. Christ commands hearers to make ready for the climactic event of encountering the all-seeing God.

Repentance is closely associated with believing or faith. In this sense, believing includes acceptance of the verity of Christ's bold claim that God's kingdom is arriving in his person, as the gospel announces. But again, there is more to conversion than acceptance of certain claims as true. Often missed is the centrality of pneumatic activity. The Holy Spirit works to convict the world of its wrongdoing (John 16:8–11). People confronted with their sin may be "cut to the heart" (Acts 2:37). The Holy Spirit convincingly penetrates the inner being with the awful reality of a life of rebellion against God and God's will. At this point, they become ready for repentance—and salvation (Acts 2:38–39). The Father through the Holy Spirit draws those

---

24. Jesus uses the verb *metanoeō*, literally meaning "to change one's mind." In pre-Christian Greek, however, it could also refer to regretting a particular act. In Jewish thought it took on the meaning of comprehensively turning back to God.

"under conviction" to the Son (Jer 31:3; John 6:44, 65; 12:32). Conviction *draws* us to repentance and salvation; it does not *drive* us there.

It would be calamitous to confuse conviction with conversion. After all, one's salvation is on the line. Paul warns against mistaking mere emotional regret for authentic repentance (2 Cor 7:10). The mark of true repentance is a changed life. Indeed, repentance in a changed heart and mind (*internal*) evokes a changed way of living (*external*) and produces a changed standing and destiny when encountering God in his righteous reign (*eternal*). In other words, a convicted sinner becomes painfully aware of his/her sin, burdened by their consequent guilt before the God to whom all are accountable for judgment, and turns from that sin to God. Believing the gospel involves trusting that in Jesus Christ we can be set right with God in spite of our history of sinful rebellion against God's law. That is good news.

A substantive Pentecostal theology of salvation includes a number of significant features. First, it affirms divine initiative and human free response of faith. Second, it confronts sin and calls forth authentic transformation. Third, its experiential nature integrates the sincerity of human emotion and volition with the priority of the Holy Spirit's agency. Fourth, its focus is not negative but positive, as it embraces the good news of God's saving offer in Jesus Christ. Fifth, it frames this present age in terms of eternity with the result of facilitating preparedness for both this life and the next.

In a word, repentance involves crisis conversion to Christ. However, repentance alone does not constitute Christian salvation. If one were to imagine salvation as a great house, then repentance would be its porch. Faith in Christ is the door by which one enters. Through repentance one approaches the house, even stands at the door. Repentance itself, however, is not salvation. Nevertheless, it is impossible to enter the door of the salvation-house without stepping onto the repentance-porch.[25] Accordingly, repentance is commanded of God and necessary for salvation. Repentance is not optional; repentance is imperative. As faith in Jesus Christ affirms God's absolute faithfulness, so repentance before God acknowledges humanity's persistent unfaithfulness; and that humbling acknowledgment prepares the heart to receive God's saving gift.

---

25. This well-known analogy was developed by John Wesley, "Principles of a Methodist Farther Explained," *Wesley's Works*, 8:414–81 (esp. 8:472).

Justification

Justification was the watchword of the Protestant Reformation. Not surprisingly, it has a long history as a hotly contested topic.[26] However, the basic meaning of justification is fairly straightforward. Justification is about forgiveness. It is about pardon or acquittal of guilty sinners before a righteous and holy God.[27] That is simple enough, is it not? Yet, unpacking how justification is accomplished and received yields an incredibly copious harvest.

The summative force of Romans 5:1–2 is particularly significant for understanding the doctrine of justification. "Therefore, having been justified by faith, we have peace with God through our Lord Jesus Christ, through whom also we have access by faith into this grace in which we stand, and rejoice in hope of the glory of God." This passage enumerates the fruits or results of justification by faith: peace with God (*relational*), access into standing in grace (*positional*), and rejoicing in hope of the glory of God (*eschatological*). It builds upon Paul's preceding argument that all the world is guilty before God due to the universality of human sinfulness (3:1–20) but can be justified by faith rather than by keeping of the Law (Jewish law/Torah) or by works of righteousness (3:21–31). Then, Romans chapter 4 provides significant examples—or better yet, precedents—indicating that the Old Testament (OT) itself bears consistent witness to justification by faith. Of course, the OT and NT do not offer rival means of salvation. Rather, the progressive revelation of the Scripture in the OT, like the unfolding of a rose beginning to bloom, gradually discloses the doctrine of justification by faith which comes to full blossom in the NT.

Paul uses commercial business language to describe justification, particularly the transactional concept of "imputation" (Rom 4:1–25; Gal 3:21–22; cp. Gen 15:6; Ps 32:2). In short, imputation means that righteousness is credited or reckoned to one's account through faith in Jesus Christ, even as the guilt of their sin was charged to Christ in his sacrificial death (2 Cor 5:21; cp. Rom 1:17).[28] The "currency" of this "exchange" is not money, but

---

26. Recently, the "new perspective on Paul" movement with its focus on clarifying the nature of justification in Pauline theology, led by major biblical theologians such as N. T. Wright, indicates that the discussion is far from finished. E.g. Wright, *Justification*.

27. The NT uses the verb *dikaioō* in a forensic or legal sense of declaring or pronouncing righteousness. One who is thus vindicated in a court of law would be said in contemporary legal terms to have been acquitted or found "not guilty."

28. Attentive readers may note that I refer to imputed righteousness of or through faith rather than the imputed righteousness of Christ. First, this terminology is more reflective of Paul's language and, I believe, his intent (e.g. Rom 3:22; 4:11, 13; 9:30). Second, Wright correctly notes that the phrase (and a body of teaching that has arisen around it) "the imputed righteousness of Christ" has been used in misleading ways,

righteousness. Paul's imputation metaphor helpfully pictures how Christ who committed no sin could be counted sin on the cross, while guilty sinners can be counted righteous because of Christ's cross.

But imputation does not mean that God "cooks the books" to make sinners come off better. That is, imputation is not an ingenious way of cheating sin and death. God is not a dishonest accountant. Rather, the doctrine of justification, and its corollary imputation, affirm that God is both just and the justifier of sinners who believe in Jesus (Rom 3:26). Think of it as if a wealthy friend picks up your dinner tab at an expensive restaurant when you cannot afford to pay. The bill has to be paid. You cannot pay it. Your friend puts it on his/her account. It is honestly paid—but not by you. The restaurant management is satisfied.[29] Yet, suppose your friend at the restaurant not only paid your tab but decided to share his/her wealth with you further. Imputation is a metaphor that helps us imagine how our friend Jesus paid our sin-debt and generously shared his righteousness-wealth with us (John 15:13). What a wonderful truth!

However, justification by faith should never be considered a mere commercial transaction in isolation from redemption's transforming power and moral implications.[30] Such carelessness has led some to misunderstand Paul's teaching on imputation. Some assume that justification by faith and imputation of righteousness suggests that one's moral conduct is irrelevant, or, at best, optional. They say, if you already have righteous standing, then why does it matter how you actually live? Incredibly, there are those who even suggest that insistence on *actual* righteousness (living right) is an obstacle to *positional* righteousness (standing in grace by faith). These aberrations are foreign to scriptural teaching. Such false teachers ignore Paul's sharp rebuke of an alarming claim that sin contributes to an increase of grace (Rom 6:1–2).

Even a casual look at Romans 6–8, as well as Galatians 5, clearly indicates that these wonderful truths of justification by faith and imputation of

---

Justification, 105 (cp. 135, 233). Third, centuries ago, James Arminius and, later, John Wesley, challenged the misuse of the doctrine of the imputation of Christ's righteousness. See Arminius,*Works of James Arminius*, 2:42–45, 2:253–58, and 2:405–08, and *Wesley's Works*, 5:238–39 and 7:312–13. Wesley, in particular, fretted against any view of justification and imputation that served as a covering for antinomianism (lawlessness, unrighteous living); *Wesley's Works*, 10:364–69 (esp. 368).

29. In various contexts Jesus uses the concept of debt to teach about sin and forgiveness (Matt 18:21–38; Luke 7:36–50).

30. Thus, I agree with what I take to be one of Tom Wright's main objections to the way imputation is often presented as *the* central model for understanding justification, *Justification*, 46.

righteousness do not issue a license to sin.[31] Some have erred in a mistaken notion that justification makes holiness unnecessary (contra Heb 12:14). Arguably, Romans 6–8 and Galatians 5 immediately follow Pauline discussions of justification and imputation as intentional qualifiers against such ungodliness. Clearly, Romans 6–8 describes the normative life in the Spirit that justification anticipates and expects (as does Galatians 5:22–26). Pauline theology presents justification with pneumatically situated participatory and transformative language (Rom 5:5). In biblical teaching, justification/forgiveness *precedes* sanctification/holiness but does not *preempt* it.[32] In essence, holiness is God's standard of living for forgiven people.

Furthermore, Romans 5:1–2 flows into Paul's immediate connection of justification by faith with spiritual formation and ethical development (vv. 3–5), as well as his extended explication of Christ's atoning death as the basis for justification by faith (vv. 6–21). Faith does not justify or save. Christ saves. Faith is the means by which we appropriate the saving benefits of Christ's work. Justifying faith expresses itself in works of righteousness, but righteous works do not form the basis of justification (Jas 2:20–24). Such a heresy would be self-righteousness or works righteousness.[33] Authentic faith, however, expresses itself in action as holy love (Gal 5:6). Accordingly, while good works cannot justify, the faith that justifies issues forth in good works—that is, in righteous conduct. As my preacher father was fond of saying, the working person is not a justified person but a justified person is a working person.

Simply put, the doctrine of justification by faith teaches that when guilty sinners put their faith in Jesus Christ, they receive forgiveness or pardon for their sins. They are acquitted and judged not guilty. They are declared or pronounced righteous before God in Christ. Of course, forgiving the sin-debt includes removing the penalty for the sin-debt. Accordingly, those who are justified by faith in Jesus Christ are no longer under the sentence of death but receive the gift of eternal life (Rom 6:23). No wonder Scripture emphatically reiterates that "the just shall live by faith" (Hab 2:4; Rom 1:17; Gal 3:11; Heb 10:38). Justification by faith is a joyous doctrine of the righteous God's pardoning of guilty sinners through faith in Jesus Christ and his atoning work, ushering in the experience of redemption's transforming power with its moral and spiritual implications.

---

31. Antinomianism is a technical term for the false teaching that Christians have no obligation to obey the moral law of God. Paul explicitly refutes that claim (Rom 3:31).

32. As Spurgeon, *All of Grace*, 46–47, said, "We need to be purified as well as pardoned. Justification without sanctification would not be salvation at all."

33. The view that obedience to a moral code, e.g., the Mosaic Law or religious, ethical, or practical commitments, forms the basis of justification is the error of legalism.

Adoption

Adoption is another legal term significant for soteriology.[34] Adoption conjoins family intimacy with legal status in terms of authority and inheritance (Gal 4:1–5; Eph 1:5). Adoption explains how those born into servitude through sin, without position or rights, become sons of God with a position of high authority and a right to inherit God's abundance. As justification portrays how the guilty are pardoned, so adoption portrays how slaves become sons. The sonship of adoption is not about male gender; it is about position. John Fogerty, after his famous protest song against class privilege, entitled "Fortunate Son" (with Credence Clearwater Revival), in which he repeatedly shouts "It ain't me! It ain't me!" testified to what a great privilege he felt it was for him to be an American.[35] Those adopted into God's family through Jesus Christ are placed in the highest privilege of all—and yet this privileged position is offered to whomever will accept it.

In ancient cultures, including Israel and the Middle East, a firstborn son was the primary heir to a father's authority and property. In ancient Rome, adoption was quite common among the upper classes, and even Roman emperors often chose their successors via adoption. When Paul describes all God's children in Jesus Christ as enjoying the highest status through the adoption of sons, he draws on well-known practice, but—significantly—develops the motif to fit the gospel, not the other way around.

Pauline theology correlates union with Christ and reception of the Spirit with adoption into sonship (Rom 8:14–17). It appears that union with Christ is the *basis* of adoption and sonship, while reception of the Spirit is the *badge* of adoption and sonship. As the firstborn Son of God, Jesus is the heir to God the Father. Adoptees become heirs of God and joint heirs with Christ—including a share in Christ's suffering and glory (8:17). The Spirit of Christ seals and signifies the sonship which adoption involves (8:16; 2 Cor 1:22). Indeed, the Holy Spirit is the initial installment and formal guarantor of the eternal inheritance God's sons have in God's Son (Eph 1:13–14). Scriptural focus here is not on charismatic dimensions of Christian spirituality (spiritual gifts); rather, it lifts up the priceless role of the Spirit in all those who become God's children and sons through faith in Jesus (Rom 8:16; Gal 4:5–6; cp. John 1:12). However, the manner in which Scripture

---

34. Adoption, *huiothesia*, signifies a legal proceeding in which an adult, who is usually not biologically related in a parent-child relationship with the adopted child, who is then entitled to all the rights and privileges of a natural child, including the rights of inheritance.

35. Fogerty, *Fortunate Son*, 6–7.

frequently weaves together the multifaceted nature in Christian experience of the Spirit into a unified whole certainly is striking.

The term *adoption*, normally applied to Christians in the NT, is applied to the people of Israel only once (Rom 9:4). Paul, there, suggestively includes adoption in a list of distinctive privileges of the covenant people, although it does not specifically appear thus in the OT. Of course, the idea of Israel becoming part of God's family as a son is included (Deut 14:1; 32:6; Jer 31:9; Hos 1:10).[36] The privileges of sonship belonged to Israel as God's "firstborn son" (Exod 4:22; cp. Hos 11:1).[37] One might describe Israel as a kind of "prototype" for the Christian doctrine of adoption. Certainly, the favored status of OT Israel among the nations is now enjoyed by every NT believer in God's unique Son Jesus—and then some. In other words, what Israel was to the Lord in the OT, every believer is in the NT—only with a better inheritance (Heb 11:13–16). The inheritance in Christ is eternal and heavenly (1 Pet 1:4). Moreover, this inheritance in and with Christ inspires confident hope and patient waiting in the present as well as for the future age (Col 1:5; Rom 8:23). It is difficult to ignore the persistent eschatological emphasis of so much of Christian soteriology, including adoption. Although believers already enjoy the benefits of salvation, there is still so much more to come that we have not yet begun to realize.

Through adoption, God grants believers a new *position* in God's family and a generous share in God's *possessions*. One usually thinks of inheritance in terms of a birthright or endowment in the form of goods or land passed down from one generation to another. But Scripture treats eternal life and other privileges of faith as an inheritance from God for those who believe in Jesus Christ. Accordingly, God forever will be unveiling the unimaginable privileges of sonship.

Talking about adoption reminds me of a family at New Harvest where I served as pastor for nearly twenty-three years. Five daughters of a relative lost their parents. Even though Danny and Paula Riffey had already raised three children of their own and were beginning to have grandchildren, they could not bear for their relative's precious children to be separated from each other and to be distributed throughout the foster care system. Therefore, though it may seem incredible, they decided to adopt all five girls. Yes, at times it was a challenge. But oh, what a blessing those children were to our congregation. A few years ago, I had the privilege of joining the oldest daughter in marriage to her beloved young man. Later, it was definitely

---

36. Morris, *Romans*, 348.
37. Mounce, *Romans* 196.

a pastor's special joy to dedicate their baby to the Lord during a Sunday morning service.

Our heavenly Father has done something most remarkable. According to Ephesians 2:3, we were "by nature the children of wrath." You and I were not sweet little children in need of a hospitable home. We were enemies of God—incorrigible, hostile sinners. We were "children" of the devil (John 8:44). But God justified us from all sin and adopted us into his own family. God gave us the highest place and then wrote us into his will to receive everything he owns.[38] All for the sake of Jesus Christ! *That* is salvation.

Looking at implications of these different salvation terms—*faith, repentance, justification, adoption,* and others—is comparable to holding a precious jewel up to the light and admiring it from various angles. It is a beautiful sight any way you look at it, but its cumulative impact is one of indescribable splendor. The doctrine of adoption is the Bible's way of expressing the truth that believers belong to God's family and that membership has its privileges. Justification abolishes the *guilt of sin*, while adoption bequeaths a *glorious destiny*.

Regeneration

Together justification and adoption address believers' new *standing* or *status* before God; the term regeneration addresses believers' transformed *state* of being with new life and a new nature.[39] The translation of *palingenesia* denotes rebirth, regeneration, or renewal. Regeneration refers to a renewed birth or beginning of a person or of the world. The Greek literally means "again birth." In the NT, it is used of the renewal both of human beings and of the whole creation. Paul says that God saved us "through the washing of regeneration (*palingenesia*) and renewal (*anakainōsis*) by the Holy Spirit" (Titus 3:5). These words closely echo Jesus' teaching in John's Gospel that one must be born (*gennaō*) again (*anōthen*) of the Spirit (3:3–8). In Matthew 19:28, Jesus uses *palingenesia* to describe the renewal of all things at the eschaton.[40]

---

38. Legitimate concerns over the aberrations of the so-called prosperity gospel, especially its central emphasis on material wealth, need not frighten believers away from the biblical truth that the Father does bless financially those whose priorities are fixed on God's kingdom and righteousness (Matt 6:33).

39. John Wesley described justification as a *relative* change (what God does *for* us) and regeneration as a *real* change (what God does *in* us). See Wesley's sermon on "The Great Privilege of Those that are Born of God," in *Wesley's Works*, 5:223–33 (esp. 5:24).

40. Simmons, "Regeneration."

Popular Christian usage rarely refers to "regeneration," preferring instead the less technical sounding "born again," which is more reminiscent of Jesus than of Paul. However, the root idea is the same. The term "new birth" is also common. All of these terms signify—etymologically, biblically, and theologically—re-*genesis*. Summarily, re-genesis is about the origin and mode of a new existence. It calls to mind Genesis, the book of beginnings. Is it not ironic that Nicodemus struggled with new birth in terms of reentering a mother's womb, when Jesus' words may have gone back even further, to the womb of creation (John 3:4, 9; cp. Gen 1:2)?

But actually, regeneration is not so much either/or as it is both/and. Regeneration is both about repentant sinners becoming a new creation in Christ (2 Cor 5:17) and about the redemption of the created order (Rom 8:22). These are complementary components of regeneration. It is no small wonder that the language of Matthew 19:28, John 3:3, Romans 8:22, 2 Corinthians 5:17, and Revelation 21:4–5 so obviously overlaps. If regeneration were an icon on our laptop screen or an app on our cell phone, more than one link would appear when it is clicked. Regeneration is marvelously multifaceted.

The doctrine of regeneration includes both salvation (soteriology) and creation (cosmology).[41] The creation, or rather re-creation concept, is determinative for understanding regeneration. Additionally, here cosmology and soteriology are strongly flavored by the future consummation of all things (eschatology). Indeed, a great deal of Christian doctrine has an eschatological orientation, at least implicitly if not explicitly.[42] In the case of regeneration, the eschatological aspect is quite direct and strong.

In Matthew 19:27–30, Jesus draws on a Jewish regal vision to describe a new world characterized by not only religious but economic and political transformation as part of "the regeneration" effectively realized via his role as Israel's Messiah (cp. Mark 10:28–30 and Luke 18:28–30).[43] This regal vision of regeneration is consistent with Jesus' insistence in John's Gospel of the necessity of the new birth for seeing or entering the kingdom of God (3:3). Harking back to Isaianic cosmological prophecies of a new creation,

---

41. It is tempting to approach Christian theology in terms of either anthropocentrism/humanocentrism (centered in humanity) or cosmocentrism (centered in the cosmos/universe/creation). However, neither is correct. Christian theology, including soteriology, is theocentric (centered in God) while reflecting God's loving concern for humanity and all creation (Gen 1:26). See Aulén, *Faith of the Christian Church*, 3, 7–9.

42. Cp. Wright, *Justification*, 11. Not surprisingly, prominent evangelical theologian Donald Bloesch, *Last Things*, 14, particularly underscores "the inseparability of eschatology and soteriology."

43. Blomberg, *Matthew*, 300–301.

Jesus pushes beyond the ontological existence of a new heaven and a new earth to announce the emergence of an entire new order ushered in by the renewal of all things in the eschaton (Isa 65:17; 66:22). In other words, Jesus does not stop with predicting that the cosmic renewal will involve *a new world coming into being* but advances to announce that the new world will include *a new way of being*.[44] Likewise, Revelation 21:1–5 weaves together physics and ethics in the rebirth of the universe, in which all that produces death has disappeared and only that which delivers life remains.

Significantly, Jesus and Paul extend regeneration language beyond the anticipated cosmological renewal at the end of the age to include present personal regeneration (John 3:3; Gal 6:15; Titus 3:5). Peter and (especially) John emphasize new birth as personal conversion (1 Pet 1:23; 1 John 2:29; 3:9; 4:7; 5:1; 5:4, 18). It should not be surprising, then, that regeneration would have both corporate and personal elements. Doubtless, deep in post-exilic Judaism's psyche—and therefore in early Jewish Christianity—were Ezekiel's prophecies to Israel, replete with precedents intertwining national and personal regeneration in exceptionally close connection (11:19; 18:31; 36:26).[45] Second Corinthians 5:17 is especially helpful in this regard. "Therefore, if anyone *is* in Christ, *he is* a new creation; old things have passed away; behold, all things have become new." Paul beautifully weaves together regeneration as present personal conversion with regeneration as anticipated eschatological cosmological renewal.[46] Those who are now born again do not live according to this old world, which is already passing away, but according to the new world that is already in the process of coming (1 Cor 7:31; 1 John 2:8, 17).

Recently, my wife, Sue, and I discussed with our granddaughter, Elizabeth, a television series she had recommended to us. Its plot focuses on a present-day story line, frequently interspersed with flashbacks and flashforwards. In these kinds of stories, I often ask myself which timeline we are in during a specific scene in order to follow the plot better. Yet, in reality, we move in more than one tense at a time (no pun intended). At any given moment the human mind is functioning in a trilateral mode. It is constantly

---

44. Thompson, "Eschatology as Soteriology," argues for a "concentric parallelism" in which individual salvation and cosmic salvation are both part of the micro/macro pattern of God's soteriological purpose, 199–200. For Moltmann, *Coming of God*, 70, "personal eschatology" does not exhaust the Christian hope of the resurrection that includes "cosmic eschatology." Although Christ's rising, like the rising of believers, is certainly "a physical happening," it is not merely "a historical event" but "an eschatological happening," 69 (cp. 1 Cor 11:26).

45. Cooper, *Ezekiel*, 316–17.

46. Garland, *2 Corinthians*, 286–88.

processing whatever is being said or done in the present moment, while drawing on memories of past experiences for input, as it anticipates possible outcomes—either desirable or not—of this or that decision or action. Even so, regeneration simultaneously involves new life now while harking back to the dawn of creation and looking forward to the day of consummation. But regeneration is not a mind game; it is a *spiritual reality*.

Theologically speaking, the regenerate presently participates in the eschatological renewal of all things, which will ultimately satisfy their partial initiation with complete consummation. The very same divine power that will in the end transform all the cosmos is already at work in those who are born again through faith in Jesus Christ, transforming them into creatures fitted for existence in that holy, eternal age. Experientially speaking, the regenerate has received new life by the Spirit. Those who are born again have a new nature animated and energized by the Spirit, just as one day their resurrected, glorified body will be animated and energized by the Spirit. Ethically speaking, the regenerate lives now according to the spiritual values of the age that is beginning, rather than the one that is passing away. For those who are born again, God's righteous reign is already the rule of the day. In short, regeneration prepares and equips believers for life in eternity by imparting unto them eternal life today.

One who repents of their sin and puts their faith in Jesus Christ as their crucified and risen Savior and Lord is justified/pardoned and becomes God's child *legally* and *positionally* through adoption and *experientially* by regeneration. However, two points warrant further mention. First, these specific features of conversion are really concomitant aspects of one "so great a salvation" (Heb 2:3). It is critical to accent the unity of redemptive experiences while excavating their diversity.[47] Second, it has already been seen that justification and adoption exhibit pneumatic, experiential elements, as does regeneration. Nonetheless, we may still describe justification and adoption as a change of *standing* or *status* before God and regeneration/new birth as a transformed *state* of being with new life and a new nature.

---

47. There is an odd tendency to view various aspects of salvation through the lens of one of its favored features. E.g., some Lutherans appear to see salvation through the lens of justification; some Calvinists through the lens of predestination; some evangelicals through the lens of new birth; and some Wesleyans through the lens of sanctification. However, salvation itself is a broad and deep concept that should not be reduced to one of its components, no matter how appealing. All redemptive experiences share a symbiotic quality.

Assurance

Over the years I have heard countless folks give testimony at church by expressing, "I am glad I do not have a 'hope-so' salvation. I have a 'know-so' salvation!" My sister, Sharon, herself a pastor, characteristically asserts: "I know that I know!" This colorful language points toward the doctrine of assurance. Perhaps I should say the *experience* of assurance, because assurance is a doctrine actualized in a believer's personal experience. Assurance speaks of complete certainty and confidence regarding one's present experience of personal salvation.[48] Notably, Fanny Crosby penned this concept so beautifully in 1873 in the opening lines of her hymn, "Blessed Assurance": "Blessed assurance, Jesus is mine! O what a foretaste of glory divine!"[49]

Yet, a great deal of confusion over assurance is common. When my wife, Sue, worked in secular business, a Christian brother in the office constantly tried to persuade her in favor of unconditional eternal security or "once saved, always saved." He became frustrated when he failed to convince her. One day he exclaimed in exasperation, "If I didn't believe in 'once saved, always saved' how would I even know that I am saved?" Sue immediately replied, calling him by name, "It sounds like you are confusing security with assurance." He was startled but only shook his head and walked away. The Bible, however, is not confused. R. T. Kendall explains, "[Y]ou do not have to reason your way to assurance. The immediate witness of the Spirit does it for you. You feel it. You know it."[50]

As far back as Isaiah 32:17, Scripture prophesied a state of assurance for God's people that promised a time of safety and security as portrayed in an agrarian setting.[51] In the NT, Paul speaks of "full assurance" in understanding (Col 2:2) and in the power of the Holy Spirit (1 Thess 1:5). Although Paul does not use the specific terminology in Romans, his declaration that the Spirit bears witness with believer's spirit that they are God's children and heirs of God with Christ clearly describes assurance (8:12–17). For the writer of Hebrews, "full assurance" inspires diligent living through hope that endures to the end (6:11) and enables one to truly draw near to

---

48. The NT term *plērophoria*, signifying complete certainty, translates as "full assurance." Cp. Col 2:2, 1 Thess 1:5, and Heb 6:11 and 10:22.

49. Written by Fanny J. Crosby in 1873 with music by Phoebe Palmer Knapp, Blumhofer, *Her Heart Can See*, 229–30. Brown, *Spirit of Protestantism*, x–xi, suggests that good theology is often better expressed in liturgy and prayer, in singing and hymns, than in precise theological statements or didactic texts.

50. Kendall, *More of God*, 197. Interestingly, Kendall is a nondenominational writer, speaker, and teacher from a Charismatic Reformed background.

51. Translated in the NKJV as "assurance," *bĕṭaḥ* describes a state of confidence arising out of a belief or feeling of safety and security.

God in faith (10:22). John describes believers as those who speak and act in love, are of the truth, and who "assure" their hearts before God with such confidence that condemnation is entirely absent (1 John 3:18-21; cp. Rom 8:1).[52]

John eloquently elaborates on the theme of assurance in 1 John 4:17-18:

> Love has been perfected among us in this: that we may have boldness in the day of judgment; because as He is, so are we in this world. There is no fear in love; but perfect love casts out fear, because fear involves torment. But he who fears has not been made perfect in love.

Love, not *fear*, defines the believers' relationship with God in Christ. Not even the appalling prospect of judgment day disturbs this bold trust. Believers filled with God's perfect love do not fear punishment. They do not dread hell. They *know* where they stand with God. They *know* they are saved. They have assurance of salvation.

Assurance is an inner confidence, amounting to complete certitude, birthed out of faith and hope in Jesus Christ and nurtured on God's perfect love, confirmed by the Holy Spirit's witness with a believer's spirit, that he/she is right with God. In other words, assurance is an abiding confidence that one is saved. There is "perfect peace" (*shalom*) sustained by trust in the Lord (Isa 26:3).[53]

Yet, as Jeremiah mournfully lamented to the Lord, there is real danger that some are deceived into a false sense of assurance through the prevalence of false teaching (Jer 14:13). It is, therefore, necessary—however distasteful or unpleasant—to talk about the possibility of apostasy. Everyday Pentecostal vernacular calls apostasy "backsliding" or "falling away."[54] Most importantly, the Scriptures say a great deal about this subject. Joshua instructed Israel against turning aside "to the right hand or to the left," and David expressed hatred for the "work of those who fall away" (Josh 23:6; Ps 101:3). Isaiah and especially Jeremiah, as well as Hosea, frequently and

---

52. John uses *peithō*, a verb meaning to persuade or to trust, as in to assure.

53. Small wonder that assurance was a favorite topic for John Wesley who, as a young man, struggled mightily over his own salvation. See *Wesley's Works*, 1:103 (cp. 3:290–83; 8:368–71; and 12:467–73). Interestingly, Josh Samuel, *Holy Spirit in Worship Music, Preaching, and the Altar*, 235–36, connects Wesley's emphasis on assurance with Azusa Street Mission pastor William Seymour's affective spirituality and theology (cp. 178).

54. "Apostasy" (*apostasia*) means rebellion or abandonment and has become a technical term for renouncing one's faith, either literally in words or by deeds inconsistent with faith (sinful living).

graphically rebuke Israel's persistent backsliding (Isa 57:17; Jer 2:19; 3:6–25; 14:7; 31:22; 49:4; Hos 11:7; 14:4). Israelite wisdom literature chimes in against backsliding (Prov 14:14).

Jesus himself sternly warns about those "who believe for a while and in time of temptation fall away" (Luke 8:13). Paul is concerned about the influence of those who once had "faith and a good conscience" but have rejected these and, therefore, "concerning the faith have suffered shipwreck" (1 Tim 2:18–20). Paul warned against the mass falling away or departure from the faith prophesied to occur at the end of the age (2 Thess 2:3; 1 Tim 4:1–3). In ominous tones, Paul describes as "estranged from Christ" and "fallen from grace" those believers who revert to Torah observance as a means of acceptance with God (Gal 5:4). He expresses strong concerns that lack of discipline or self-scrutiny could result in a believer becoming "disqualified" in Christ's service (1 Cor 9:27; 2 Cor 13:5–7; Titus 1:6).[55] Hebrews warns against irreversible damage of falling away as a kind of re-crucifying and public shaming of the Son of God (6:3) and a falling short of God's grace (12:15). Second Peter warns readers about the possibility that they may "fall from [their] own steadfastness" (3:17)—a warning preceded by a graphic description of those who knew Jesus Christ but became "again entangled" in the world so as to "turn from the holy commandment" (2:18–22).

In plain English, it is possible for someone who has been saved, perhaps enjoyed a high degree of assurance, to subsequently backslide or fall away from Christ (to apostatize), thereby forfeiting their status in Christ and all its attendant privileges. No one can use Christian liberty as a "cloak" to excuse sinful living (1 Pet 2:16; Gal 5:13). If such a person were to pass from this life in that state, that is, without restoration (Gal 6:1), they would be forever lost. Assurance is not automatic. Assurance, like all of salvation, is relational. So long as one is in right relationship with Christ, they have full assurance. They need not fear judgment or its just punishment.

Having stated the discomfiting truth about apostasy, there is yet more to say. Now, we may consider God's keeping power. Thank God! If anyone wonders what is positive about assurance if apostasy is possible, then God's keeping power is the reassuring answer. Arising directly out of a doxology celebrating salvation, Peter moves smoothly into a description of Christians' heavenly inheritance and then flows directly into a specific affirmation of God's keeping power (1 Peter 1:3–5). A key statement for this discussion is Peter's explanation that those who have their hope in the risen Christ "are kept by the power of God through faith for salvation ready to be revealed in the last time" (1:5). The word for "kept" is *phroureō*, meaning to "keep under

---

55. "Disqualified" (*adokimos*) signifies worthless, failing the test, unfit.

watch" or to "guard," and is well translated "protected" (cp. NASB).[56] In short, God's power keeps/guards or protects believers until final salvation is realized. While Peter's qualifying phrase "through faith" prohibits any position that those who are unfaithful—casting off faith—will still be inevitably saved, this verse offers great comfort and encouragement. Human stamina is not the determinative factor for final salvation. Rather, God's power enables enduring steadfastness.

Similarly, Paul affirms both God's keeping power and the critical importance of a believer keeping faith (2 Tim 1:12; 4:7).[57] Further, Jude indicates that believers are "preserved" or kept by God "in Christ" (v. 1).[58] Just as Peter and Paul do not teach that one who dispenses with personal faith will still be saved, neither does Jude teach that one who abandons Christ will still be saved. Yet, they all clearly teach that God's keeping power enables enduring steadfastness—as does Jesus (Matt 24:13; John 10:28). Accordingly, believers who continue in a faithful relationship with Jesus Christ should be encouraged and strengthened that their final salvation is in God's hands. Therefore, the doctrine of assurance, the possibility of apostasy, and the confidence in God's keeping power are completely congruous.

A spiritually healthy doctrine of assurance carefully navigates treacherous waters amid the dangerous extremes of delusion and phobia concerning personal salvation. On the one hand, unwise acceptance of the idea of "once saved, always saved" can lull one into a sense of false security not based on scriptural reality. That could lead someone to assume wrongly that they are saved, when in reality they are not prepared for eternity. On the other hand, constant anxiety or uncertainty over whether one is saved or not, or whether one can remain so, can strain any sensitive soul to the breaking point, perhaps driving them into despair. At best, they would be robbed of the joy and peace of a satisfying Christian life; at worst, they might give up altogether. A proper theology of assurance grants confidence to face eternity without fear, while still calling believers to diligence in their manner of living in this present age. Assurance holds *confidence* and *diligence* together as a well-matched pair.

This chapter has looked at soteriological assumptions or basic ideas about salvation. It suggested that Pentecostal soteriology arises out of biblical commitments within the historical and theological trajectories of Evangelical Protestantism and Wesleyan-Arminian movements. Recognizing

---

56. New American Standard Bible: 1995 update. Cp. to the New Living Translation as well.

57. In 2 Timothy 1:12 Paul uses *phylassō*, to guard or to keep.

58. Again, *tēreō* means to keep or to guard.

that salvation is part of a broad doctrinal complex, this chapter then surveyed specific conversion experiences such as faith, repentance, justification, adoption, regeneration, and assurance with scriptural insights from a Pentecostal perspective uppermost in mind. The introductory nature of chapter 1 should helpfully set the stage for subsequent chapters; and hopefully, it has allowed the reader a glimpse at the profound nature of the Christian doctrine of salvation. Soteriology reminds me of an ocean. I have often admired the surface of the sea from the deck of a ship while wondering at the vast mysteries lying in the fathoms deep beneath. Is it not so with salvation?

2

Soteriological Foundation

(Place of Grace in Salvation)

Andrew Richie was bi-vocational for much of his ministry. While my father's life calling was evangelism and church planting, he often did carpentry work to support a family of eight. My brother and I, and sometimes my four sisters, provided a ready-made labor force. One important lesson we learned from him about building homes was the vital importance of a good foundation. The foundation is the load-bearing part of a building. Everything else rests on it. It has to be right. If the foundation is not right, everything else will be wrong. There are many important interrelated themes regarding salvation, but in the end, it all rests on God's grace. In this sense, Pentecostals can fully agree with yesteryear's great Baptist preacher Charles Spurgeon that "salvation is all of grace."[1] Not surprisingly, Anglican cleric and poet John Newton's eighteenth-century hymn "Amazing Grace" remains an all-time favorite for Pentecostals.[2] Therefore, this chapter briefly delves into a topic that could easily take up the whole book—and then still not do it justice: the soteriological significance of grace.

---

1. Spurgeon, *All of Grace*, 10.
2.. At least in my circles! John Newton, "Amazing Grace," in *Church Hymnal*, 57.

SEVERAL INTERRELATED INDISPENSABLES

Shortly, I will address grace directly. First, however, for Pentecostal soteriology, several indispensable features preface and inform a discussion of the place of grace in salvation.[3] First is the christological center. Pentecostal Christians are committed to the absolute uniqueness of Jesus Christ. Jesus is at the heart—literally at the center—of who Pentecostals are, of what they believe, and of what they do.[4] They believe Jesus preexisted from all eternity, that he is God incarnate, fully divine and fully human, that his sacrificial death provides atonement for sins, and that he rose bodily from the dead and is coming again.[5] In a capsule, Jesus alone is Lord and Savior (John 14:6; Acts 4:12). Christian soteriology arises out of the identity of Jesus Christ (Matt 16:13–17).

Then, there is the pneumatological basis to Pentecostal theology. Below I address a number of pneumatological dynamics of salvation specifically, but here a more general affirmation of the importance of pneumatology (doctrine and experience of the Holy Spirit) appears in order. Pentecostals unabashedly affirm the continuing validity of the day of Pentecost for encounter with the Holy Spirit today (Acts 2:1–4). As Keith Warrington asserts, "That which is central to being a Pentecostal is the desire to encounter the Spirit."[6] Of course, Pentecost encounters may include intense emotion, but encountering God's Spirit experientially affects personal and moral transformation.[7] Pentecostals' experiencing of the Holy Spirit includes, but is not limited to, Spirit-inspired worship and the exercise of spiritual gifts such as speaking in tongues, interpretation of tongues, prophesying, healing, and others.[8] As shall be seen, the Holy Spirit is vigorously active in salvation as well.

---

3. See Richie, *Toward a Pentecostal Theology of Religions*, chapter 2, for a fuller discussion of these key issues.

4. Arrington, *Christian Doctrine*, 2:25–26. Interestingly, Stephenson, *Types of Pentecostal Theology*, 56–57, critiques Steven Jack Land's traditional employment of the "fivefold gospel" or "full gospel" paradigm (Jesus as Savior, Sanctifier, Spirit Baptizer, Healer, and Coming King) in Land, *Pentecostal Spirituality*, out of concern for potential christological displacement, or at least, diminishment, of pneumatology. Yet even so Stephenson's intent, in my reading, does not seem to be so much a desire to conversely displace or diminish Christology as to provide an appropriate theological entry point for authentic Pentecostal pneumatology in the context of a robust Trinitarianism.

5. Arrington, *Christian Doctrine*, 2:25–116.

6. Warrington, *Encounter*, 130.

7. Cross, *Answering the Call*, 14–16, 107.

8. Kärkkäinen, *Pneumatology*, 89–92. An excellent resource on Pentecostal worship is Josh Samuel, *Holy Spirit in Worship Music*.

Next is Pentecostal theology's ecclesiological locus. For Pentecostals, no human institution or organization can begin to compare to the church for its unparalleled place in God's eternal purpose for human beings. Pentecostals do not think of the church as an organization but as an organism—a living body with Christ as its head (Eph 1:22–23).[9] The church as an institution is created by God and progressively formed throughout redemption history by saving grace in Christ.[10] The church is a fellowship with the Triune God (1 John 1:6; 1 Corinthians 1:9; 2 Corinthians 13:13). This divine fellowship goes much deeper than close association or camaraderie; it is *koinonia,* a reciprocal sharing, a mutual participation, in the life of God by believers, made possible by redemption in Jesus Christ and given and sustained by the Holy Spirit.[11] God's church is, therefore, set apart from all other religious institutions or organizations. While the church is not the way of salvation—only Jesus is the Way—it is a vehicle of salvation. The church delivers the saving message of the gospel to a world of lost sinners. Therefore, the church expresses and embodies redemption in Jesus Christ.

There is a missiological setting to Pentecostal theology. For Pentecostals, mission is the chief reason the church exists. The doctrine of the church (ecclesiology) and the doctrine of the church's mission (missiology) are inseparably linked. Likely, it would be close to impossible to overstate the importance Pentecostals attach to the mission of the church. Pentecostal missiologists Julie Ma and Wonsuk Ma affirm that, ultimately, mission belongs to God (*missio Dei*), describing God's plan to restore fallen creation, including humanity, through God's invitation to humans to participate in the outworking of that divine purpose (Matt 16:18).[12] Saving the lost represents the heart of what Jesus came to do and of what he sent his church to do (Mark 10:45; John 20:19–23). For Pentecostals, getting saved is not only about the hereafter but the here and now as well. Pentecostals believe a person who gets saved is called to bear witness so that others may come to know Christ.

Pentecostal theology obviously has a soteriological focus. Emphatically, Pentecostal theology affirms the distinctive nature and necessity of Christian salvation. It roundly rejects the ideology of religious pluralism with its dangerous tendencies to redefine Christian salvation in ambiguous

---

9. Menzies and Horton, *Bible Doctrines,* 175.

10. Duffield and Van Cleave, *Foundations of Pentecostal Theology,* 417–20, and Arrington, *Christian Doctrine* 3.166.

11. Arrington, "Ecclesiology and the Great Commission," 107–9.

12. Ma and Ma, *Mission in the Spirit,* 6 (see also 286).

terms acceptable to unbelievers.[13] Pentecostals believe that salvation from sin and from its consequences is essential, that it is the provision of Christ's atonement personally experienced through faith, and that it graciously imparts the gift of eternal life while including present commitment to lived discipleship (John 3:16; Matt 28:19).[14] Christian salvation, to state yet again what cannot be said too much, is always inextricably tied to Jesus Christ as Savior (John 3:18; 20:31).[15] For Pentecostals, Christianity is not merely a philosophy of life or worldview, nor is it simply an ethical system or set of moral values; it is eternal salvation.

Further, note an eschatological lens in Pentecostal theology. Pentecostals believe fervently in the literal coming again of Jesus Christ, with the consummation of history according to God's eternal purpose for creation. Eschatology (doctrine of the last things) is more than a key doctrinal category for Pentecostals. It is a driving force in their theology and spirituality as well as their missiology. The whole Pentecostal worldview is shaped by a self-understanding that they are humble recipients of "the last days" outpouring of the Holy Spirit (Acts 2:14–21).[16] In other words, eschatology is a lens through which Pentecostals view reality. Eschatology was critical in the origins of the Pentecostal movement and remains essential for its ongoing development.[17] No Pentecostal theology is complete without accounting for its eschatological aspects and their implications. Pentecostals' view of last things is not "pie in the sky" escapism.[18] Pentecostal eschatology is the telos—the inherent logic, the guiding rationale—for Christian faith and service. Pentecostal soteriology has an irreducible eschatological element. It does not embrace a pitiful hope limited to this life only but eyes eternity with expectant anticipation (1 Cor 15:19).

---

13. Copan, "Following a Unique Christ in a Pluralist Society."

14. Arrington, *Christian Doctrine*, 2:159. Bloesch, *Essentials of Evangelical Theology*, 172–75, is right that the atonement is one of the most misunderstood doctrines in modern theology but that its critical importance and meaning stand up well under close scrutiny.

15. See Sterling, "Our Only Hope in a Pluralistic World."

16. Similarly, an interesting story concerning Niko Njotorahardjo, an Indonesian pastor and global leader among Pentecostals, related by Djohan Handojo and Himawan Leenardo, in Njotorahardjo, *Messenger of the Third Pentecost*, 147, recounts his regular retirement to an obscure fishing spot with plain accommodations to remind himself of his humble beginnings.

17. The gist of Faupel, *Everlasting Gospel*.

18. Arrington, *Spirit-Anointed Jesus*, 352, argues from Luke 21:36 that Jesus provides the hope of "escape" as encouragement for believers to adopt an attitude of alert expectancy that becomes a source of strength during temptations and trials in this life.

Next is the biblical structure for Pentecostal theology, including soteriology. It bears repeating that Pentecostals believe the Bible to be the inspired and authoritative Word of God. Every doctrine and practice must be either evaluated and endorsed by the light of the Scriptures or firmly rejected as unreliable. Early Pentecostals reacted against an intellectual climate that placed the views of rationalists above faith in the Bible.[19] John Wesley famously said,

> I want to know one thing, the way to heaven; how to land safe on that happy shore. God Himself has condescended to teach the way; for this end He came from heaven. He hath written it down in a book. Give me that book! At any price give me the Book of God! Here is knowledge enough for me. Let me be *homo unius libri*.[20]

In Latin the preceding phrase means "Let me be a man of one book!" Only the Bible should hold supreme sway over one's life. Thus, Arrington asserts that just as Pentecostals have been called "people of the Spirit," even so they are justly called "people of the Book."[21] Pentecostals believe that the Bible is the book of salvation, and that it is the inspired narrative and explication of God's saving acts toward a world of lost and dying sinners. Even greater, it's very words when received in faith impart life to the human soul.

In chapter 1, I argued for the Wesleyan-Arminian orientation of Pentecostal theology. Here, I reiterate that theological consistency is essential. Thus said, Pentecostalism is clearly part of a particular historic theological stream; therefore, its theology should reflect this identity for purposes of consistency.[22] Specifically, John Wesley's emphasis on sanctification as a deeper experience beyond justification and on the agency of the Holy Spirit in the Christian life not only resulted in the founding of Methodism and contributed to the Holiness Movement, but eventually "became a major

---

19. Conn, *Like a Mighty Army*, xx. Contemporary Pentecostals can echo Bloesch, *Last Things*, 15, as he combats "a rationalistic spirit" but affirms "the paradoxical unity of the scriptural word and the illumination of the Holy Spirit, which brings the written Word of God to life in a divine-human encounter." Nevertheless, Bloesch, *Last Things*, 292, thinks Pentecostals tend to subordinate the Word to the Spirit, a charge that shocks Pentecostals with their characteristic commitment to a high view of scriptural inspiration and authority and insistence on a consistent hermeneutic—see Arrington, *Christian Doctrine*, 1:23–24 and 1:73–83. McGrath, *Christian Theology*, 82, comes closer than Bloesch when describing Pentecostals as suspicious of theology that "[places] too much emphasis on rational reflection . . . thereby neglecting its experiential aspects."

20. Wesley, *Wesley's Works*, 5:62.

21. Arrington, *Christian Doctrine*, 1:25.

22. Snyder, "Wesleyanism," 931.

factor in the rise of Pentecostalism."[23] While contemporary Pentecostal organizations may claim this heritage to varying degrees, and global Pentecostals are diverse and distinctive in their own identities, nevertheless, the significance of this historical trajectory is nearly universally acknowledged. Significantly, Wesleyan-Pentecostal theology turns on the pivot of grace, and Wesley unequivocally stressed the unqualified necessity of grace for salvation.[24]

BASIS IN GOD'S GRACE

One point that we discover in great theologians as diverse as Origen, Augustine, John Calvin, John Wesley, and Jonathan Edwards is the idea that salvation is grounded in the centrality of divine grace.[25] Pentecostal soteriology heartily concurs. Even so, the biblical testimony is the decisive factor. Essentially, salvific conversion occurs by God's grace through faith in Jesus Christ as crucified and risen Lord and Savior (Rom 10:9; Eph 2:8–10; Titus 2:11–14).[26] We can consider Ephesians 2:8–9 as a kind of golden text on grace.[27] It may be the most oft-quoted scriptural statement on grace by many Pentecostals (and others). Although not exhaustive by any means, a closer look at this passage serves well to introduce the topic of grace.

In the first seven verses of Ephesians chapter 2, Paul describes how those who were dead in sin have been made alive in union with Christ out of the abundance of God's mercy, love, and kindness. He has already twice mentioned grace (vv. 5, 7). Subsequently, in verses eight and nine he elaborates on grace more fully. "For by grace you have been saved through faith, and that not of yourselves; *it is* the gift of God, not of works, lest anyone should boast." A straightforward summary reading of this passage indicates that, positively speaking, salvation from death and wrath is accomplished on the basis of divine grace through the means of faith.[28] Nega-

23. Snyder, "Wesleyanism," 936.

24. Snyder, "Wesleyanism," 933. Cf. *Wesley's Works,* 2:500.

25. Even for Origen, who arguably had some inconsistent or irregular ideas about grace, grace is, nevertheless, of paramount importance. See Drewery, *Origen and the Doctrine of Grace.*

26. Arrington, *Christian Doctrine,* 2:209–27. Therefore Bloesch, *Last Things,* 15, who argues that "God's grace knows no limits in its outreach to a lost world," nevertheless insists that "it always directs'" everyone "to the cross and resurrection of Christ, for only here does God meet us as redeeming Savior and Lord."

27. This succinct statement captures and summarizes "the heart of Paul's gospel," O'Brien, *Ephesians,* 174.

28. The context makes it clear that this faith is in Jesus Christ.

tively speaking, salvation is not a result of human endeavor, which even if it were possible, would merely feed human pride; rather it is received as God's generous gift.[29]

The keyword is of course *grace (charis)*. It conveys *"the sense of a gift of kindness and favor."*[30] Interestingly, Paul uses *dōron*, which signifies a gift or a present in close proximity to *charis*, as if to further clarify, even amplify, his previous usage of grace. The emphasis is definitely on God's efficacious generosity, in contrast to the insufficiency of human works (*ergon*) or acts for obtaining salvation. We can well describe "grace" in this sense as unearned, undeserved, unmerited. God's extraordinary act of kindness is the basis for human salvation. God's grace is the antithesis of human accomplishment or achievement. No human being ever has nor ever will deserve to be saved. Salvation is by *divine favor*.

Although verses eight and nine are often quoted as a pair, verse ten is closely linked with them grammatically and thematically. "For we are His workmanship, created in Christ Jesus for good works, which God prepared beforehand that we should walk in them." It is interesting that both verses eight and ten begin with an explanatory conjunction. Translated as "for," *gar* introduces an explanation of a previously mentioned sentential element.[31] Thematically, this means that the statement on salvation by grace through faith in verses eight and nine makes clear the use of grace in verses five and seven; then, verse ten makes clear the proper relation of works to grace in view of verses eight and nine. To the point, Paul carefully explains that salvation is an unearned gift that transforms recipients.

Further, the doubled "for" statements of verses eight and ten add an emphatic element. Paul stresses the significance of the nature of salvation by grace in relation to works. The grace of God that grants salvation apart from human works creates recipients anew according to the divine design and purpose, both anticipating and enabling righteous living, thereby producing believers whose lives are characterized by good works which, nonetheless, have their origin in God and God's grace. Righteous works do not and cannot *precede* grace as a basis or grounds for receiving salvation; yet good works necessarily *succeed* the re-creative and transforming influence of the reception of saving grace. In this sense, grace is divine power for faithfully living a fruitful Christian life. Yet, grace as *divine power* is no less grace as

---

29. Again, the implication is that faith is the means through which the free gift of salvation is appropriated or personally received.

30. Mathews, "Blessing." Italics are original.

31. Lukaszewski, notes on Ephesians 2:8 and 2:10, *Syntactic Greek New Testament*.

divine favor, as it likewise finds its origin and energy in the incomparable generosity of God's extraordinary kindness.

In trying to understand Paul's teaching that grace is both divine favor and divine power, both free gift and active working, we might look at Paul's description of how grace works in his own life.[32] "But by the grace of God I am what I am, and His grace toward me was not in vain; but I labored more abundantly than they all, yet not I, but the grace of God *which was* with me" (1 Cor 15:10). In the fifteenth chapter of 1 Corinthians, Paul launches a defense of the Christian doctrine of bodily resurrection via an affirmation of the risen Christ according to the Scriptures and to eyewitness testimonies, including his own (vv. 1–8). His exalted status as an eyewitness of the risen Christ reminds Paul of his deep sense of personal unworthiness (v. 9). Yet, his humble acknowledgment practically compels him to explain his remarkable effectiveness as an apostolic minister (v. 10). Paul attributes it all to God's grace.

Paul begins verse ten with an adversative conjunction. Translated as "but," here the use of *de* expresses contrasts between the immediate clause and the one preceding it.[33] Paul thus draws a sharp contrast between his personal unworthiness acknowledged in verse nine and the effectiveness of God's grace in his life and ministry affirmed in verse ten. If I were preaching, I would probably ask for an "Amen!" right about here. Who among Christ's ministers does not sense this sharp contrast in themselves? For the purpose of this discussion, I wish to hone in on the operative agency of God's grace.

Though the passage is brief, Paul uses the word *grace* three times in verse ten. While the idea of grace as divine favor is certainly present, his accent is on grace as divine power or enablement. The word Paul uses for labor (*kopiaō*) signifies intense, extreme, arduous activity. He has worked hard for his Lord. He goes so far, apparently without any fear of rebuttal, as to flatly claim that he has worked harder than all others (that is, he has worked to a greater degree or a to greater extent). Yet, he honestly attributes this work and its effectiveness to God's enabling grace. In short, God's grace operated as divine power within him to effectively accomplish God's calling and purpose in his life and ministry. Significantly, Paul repeatedly presents this gracious divine working as a pattern for himself and for others (Eph 3:7–8; Gal 2:8; Phil 2:13).

Let us draw together the threads of this discussion so far. The salvation of sinners accomplished in Jesus Christ and appropriated by faith in

---

32. Ordinarily, "free gift" would be redundant because a gift is by nature free. However, Scripture uses this phrase to emphasize the inexpressible generosity of divine grace (Rom 5:15, 16, 18).

33. Lukaszewski, notes on 1 Corinthians 15:10, *Syntactic Greek New Testament*.

him is possible only by the agency of God's grace. God's grace arises out of the infinite abundance of God's attributes of mercy, love, and kindness, and is expressed as God's incomparable generosity in freely giving salvation to those who put their faith in Jesus. Performing righteous works does not and cannot merit or earn salvation. The nature of grace breaks human arrogance. Salvation is received only as God's generous gift. Salvation transforms sinners into a new creation, and that transformation reflects God's gracious purpose in their lives through their good works or righteous lifestyle.

More technically, Paul's declaration refutes two incorrect views. On the one hand, Paul contradicts a soteriological meritocracy based on human performance as the basis of salvation. On the other hand, he contradicts a negation of human moral accountability and culpability which would, in effect, make the ethical lives of the saved both irrelevant and optional. Negatively, Paul's doctrine of grace refutes legalism—that one can be saved by obeying laws or rules—and antinomianism—that one who is saved need not keep the commandments.[34] Grace is not reactive, it is not received as a reward for anything prior to its own reception. Grace is evocative; grace received calls into being and brings forth good works.

Positively, Paul's doctrine of grace places the initiative and accomplishment of salvation squarely with God. God freely offers the gift of salvation accomplished through Jesus Christ to whomever will freely accept by putting their faith in the crucified and risen Lord and Savior. Salvation is by God's grace, and grace is a free gift; so then, salvation is God's free gift.

THE SHAPE OF GRACE

The preceding section provided biblical understanding of the foundational nature of grace for salvation. The present section surveys foundational theological categories of grace. It is important to state that all God's grace is of a whole; that is, it is one divine grace. Even though grace can and does work in variegated ways and can be described in terms of its working—for example, justifying grace or sanctifying grace—it is, nevertheless, God's gracious working in specific fashion rather than attributable to different kinds of grace (1 Pet 4:10).

Another way of thinking about various aspects of God's one unbroken grace is in terms of human experience. A believer may experience, and therefore subsequently describe, grace differently in terms of a particular need. For example, in describing God's grace in conversion, one speaks

---

34. Although Paul develops the doctrine of grace most fully, it is also quite apparent in other canonical writers (e.g., Exod 33:12–17; 34:9; 1 Pet 1:10, 13; 4:10; 5:10, 12).

of "saving grace." When describing divine aid in a crisis, one speaks of "strengthening grace" or "sustaining grace" (2 Cor 9:8; 12:9). Moreover, in such circumstances we are describing how we experience grace in a particular manner at a particular time to match a particular need. We are not actually describing kinds of grace so much as how God applies his grace to our lives in a certain fashion. I wish to firmly assert that God's grace is not divided or fragmented; it is one; it is a whole. To illustrate, it is, of course, possible to describe a human body as a collection of several anatomical systems (e.g., cardiovascular, pulmonary, musculoskeletal, nervous, digestive). Yet, all the systems comprise one body with various functions. Similarly, God's one grace can function differently, but it is, nevertheless, undivided.

Theologians have developed technical vocabulary for describing the temporal (the when) and effectual (the how) aspects of grace at work in salvation. Grace may be described in terms of its working in people *before* they are converted, described as prevenient/preceding grace; *during* conversion, or justifying/saving grace; and *after* conversion, subsequent sanctifying grace.[35] Prevenient grace or grace that goes before (from Latin *praevenire* "to come before" or "to anticipate") describes grace at work before conversion, leading and enabling one to respond to God's offer of salvation in Christ if they will (Rom 2:4; Rev 22:17). It is different from what some call "common grace," or God's goodness toward the just and unjust, which actually may be better described as divine providence (Matt 5:45; Acts 14:17).

As it is commonly used, saving grace, also called justifying grace or converting grace, refers to grace at work in one becoming a Christian, that is, in conversion (Titus 3:4–7). The focus of saving grace is on forgiveness of sins and the gift of eternal life. Even though Protestant traditions tend to emphasize justification, so-called "justifying" grace includes, as previously stated, all that is involved in experiencing Christian conversion. Conversely, sanctifying grace refers to grace at work in renewing the image of God in converted sinners and transforming them into Christlike disciples—in other words, making them holy (Rom 15:15–16; 1 Pet 1:15). Some describe regeneration as "initial" sanctification, even though it is a conversionary experience, because it involves impartation of new life with its implanting of a new nature having holy affections or dispositions. According to this type of nomenclature, "entire" sanctification describes an experience subsequent to new birth of becoming completely or fully consecrated to God in all one's being (1 Thess 5:23). In between initial and entire sanctification is a

---

35. Another way of exploring how grace functions, popular since Augustine, is "prevenient grace" (God's grace before conversion), "operative grace" (God's grace accomplishing conversion), and "cooperative grace" (God's grace working with the renewed human will for growth in holiness), McGrath, *Christian Theology*, 369.

more or less indefinite period of spiritual formation and development that may be called "progressive" sanctification or growth in grace (2 Pet 3:18).[36] Indeed, the pursuit of holiness is (or should be!) the lifelong endeavor of every believer in continuing commitment to the standards of God's grace (Heb 12:14–15).[37]

Finally, there are long-standing debates—and as yet unresolved, at least with any satisfactory consensus—on the relation between nature and grace, especially whether divine grace is superimposed upon human nature or completes and enables human nature. This controversy is often described as "the nature-grace dialectic."[38] Although there are many thorny theological problems here, it is not really the kind of topic that attracts (or distracts!) Pentecostal theology a great deal. At the risk of oversimplification, generally it is enough for Pentecostals to understand that grace comes *from* God *to* lost humanity, *bringing* salvation (Titus 2:11–13).

However, I do not want to sound dismissive. A number of considerations are of cardinal importance. First, grace is divine in origin and action. Grace is always *God's* grace. Second, grace respects human nature as created by the God of all grace. The Creator never violates his creature. In other words, grace is not coercive. Third, human nature in its fallen, sinful state is lost and undone. We cannot save ourselves. Fourth, the image of God in human beings has not been erased and must not be ignored. Even lost human beings—although certainly not what they were created to be—are still human beings after all. Finally, the doctrines of prevenient grace and synergy address underlying concerns of the nature-grace dialectic. Prevenient grace explains how God works with lost humans to bring them to salvation; synergism explains how converted human nature responds to God's gracious working in cooperation with the Spirit of grace. In plain language, we must discern who God is and what God does without destroying our own identity, liberty, and responsibility.

However, the preceding discussion does bring us to a relevant but neglected topic: *the means of grace*. One of the reasons the topics of the relation of nature and grace and the means of grace are related is because it is critical in both to avoid any hint of human merit and to affirm fully the

---

36. See Bloesch, *Last Things*, 232.

37. Unfortunately, nineteenth-century proto-Pentecostal Andrew Murray, *Inner Life*, 47, was all too correct that a prevalence of false teaching denying the ability of the grace of Christ to make disciples holy has eroded the determination of many to pursue a life of radical obedience.

38. For a great summary of the main issues at stake see Olson, "Dialectic of 'Nature and Grace' in Christian Theology."

role of human responsibility before God in Christ.[39] The "means of grace" are those ways that God uses to work in believers to cultivate and nourish grace in their lives, confirming and strengthening them in the faith and in their faith walk. Specific means of grace include prayer, fasting, Bible reading, corporate and private worship, and observance of the ordinances or sacraments. They also include good works of all kinds, such as visiting the sick and the incarcerated, feeding and clothing the needy, honest labor, and generally loving God and neighbor in word and in deed.

Pentecostals have not traditionally utilized "means of grace" language. Although this nomenclature has a strong Wesleyan background, it likely seems a bit too formal and liturgical for many Pentecostals.[40] Pentecostals rather tend to think and to speak more in terms of spiritual disciplines or, even more so, of spiritual practices.[41] Nurturing Pentecostal spirituality are several spiritual practices, including uninhibited worship, tarrying in prayer, seasons of fasting, caring for one another, bearing witness to the world, sharing testimonies, living a life of self-sacrifice, preaching the whole gospel, healing the sick, immersing oneself in God's Word, and seeking spiritual gifts. All of these spiritual practices occur in the context of "a sense of urgency and longing in light of the soon return of Jesus."[42] The connecting point is that Pentecostals ardently insist that a strong devotional life and personal piety help one spiritually grow and stay strong as Christ's disciple. Explicitly, that is really what the means of grace are all about, too.

What Pentecostal theology needs to elucidate more consistently is that spiritual growth and formation are the work of God's grace (2 Pet 3:18; Eph 4:15). Accordingly, whatever the church or a congregation or an individual believer does to cultivate and nourish spiritual formation and growth actually commences as a response to God's grace and is, always significantly, subsequently dependent on God's grace for effectiveness or fruitfulness. I do not doubt that this plain truth is largely what Paul meant in his statement (taken by many to be cryptic) to the Christians at Philippi:

> Therefore, my beloved, as you have always obeyed, not as in my presence only, but now much more in my absence, work out your own salvation with fear and trembling; for it is God who works in you both to will and to do for *His* good pleasure. (Phil 2:12–13)

---

39. Cp. Bloesch, *Essentials of Evangelical Theology*, 212–15.

40. Anecdotally speaking, I think I hear "means of grace" terminology more today than was once the case.

41. See Richie, *Essentials*, 110.

42. Martin, *Spirit-Filled Worship*, 198.

Therefore, whether we call it "the means of grace" or "spiritual practices," let us obediently allow God's grace and power to *work in us* that we may well *work out* our salvation.

PNEUMATOLOGICAL DYNAMICS

Recently Pentecostal theologians are coming to place more emphasis on pneumatological dynamics of soteriology. For example, Frank Macchia argues in support of the Holy Spirit's participatory role in justification.[43] Of course, linking pneumatology with justification without denying Protestant Reformation views on forensic or transactional elements can be a viable approach for Pentecostal theology (1 Cor 6:11; 1 Tim 3:16). Indeed, others are coming to similar conclusions. N. T. Wright has had some personal Pentecostal experiences but is widely known primarily as an Anglican theologian. He argues that much of post-Reformation theology has simply left the Holy Spirit out of the equation on salvation. This pneumatological lacuna is particularly problematic, because it alters understanding of the means of salvation and the Christian life.[44]

Veli-Matti Kärkkäinen, a Pentecostal theologian, has argued that Western Pentecostal soteriology has some surprising similarities to Eastern Christianity's emphasis on the role of the Holy Spirit in salvation.[45] He contends that conceptions of union with God and participation in the divine nature common among Eastern Christians bear resemblances to Pentecostal understandings of sanctification and Spirit baptism (Acts 2:4; 2 Peter 1:4).[46] At least some of these similarities may be traceable to the influence on Pentecostals of John Wesley's openness to "a pneumatological understanding of the concept of grace."[47] In any case, for Pentecostals, pneumatology and soteriology are not tightly compartmentalized theological categories. Indeed, in Pentecostal theology, the Holy Spirit and salvation are more related than separated. Not surprisingly, therefore, Wright's reminder to Anglicans and

---

43. Macchia, *Justified in the Spirit*, 14, 75, 86, 202, and Bernard, *Justification and the Holy Spirit*, 11–12, 112–15, 117, 121.

44. Wright, *Justification*, 10–11.

45. Kärkkäinen, *One with God*, 4, 6, 108–114, 120, and 127.

46. With cultural and linguistic allowances. Eastern or Orthodox Christians speak of *theosis* or "divinization" where Pentecostals speak of sanctification and Spirit baptism. But both are speaking a pneumatological language. Of course, there are important caveats, such as Orthodoxy's sacramental soteriology, which is soundly rejected by Pentecostals, Kärkkäinen, *One with God*, 113–14.

47. Kärkkäinen, *One with God*, 72–80 (esp. 76). Cp. 111 and 113. See also Macchia, *Justified in the Spirit*, 68–69.

to the broader Christian community of the operative role of the Holy Spirit in God's redemptive narrative and in all of Christian faith and life resonates strongly with many Pentecostals.[48]

Chapter 1 of this volume noted that there are remarkably strong pneumatological elements in the several redemptive experiences of conversion, including repentance, justification, adoption, regeneration, and assurance. Chapter 2 has already noted that divine grace is God's favor and power or generous disposition and benevolent action. How does God's gracious disposition translate to God's benevolent action? It is by the agency of Holy Spirit. The working of the Holy Spirit is God's grace in action. Grace is both benevolent and active. The Holy Spirit lavishly conjoins these two aspects of divine grace.

Both Testaments describe the Holy Spirit as "the Spirit of Grace" (Zech 12:10; Heb 10:29). The phrase "the Spirit of Grace" is descriptive of the Spirit's direct role in actively implementing the grace of God in Christian experience. Thus, the Holy Spirit is "the gracious Spirit" or even better, "the grace-giving Spirit." In other words, the "Spirit of grace" is "the Spirit from whom we receive grace."[49] The Holy Spirit unites the divine *attribute* of grace as generous and kind disposition, that is, grace as unmerited favor, with the divine *action* of grace, that is, grace as power. As divine attribute, grace describes that which the Holy Spirit *is* (that which is true of the Holy Spirit's nature and character). That is to say, grace in this sense describes the *person* of the Holy Spirit. As divine action grace describes that which the Holy Spirit *does* (that which is true of the Holy Spirit's acts). That is to say, grace in this sense describes the *work* of the Holy Spirit.

Now it is necessary to emphatically state a fundamental principle of grace: *all grace originates in and derives its nature and character from the incomparable generosity and kindness of unmerited divine favor*. God's marvelous deeds consistently reflect the excellence of God's eternal being (Ps 150:2). What God *does* manifests who God *is*. Grace as divine power is the outflow and overflow of God's divine favor. It is not the other way around. In no manner can grace by any means be earned. Grace never takes on the qualities or traits of reward or wage. Divine grace is by definition always God's free gift. What is true of the definition is true of the implementation—grace in action is always God's free gift. God does not give grace in recognition of effort or achievement. God does not give grace as payment for service. Grace is always divine gift. Grace as divine gift is a revelatory

---

48. Wright, *Justification*, 96, 239 (cp. 247).
49. Cp. Ellingworth, *Epistle to the Hebrews*, 541.

manifestation of the graciousness of the divine being. Grace is first *who* God is and then *what* God does.[50]

Given the gift nature of grace and the association of the Holy Spirit with the work of grace, it is fascinating that the language of Scripture frequently couches reception of the Holy Spirit in the category of gift. Jesus describes reception of the Holy Spirit as the Father's gift to his children (Luke 11:13). Repentance of sin followed by baptism in water includes the promise of receiving the gift of the Holy Spirit (Acts 2:38-39). When a sorcerer sought to purchase the ability to impart the Holy Spirit, Peter rebuked him for thinking God's gift was for sale (8:20). Without partiality, both Jews and Gentiles who believe in Jesus receive the gift of the Holy Spirit (10:45; 11:17). Those who have "tasted the heavenly gift" are "partakers of the Holy Spirit" (Heb 6:4). Obviously, the Holy Spirit and the concept of gift are closely associated.

In Luke 11:13, Jesus uses the plural *domata* for gifts in a general sense of presents or that which is transferred to a person without prospect of compensation or payment. This is understandable, since Jesus is directly speaking of parental gifts of a general nature before moving to apply parental generosity to the heavenly Father's superabundant gift of the Holy Spirit. Here, Jesus does not use "gift" in direct reference of the Holy Spirit. However, the Acts references (2:38; 8:20; 10:45; 11:17) and the Hebrews reference (6:4) use *dōrea* as directly descriptive of the gift of the Holy Spirit. Two implications are important. First, *dōrea* often signifies a more formal endowment. Here, we may understand that the gift of the Holy Spirit is not a casual or impulsive gift in an informal relationship of one kind or another; rather, the gift of the Holy Spirit is God's formal or official endowment or presentation marking and ratifying God's redemptive relationship with recipients.

Second, in the NT *dōrea* always implies the grace of God.[51] Here, we return to the topic of the relationship between the Holy Spirit and God's grace. The gift of the Holy Spirit, through the risen Savior, is granted and received "as the grand blessing of the new covenant."[52] That is to say, the Holy Spirit who shares in the gracious divine disposition and acts graciously in

---

50. How might this relate, though, to the injunctions to pray, worship together, and generally practice spiritual disciplines, which we have spoken of earlier in this chapter? Do not these disciplines engender more grace for the believer? Even these may be best thought of as continuing responses to grace through faith and active obedience (Acts 13:43; Rom 1:5; 1 Cor 3:10; 2 Cor 6:1; 9:8; 1 Pet 4:10; 5:5, 10, 12; 2 Pet 3:18). These connections indicate a journey of going from grace to grace that is always initiated and enabled by the God who calls for responsive faith and obedience according to grace.

51. See Friedrich Büchsel on *dorea* and cognates in Kittel et al., *Theological Dictionary*, 2:167.

52. Jamieson et al. in *Commentary on the Whole Bible*, 2:176.

human lives is given by the Father through the Son to believers on the firm basis of grace. The Holy Spirit *is* grace; the Holy Spirit is *given* by grace; and the Holy Spirit *gives* grace. In any case, it is all of grace. The Spirit of grace! See how wonderfully appropriate is this splendid title?

In its use of the term "the gift of the Holy Spirit," scriptural consideration is not confined to charismatic manifestations. Clearly, the gift of the Spirit also "denotes the gift of grace and salvation which is always present in the heart which the Spirit enters"; but it is a serious mistake to conclude that there was (is) not room for a subsequent experience of the Spirit or that the churches both control (limit) the giving of the Spirit through Word and sacrament.[53] The contexts of Acts 2:38, 8:20, 10:45, and 11:17 as well as of Hebrews 6:4 strongly militate against such a possibility. In each of these cases, spiritual gifts were present in a prominent manner. If it is an error to limit the gift of the Spirit to charismatic manifestations—and it is—then it is the same class of mistake to limit the gift of the Spirit to salvation.[54] However, what is crucial for the present discussion of a Pentecostal theology of salvation is clear recognition of an inseverable relation between the grace of God and the gift of the Holy Spirit in both its reception and in its work in Christian faith and life.

A NEW RELATION AND A NEW CREATION

As we have seen, for Pentecostals, conversion involves making peace with God (reconciliation) through faith in Jesus Christ and becoming a new creation by the Spirit's life-changing power (Rom 5:1; 2 Cor 5:17). Yet salvation is not limited to conversion—that is, to forgiveness and entry into a new relationship with God in Christ.[55] Although we are addressing different issues from different angles, I nevertheless find much to commend in Tom Wright's insistent assertion that "Any attempt to give an account of a doctrine which screens out the call of Israel, the gift of the Spirit and/or the redemption of all creation is doomed to be less than fully biblical."[56] Obviously, being less than biblical leads inevitably to distortions. Howard Snyder and Joel Scandrett help to restore that biblical note in rather decisive fashion

---

53. Unfortunately, Lenski, *Interpretation of the Acts of the Apostles*, 109, errs here.

54. Surely, it is not inadmissible to note that spiritual gifts most commonly known as "charismatic" manifestations, the *charismata* (1 Cor 12:1–10; Heb 2:4), are literally "gifts of grace" or "grace-gifts." How could they be dismissed from a discussion of grace and the Holy Spirit?

55. Constantineanu and Scobie, eds., *Pentecostals in the 21st Century*, 5.

56. Wright, *Justification*, 250.

with their emphasis on salvation as the healing of creation, including earth and heaven and encompassing the restoration of the broken relationship between God, people, and the land.[57]

Chapter 1 looked just a bit at regeneration in terms of both an individual believer's new birth and the ultimate regeneration of the created order (re-genesis). Chapter 2 has thus far briefly addressed sanctification, both initial and entire, in terms of sanctifying grace. There remains to consider glorifying grace or glorification. The glorification of believers occurs in the context of "the redemption of all creation." Glorification is the final stage in Christian salvation. Admittedly, I say "final stage" with some slight reservation. I am reminded of a recurring experience that my wife and I have had when taking long flights involving several connections. Almost inevitably a flight attendant or a co-passenger would ask if the next stop was our "final destination." Even if the next stop were the last leg of that particular trip, Sue and I often would respond with a smiling qualification about our *final* destination from the perspective of *eternity*.[58]

Who knows what God has in store for his people throughout eternity? Even though God has revealed by his Spirit that which this world's eyes cannot see and its ears cannot hear, is there not yet more than we presently can comprehend (1 Cor 2:9–10; Rom 11:33–36)? Yet, I suppose, we do not consider "beyond glorification" (if there even is such a notion) as salvation, so much as our eternal enjoyment of the fruits of salvation. With that qualification in mind, the doctrine of glorification is where soteriology and eschatology meet and merge—an exceptionally exciting conjunction. The term *glorification* derives from the biblical teaching that believers will participate in and be transformed by divine glory (John 17:22; Rom 8:30). Eschatologically, it is directly linked to the hope of the resurrection (Ps 49:15; Dan 12:2; John 11:23–24; 1 Cor 15:20).

However, resurrection means much more than receiving a body that lives forever—although it certainly includes that much at the least (1 Cor 15:42–44). In glorification believers are completely conformed to the image of Christ (Phil 3:21). Glorified saints become just like Jesus forever (1 John 3:2). As the perfect conformity of the believer to the image of Jesus Christ, both in body and soul, glorification is the completion of sanctification as the gracious power of the Holy Spirit eventually culminates a transformative

---

57. Snyder and Scandrett, *Salvation Means Creation Healed*.

58. As Christopher Wright in *Salvation Belongs to Our God* puts it, "Biblical salvation impacts the whole of life and death in its scope. It affects time and eternity, this age and the age to come. It is above all salvation from the wrath of God so that we may live eternally with him in the new creation. But it includes many other dimensions of the saving blessing of God in this life," 195.

journey of moving "from glory to glory" (2 Cor 3:18).[59] In effect, God removes all sin from the life and presence of the redeemed and fits them for existence in the eternal estate (Eph 5:7).[60] Therefore, in a sense glorification is the end goal or telos of salvation itself (2 Tim 2:10).[61]

Salvation involves justification, adoption, regeneration, assurance, and sanctification in this life. In the age to come, it means the glorification of the inner person and the resurrection of the body in glory. Glorified persons are fitted for a glorified environment. Scripture climaxes the course of salvation history with a glorious new heaven, new earth, and new Jerusalem (Rev 21:1–5). Believers' glorification is, therefore, set within the context of the redemptive renewal of terrestrial and celestial, indeed, of cosmological, existence. Those who have believed in Jesus during this life will literally share in his glory for eternity. Succinctly, "glory" (*doxa*) refers to God's majestic honor and splendor as well as to the brightness and power of his divine presence. Glorification, therefore, denotes that upon resurrection Christians will enter into a state of glory in which they will experience God's immediate glory and enjoy Christ's abiding presence. The *glory* of *glori*fication is God's glory.

Theologically speaking, glorification is an extremely important aspect of Christian soteriology. First, the doctrine of glorification testifies to the ultimate power of God's grace to completely and permanently overcome sin and death. Second, the doctrine of glorification testifies to the incomparable splendor of God's eternal purpose for all creation and, especially, for redeemed humanity. Third, the doctrine of glorification inspires and energizes the entire Christian life in this present age with its invigorating vision of the eternal state. Fourth, glorification climaxes Christ's incarnation as his temporal self-emptying accomplishes eternal splendor for his disciples. Further, glorification fulfills Pentecost as the initial infilling of the Spirit as it will be finally experienced in its full glory.

Points one through three (above) have received some attention already, but four and five exact further comment. John's Gospel begins with a

---

59. Kendall, *More of God*, describes this journey as a series involving increasing "increments of glory," driven by the ultimate "hope of glory," 199, 200 (cp. Col 1:27). Bloesch, *Last Things*, 122, says "Sanctification as a present experience leads into glorification as a new reality."

60. Thus, all redemptive experiences, including conversion and entire sanctification, flow into and find ultimate fulfillment in glorification.

61. One is reminded of Moltmann's discussion of "the future of the spoiled life" in *Coming of God*, 116–18. Is not there a sense in which every life ending its sojourn in this world is unfinished and unfulfilled? Yet eternal life grants that each one may become the person God meant us to be, that our life reaches its "proper realization" in "its successful and completed form," Moltmann, *Coming of God*, 117.

dramatic statement of the glory of the Divine Word dwelling, literally coming to "tabernacle" among us (Christ's incarnation) (1:14). John subsequently declares, repeatedly, that Jesus became glorified in his death and resurrection (7:39; 12:16, 23; 13:31–32). In John 17:5, Jesus petitions for his return to divine glory: "And now, O Father, glorify Me together with Yourself, with the glory which I had with You before the world was" (v. 5). Therefore, the Son of God—crucified, risen, and ascended—is now "glorified." The Johannine emphasis on the glorified Christ is vividly depicted in the first chapter of Revelation (vv. 9–20). Similarly, we learn from Paul that as Jesus bore the image of humanity before being glorified, so redeemed humanity will bear the glorious image of his divinity (1 Cor 15:49). Humans, at least redeemed humans, can finally fully become what God intended when he created them in his image: *bearers of divine glory*. Thereby, the glorification of believers is the ultimate result of the incarnation and glorification of Jesus himself.

As for point five, the church's infilling with the Holy Spirit at Pentecost promises believers that the day will come when they will hear "a loud voice from heaven saying, 'Behold, the tabernacle of God *is* with men, and He will dwell with them, and they shall be His people. God Himself will be with them *and be* their God'" (Rev 21:3).[62] As Yahweh dwelled in a tabernacle made of skins among ancient Israel, as Christ came as a living tabernacle during his incarnation, as the Holy Spirit now tabernacles with the church, the Temple of the Living God, so the Lord God himself will tabernacle among all the redeemed of the ages in the eschaton.[63] Lukan and Pauline emphases on the Holy Spirit as the divine promise that began to be fulfilled at Pentecost and continues to be fulfilled in the present will be finally and fully accomplished in glorification (Luke 24:49; Acts 1:4; 2:33, 39; Gal 3:14; Eph 1:13).

At that time, the oracle of the old Hebrew prophet will come to pass: "'The latter glory of this house will be greater than the former,' says the Lord of hosts, 'and in this place I will give peace,' declares the Lord of hosts." (Hag 2:9 NASB).[64] God's people can finally fully become what God intended when God first called them out and gathered them in his name: *a habitation of divine glory*. Until that time, may all who are "reproached for the name of

---

62. Thus, Bloesch, *Last Things*, 78, states: "Pentecost is a present reality, and what remains is for this glorious and incomparable salvation to be revealed to the whole creation through a final outpouring of the Holy Spirit on all flesh (Joel 2:28; Acts 2:17)."

63. Yahweh, sometimes inaccurately transliterated as *Jehovah*, is the proper name of Israel's God (cp. Exodus 3:14).

64. The Hebrew word for glory, *kā·bôd*, describes a heaviness or weightiness figuratively signifying honor, power, splendor resting upon a person or place, but particularly upon the Lord God. Indeed, "the Glory" is a title for God (Ps 106:20; Jer 2:11; Hos 4:7).

Christ" be blessed and may "the Spirit of glory and of God" rest upon them (1 Pet 4:4); for the glorification of believers is the ultimate fulfillment of the promise of the Spirit of Pentecost.

Presently therefore, we can say that when the Spirit of grace first begins drawing a lost sinner to repentance and faith, that his/her glorification is already in the divine mind as that consummation toward which all the work of grace in that person's whole life is ever directed. Christianity is an eschatological religion, and the Christian doctrine of salvation is no exception. Quite to the contrary, salvation is from beginning to end about preparing for and finally entering eternity in glory. Many believers describe passing from this life to the next as "going to glory"—and so it is, although glorification awaits resurrection.

Focusing on eternal glory does not lessen responsibilities for life in this present age, but it does put them into proper perspective. The present world is penultimate. I grew up hearing Pentecostals enthusiastically sing:

> I do not want to get adjusted to this world, to this world;
> I've got a home that's so much better,
> I want to go to sooner or later,
> I do not want to get adjusted to this world.[65]

Admittedly, I wondered then why they would adopt this attitude. Now I know. Christians are "sojourners and pilgrims" traveling through this world on the way to a better place (1 Pet 2:11; Heb 11:13-16). I remember hearing my Pentecostal mothers and fathers in the faith say that this world is "a rehearsal" for eternity. Of course, we might add, the rehearsal is important; it is where we all get ready—agreed; but let's not get it mixed up with the real thing. It certainly must not become all-important or most important. Although, wouldn't that be like us? To get all caught up in the rehearsal but miss the play or the wedding, that is, to miss the main event? Eternity is real! How we live in this world is vitally important not because it is all there is to life, but precisely because there is more to come. There is *glory* to come.

Preceding grace. Justifying grace. Sanctifying grace. Glorifying grace. It is all *saving grace*. Therefore, the Bible says, "You are saved by grace"!

In his classic text on God's attributes, the great devotional theologian A. W. Tozer observes that all human language falls far short of describing exactly what God is like. The best we can do is "to use a great many 'like' words" in an attempt to make the unfamiliar and incomprehensible a bit more familiar and comprehensible, that is, a bit more knowable. In some sense, God is "like" this or like "that," but then of course, we confess that

---

65. Sanford J. Massengale, "I Do not Want to Get Adjusted (To This World)," in *Church Hymnal*, 218.

"slavish literalism" toward our analogies would be yet another and perhaps more grievous error.[66] Our comparisons are always incomplete and partial. Our analogy is always imperfect. God is ultimately incomparable.

For me, the working of the Holy Spirit and the power of God's saving grace in Jesus Christ is like a great river (cp. John 7:37–39). Perhaps this analogy suits me, partly because boating, canoeing, kayaking, and rafting are family hobbies. On the other hand, maybe it is because a river is such a universal symbol of life and power. In any case, a river system has headwaters, a main trunk, branches, and tributaries that nevertheless flow together as one. Eventually, all this water from rivers and streams runs into the ocean or into an inland body of water such as a lake. Personally, it helps me to remember this analogy when I am attempting to trace out the myriad workings of God's ever-amazing grace, that grace always comes down to God's ultimate purpose in Jesus Christ of saving lost humanity and of restoring broken creation.

Ephesians 1:7–10 really sums up the indescribable, unfathomable, immeasurable "riches of His grace":

> In Him we have redemption through His blood, the forgiveness of sins, according to the riches of His grace which He made to abound toward us in all wisdom and prudence, having made known to us the mystery of His will, according to His good pleasure which He purposed in Himself, that in the dispensation of the fullness of the times He might gather together in one all things in Christ, both which are in heaven and which are on earth—in Him.

Ultimately, and by design, grace all comes down to God's saving purpose in Jesus Christ. Accordingly, I utter a hearty "Amen!" to Spurgeon's fervent prayer: "O blessed Spirit of all grace, make it so!"[67]

---

66. Tozer, *Knowledge of the Holy*, 6–7.
67. Spurgeon, *All of Grace*, 11.

3

Paradigmatic Soteriology

(Models of Salvation)

One of the many strengths of Pentecostal movements is their incredible versatility. Pentecostals are able to adapt to vastly different environments, functions, or activities. However, Pentecostal versatility is not due to changeableness or inconstancy. It is rather like my wife's prized kitchen mixer, which has several different attachments and, therefore, a wide variety of culinary uses, but never becomes other than what it is. Pentecostals, moreover, at their core are established on a clear underlying unity. Thus, we can discern certain models of salvation that distinctively coalesce in Pentecostal understandings of salvation. Paradigmatic models serving as primary indicators of distinctive Pentecostal soteriological emphases include the exodus of Israel, the ministries of Jesus and of the apostles, and *Christus Victor* atonement theology.[1] This chapter will examine and expound on the meaning and significance of these models for a Pentecostal theology of salvation.[2]

1. *Christus Victor* is Latin for "Christ the Victor." A concept of Christ's atonement as a victory over evil will be clarified further in the following pages.

2. McGrath, *Christian Theology*, 349, helpfully explains that throughout Christian history and in the present, "the notion of salvation" has involved *contextualization* via a *receptor-orientation* in which various emphases have come to the fore based on specific needs in a given culture or time. As McGrath also notes, 349, a difference of *emphasis* is consistent with the authentic nature of salvation; indeed, it would be a mistake to truncate salvation by reducing it exclusively to any one model.

AN EXODUS SALVATION MODEL

Historic Christianity has long drawn on the exodus tradition in its self-definition regarding typological implications of the incarnation and atonement of Jesus Christ.[3] Similarly, African American spirituality and theology, immensely influential in the Pentecostal movement, draws from the liberative elements of the biblical narrative in an embrace of God as emancipator.[4] These historic trajectories are firmly rooted in Scripture. Pentecostal NT commentator James Shelton explains that Matthew's Gospel presents the ministry of Jesus in terms of fulfillment of the exodus deliverance and as an indicator of the nature of God's saving acts.[5] Arrington delineates parallels in Acts between Moses and Jesus with Israel's deliverance prefiguring "God's mighty saving act from our bondage through Christ."[6] Pentecostal theologian Daniel Pecota stresses the nature of Christian salvation as rooted in the experience of deliverance arising out of the exodus event and in ongoing deliverance themes throughout Israel's subsequent salvation history.[7] Divine deliverance, emancipation if you will, occurs in natural/physical, legal, or spiritual contexts but with emphasis on the spiritual. Yahweh's deliverance or salvation of Israel out of the hands of the Egyptians is prototypical of Christian salvation and anticipates the mission of Jesus Christ to seek and to save and deliver the lost by setting rescued captives free (Luke 19:10; 4:16–19).

Pentecostal soteriology largely "spiritualizes" the exodus tradition. This does not mean that Pentecostals question the historicity or literalness of the exodus event. Quite the contrary. Rather, it is a normal application of an already evident emphasis alluded to above. Pentecostals interpret the exodus primarily in a spiritual sense. Thus, *Israel's exodus represents rescue from bondage to sin and death in order to worship the Lord in freedom and to receive a heavenly inheritance.* I agree that this is a correct application of the exodus event for Christians.[8] I add, however, that it is not complete in and of

---

3. Kärkkäinen, *Spirit and Salvation*, 291. As Moltmann, *Coming of God*, 67, notes, "Israelite faith in God was determined by the Exodus experience." It should not be surprising that it would have important implications for the Christian faith as well.

4. Alexander, *Black Fire*, 39, 40. The exodus tradition is particularly prominent in this emphasis, portraying a God of freedom who befriends and defends the oppressed and sends his Son as liberator even as he calls forth obedience from his people. See Fields, *Black Theology*, 18, 31, 87–88.

5. Shelton, "Matthew," 139–40.

6. Arrington, *Spirit-Anointed Jesus*, 146.

7. Pecota, "Saving Work of Christ," 325–29.

8. For McGrath, *Born to Wonder*, 93, "The Passover celebration recalled the events of the Exodus and their significance, thus becoming a focus for Israel's memory of its

itself. First, I will unpack the spiritual application of the exodus event; then, I will offer suggestions for its expansion.

A number of questions quickly come to mind. What is bondage to sin and death? In what sense does "rescue" describe "salvation"? Is freedom a necessary requirement for divine worship? Why is a believer's inheritance couched in terms of the "heavenly"—and what does that mean anyway? There are other questions that could be raised, but these will serve to discuss a Pentecostal appropriation of the exodus theme for its understanding of soteriology.

First, what is bondage to sin and death? Of course, this nomenclature owes its existence to the fact that ancient Israelites were literally slaves in the ancient Egyptian empire until the Lord set them free, and that this redemptive liberation formed the basis of their covenantal relationship—of which the Hebrew prophets reminded their descendants (Jer 34:13; Mic 6:4). Jesus, in turn, disturbed some Jewish religious leaders by applying this theme to slavery to sin with its consequences and to the need for liberation by the Son (John 8:34–36). The apostles, subsequently, continue and develop this theme of bondage to sin and death with redemption as freedom unto life (Rom 6:15–23; 2 Pet 2:19).

In terms of Pentecostal soteriology, I suggest that bondage to sin and death describes sin's enslaving nature with its damnable consequences.[9] Sin dominates, destroys, and, ultimately, damns human beings. In chapter 1, we talked about the Genesis account of human beings falling into sin, thus becoming distorted, twisted, and lost. Fallen human beings are controlled by sin's addictive and forceful influence in their lives. Sin's control may manifest itself overtly in some cases as openly profligate behavior. In other cases, it may appear in a more covert manner through insidious attitudes and surreptitious actions. In either case, the damaging impact of sin on human existence occurs. At best, human flourishing is dampened; at worst, individuals, marriages, families, even entire nations, and, actually, the whole world, exists in self-destruct mode. In reality and by far the worst of all, sin places humanity in violent opposition to God's righteous will thereby

---

past and its hopes for its future."

9. Slavery, in comparison to indenture, means that slaves are unable to liberate themselves legally. Even if they were to run away, they are technically still under the bondage of slavery. Understanding sin as slavery also emphasizes its structural and societal nature, rather than just individual and personal nature and behavior. And yet, another aspect of a slave is that they cannot choose their master nor choose to serve another master. This was the whole purpose of the exodus—while Israel was enslaved to Pharaoh (considered a demigod and, therefore, they were enslaved to idolatry) then they could not choose to worship Yahweh. Only once Yahweh defeated Pharaoh and rescued them were they free to worship Yahweh.

incurring the just condemnation (judgment) of eternal punishment. Every January, the President of the United States gives a State of the Union address to a joint session of Congress. More important to recognize is the bondage to sin and death that describe the state of a lost and dying world.

Second, in what sense does "deliverance" describe "salvation"? The Lord's intent and subsequent deliverance or rescue of Israel from Egyptian bondage (Exod 6:6) became an identifying characteristic of Israel among other nations and a guiding motivation for their trust in the Lord—as well as a basis of reproof for lack of trust (Exod 18:10; Judg 10:11). As it did with many poets and prophets, the Lord's role as deliverer became a central image in the Psalms (18:2, 50; 32:7; 40:17; 70:5; 144:2).[10] In fact, the prophet Joel links last days deliverance and salvation in a key text for Peter's Pentecost Day sermon (Joel 2:32; Acts 2:21). Paul aptly understands salvation to include deliverance from this present evil age (Gal 1:4), from the power of darkness (Col 1:13), and from the wrath to come (1 Thess 1:10).

In terms of Pentecostal soteriology, deliverance describes the divine act of abolishing and breaking the overwhelming power of sin's domination of human life with its restrictive and debilitative effects.[11] God's redemptive act in Jesus Christ has formally ended sin's authority. It has functionally severed sin's shackles for the redeemed. Sin no longer has the authority or ability to control human lives. Believers can begin to live the full, and fulfilling, life for which God created them. As chapter 1 of this volume indicated, salvation is multifaceted. Certainly, forgiveness and justification are pivotal. Yet, any salvation that leaves believers "under the heel" of the oppressor is hardly worthy of the name. That is where deliverance comes into the soteriological picture. The Lord delivers—rescues—from sin. Christians are not merely "saved sinners"; they have been rescued from sin. Christians are not saved *in* sin but *from* sin (Matt 1:21).

Salvation as deliverance has significant implications for life in this age as well as in that which is to come. Believers may now live an overcoming, victorious life, because they are no longer controlled by sin. True, the battle is not over. Indeed, it is far from over. Yet, the decisive victory has been won. Pharaoh chased Israel to the Red Sea. However, on the other side of the Red Sea they encountered other obstacles to their progress that had to be

---

10. Also, this theme occurs in Isaiah 40–55 (e.g., Isa 43:16–21). While these texts point to a second exodus, it is on the basis of the consistency and sovereignty of God as deliverer.

11. It is a very combative idea in the Exodus and other OT texts. It points to God as a warrior defeating the other gods. E.g., see the Song of Moses and Miriam (Exod 15; Isa 51:9–11). In this sense, the exodus in the OT is also very cosmological—which lends itself well to *Christus Victor* atonement theology.

confronted and overcome. Even in Canaan (the promised land!), they fought to root out resistant enemies. Yet the Lord, who had decisively acted to deliver them from Egypt, continued to deliver them as further needs arose—so long as they trusted him. It is so with believers today. In this life, we continue to encounter trials and tribulations; but the Lord continues to deliver. Sin no longer has the upper hand. Sin is not in control. The Lord delivers!

Third, is freedom a necessary requirement for divine worship? Salvation as deliverance clearly indicates that salvation brings freedom. To put it more directly, salvation bestows freedom on believers. In terms of negation, believers are no longer slaves to sin, no longer subjugated to its tyranny. Believers have been released from sin's restraints. Affirmatively, believers are free to be and do according to God's will. In a word, they are *free* to worship the Lord as they ought. In the canonical account of Israel's exodus, the Lord repeatedly declares some variation of "Let my people go that they may serve me" (Exod 8:1, 20; 9:1, 13; 10:3; cp. 5:1; 7:16).[12] The Lord's stated objective or purpose for Israel's liberation was that they might be *free* to serve or worship him.[13]

In terms of Pentecostal soteriology, I suggest that the telos of Christian liberty has a doxological or liturgical orientation. Redemption's end goal or ultimate purpose is freedom *from* sin's tyranny *for* divine service. Christian freedom is not licentiousness. Christian freedom may be properly described as principled liberty. But even that principled liberty has a specific directive. "Orientation" describes the direction toward which an object or interest is turned. For example, a particular blog may be oriented toward the business community or entertainment industry or medical field. Everything on its site will be directed toward the furtherance of its focused interest among readers. So, everything in the Christian life is directed toward or oriented to the purpose of serving the Lord. Even more specifically, serving the Lord has a liturgical nature. Although liturgy is frequently understood to refer to formal aspects of ritual worship, the term itself connotes an idea of ministry or service to or for the divine. In other words, liturgy is worship.[14]

Another way to put it would be to say that Christian freedom is doxological in nature. That is, redemption frees believers from sin *in order to* serve the Lord through a life of praise.[15] Doxology, or giving praise to God,

12. Being enslaved meant they did not have this freedom. Even though they were descendants of Abraham and were the covenant people, freedom to freely worship Yahweh for this enslaved generation only occurred as a result of the exodus deliverance.

13. The Hebrew (ʿābad) signifies work of various kinds, including ritual service or divine worship.

14. Cairns, "Worship," 265.

15. This is also observed in the exodus as the people enthusiastically sang the

involves both specific acts in corporate and private worship and an entire lifestyle dedicated to glorifying God. Pentecostals are all about worship. We are widely known for enthusiastic worship in our corporate gatherings. That is good, for we are redeemed in order to worship the Lord. Salvation sets us free to worship the Lord. Yet, worship also includes serving the Lord in the beauty or splendor of holiness (Ps 29:2; 96:9). Worship is both a corporate act before God and a personal way of being with God in this world. Worship is a way of life.

Fundamentally, Christians are delivered from sin for service to the Lord. Believers are set free from sin's oppressive tyranny in order to serve the Lord freely in love. Salvation is not merely a "get out of hell free card." It is not merely "a ticket to paradise." Salvation is being set free from the bondage of sin in order to freely and lovingly serve and worship the Lord who is the Deliverer.

Fourth, why is a believer's inheritance couched in terms of the "heavenly"? And what does that mean anyway? In the exodus event, the Lord promised Israel an earthly inheritance consisting of the land of Canaan (Lev 20:24).[16] Jesus affirmed an earthly aspect of inheritance (Matt 5:5) but extended inheritance to include eternal life (19:29; cp. Mark 10:29–31) and the kingdom of God (Matt 25:34). Paul proclaimed an inheritance for those who are sanctified by faith in Jesus (Acts 20:32). Like Jesus, his summary descriptive term for the Christian's inheritance is the kingdom of God (1 Cor 6:9–10; 15:50; Gal 5:21; Eph 5:5). This inheritance, obtained in Christ (Eph 1:11) and guaranteed by the Holy Spirit (1:13), is the "riches of glory" received by the "saints in the light" (1:18; Col 1:12). It is a reward for serving the Lord Christ (Col 3:24). Hebrews describes the believer's inheritance as "salvation" in fulfillment of God's promises (1:14; 6:12). It is eternal in nature (9:15). Peter directly declares that believers have "an inheritance incorruptible and undefiled and that does not fade away, reserved in heaven" (1 Pet 1:4). God himself sums it all up in Revelation: "He who overcomes shall inherit all things, and I will be his God and he shall be My son" (21:7).

In terms of Pentecostal soteriology, a heavenly inheritance signifies the transcendent quality of the believer's eternal state. What believers will receive from God through the Lord Jesus Christ is above and beyond the range of human comprehension and experience. It is divine in origin. It is

---

praises of Yahweh to celebrate his victory over Pharaoh (see the Song of Moses and Miriam in Exodus 15).

16. The victory of Yahweh was cosmological (Exod 15:11) and universal (15:14–15). In one sense, the exodus functions as a paradigm or architectural model—what God did for one small people group (the Israelites), he will then do for all people through Christ (the world).

everlasting in duration. It is indescribable. "I Can Only Imagine" by Mercy Me is one of my all-time favorite songs.[17] We played it at my father's funeral. But really, I cannot even imagine heaven. It is beyond me. Yet, "heavenly" means more than location. Although Pentecostals believe their spirit will go to heaven when they die, they do not see themselves spending eternity in an ethereal existence (as cherubs floating on a cloud playing a harp). Belief in a literal new heaven and new earth in the eschatological consummation of history provides the basis for a conviction that their eternal existence will involve transitioning into this real mode of being in resurrected, glorified bodies (see chapter 2). Israel's inheritance of a new land transposes into the Christians' inheritance of a new world (Heb 12:18–22). Most of all, in its central and primary aspects, the believers' heavenly inheritance or reward means enjoying God's immediate presence and unfathomable blessings forever.

According to Revelation 21:4, "God will wipe away every tear from their eyes; there shall be no more death, nor sorrow, nor crying. There shall be no more pain, for the former things have passed away." This is a nullifying definition of eternal existence. Eternity will be good because of all the bad that is *not* there. Positive descriptions of the heavenly city or new Jerusalem with gates of pearl and a street of gold with walls of jasper (21:9–21), and so on, portray the brilliant splendor of heavenly existence. Even more importantly, the glory of God and of the Lamb will be there (21:22–27). Finally, the river of life (22:1–5) speaks of an unending life of unimaginable flourishing.

Pentecostalism is a hopeful faith. It entertains expectations that reach beyond this present age to lay claim on eternity itself. It anticipates a heavenly inheritance. Pentecostal soteriology is forward-looking; it is future-oriented. However, hope for eternity transforms the present, infuses it with fresh energy, and fills it with amazing stamina. Pentecostal soteriology enables believers to cross the deserts of this world, fighting giants all the way, without turning back or quitting, because they are headed toward a better time and place that they will inherit from their Lord.

In the previous paragraphs I have asserted that Pentecostal spiritualization of the exodus theme for soteriological understanding is correct. I now suggest that it is incomplete. Accordingly, what follows does not intend to invalidate that which has preceded it. However, it does intend to develop it further. In reality, I am not saying anything new, not even for Pentecostals. Black Pentecostals, as already alluded to above, have long recognized and emphasized the point I wish to make now. My main point is that the exodus

---

17. See Millard, *I Can Only Imagine*.

event, while primarily a spiritual event, was not solely a spiritual event. It was also an ethical, political, even an economical, event. Perhaps it would be better to say that the exodus had a social nature.

One nation or race of people had been enslaved and oppressed by another. The Lord, through Moses, set them free and, in due time, gave them their own land, their own country.[18] I suggest that the exodus event demonstrates that the Lord is opposed to the oppression of any group of (apparently) powerless people by any other (superficially) powerful group of people. I further suggest that the Lord sends "deliverers" to lead the oppressed into freedom. I also suggest that salvation should include commitment to the liberty of ourselves and of others in this world, as well as in the next. Finally, the liberation of the oppressed includes commitment to establishing them in their own place.

I am arguing that the implications of the exodus are not only spiritual but also social (*slavery* of a people group indicates a social construct and social control). I am not arguing that the latter should subsume the former. However, I am arguing that the spiritual should include the social. John Wesley is well known for his insistence that Christianity is a "social religion" and that to turn it into a "solitary religion" destroys it.[19] He was right. Christianity is relational. It involves our vertical relationship with the Lord and our horizontal relationship with our neighbors—and both relationships are rooted in holy love (Matt 22:37–40). Incontrovertibly, the spiritual experience of salvation should extend to its social implications.

If the spiritual experience of salvation extends to social responsibilities, then it is evident that the spiritual is first and not the other way around. In describing the order of creation and incarnation and their implications for the doctrine of the resurrection, Paul says the natural comes first and then the spiritual (1 Cor 15:46). And truly, as unregenerate human beings, we were natural before we became spiritual. However, when it comes to

---

18. Arguably, God liberated the Israelites not merely because God hates slavery—although he does hate slavery—but because of God's commitment and faithfulness to covenant. The Israelites cried out, and God responded on the basis of covenant (Exod 2:23–25). Then, in the giving of the law, slavery of others was included in the law. While an Israelite could be enslaved, there was provision for liberation. Apparently, the care for slaves included in the Decalogue indicates a trajectory towards liberation (Deut 5:15). In a paradigm or architectural model, what God did with the Israelites in the micro points to God's heart for the macro, that is, for social transformation of all people groups so that liberation is possible for all.

19. Wesley, "Upon Our Lord's Sermon on the Mount." While we are on the subject, Peter Althouse, *Spirit of the Last Days*, is on the right track when he concludes that Pentecostal theology needs revisioning away from dispensationalist fundamentalism in a manner that recovers prophetic elements of early Pentecostalism and invites social engagement yet remains "personal and social in breadth," 193–97 (esp. 196–97).

the priorities of regenerate believers, the spiritual must always eclipse the natural (Matt 6:33). Accordingly, we receive the apostolic injunction not to love the things of this world but rather to the love God the Father (1 John 2:15–17).

To be clear, helping oppressed people experience liberty and abundance is not loving this world over God the Father. However, focusing on peoples' needs in this world rather than for the next is a grievous and serious displacement of priorities. If it is contrary to true faith to say casually to someone in dire straits, "Depart in peace, be warmed and filled" (Jas 2:16), without attempting to minister to their physical needs, what would it be to give them physical and temporal warmth and fullness but to leave their spiritual and eternal needs unmet? Should their souls be left naked and hungry while their bodies are covered and nourished? By no means! Nevertheless, as Jesus said on another topic, we ought to do the spiritual first without leaving the other undone (Matt 23:23).

This section has presented an exodus model of salvation as uniquely viable for Pentecostal soteriology. It does not deny that other Christians utilize this model in some sense. Rather, a Pentecostal appropriation of the exodus distinctively emphasizes the deliverance nature of salvation with significant implications. Neither does it imply that an exodus model emphasizing salvation as deliverance should exclude a forensic justification model or a therapeutic/transformative regeneration/sanctification model. Rather, a Pentecostal appropriation of the exodus complements these other salvation models—and vice versa. Yet, the deliverance element of salvation must not be assimilated into others. Salvation *is* deliverance.

As we have already seen, an exodus deliverance theme encountered in the OT extends into the NT through the ministry of Jesus Christ and of the apostles. Restorationist aspirations regarding NT apostolic Christianity likely account for, at least in large part, Pentecostals' strong attraction to this model.[20] Nevertheless, a specific theology of the atonement undergirds and extends Pentecostal soteriology consistently with its understanding of Jesus Christ as the Ultimate Deliverer of those who put their faith and trust in him. The following section begins to delve into that salvation model.

---

20. Interestingly, Indonesian Pentecostal Niko Njotorahardjo, who emphasizes miraculous healings in his ministry, stresses in *Messenger of the Third Pentecost*, 123–24, that "The restoration has already started since now, but when [Jesus] comes back, the restoration will have been finished perfectly." Cp. *Messenger of the Third Pentecost*, 159–60 and 170, 173.

A *CHRISTUS VICTOR* SALVATION MODEL

Christ's atoning death is of central significance for Christian doctrine. It may be appropriately grouped with foundational truths regarding the triune God's sovereign majesty, with Christ's deity, bodily resurrection, and coming again, with the Holy Spirit's ministry, with scriptural inspiration and authority, and with biblical mandates on personal integrity and sexual morality.[21] Accordingly, we should approach it circumspectly.

Predominant during patristic times, *Christus Victor* theology is a comfortable fit for contemporary Pentecostals.[22] *Christus Victor* emphasizes the nature of Christ's atonement as a ransom (Mark 10:45; 1 Tim 2:6). Christ's atonement effectively defeated the devil (Heb 2:24; Col 2:15; Rev 5:5); death and hell have been conquered (1 Cor 15:54–57; Rev 1:18). As promised by God, the seed of the woman (the Messiah) has crushed the head of the serpent (Satan) (Gen 3:15). For Pecota, "Seeing the Atonement as the victory over all the forces of evil must always be a vital part of our victorious proclamation of the gospel."[23] Likewise, Larry Hart underscores that "the concept of the atonement as a cosmic conflict and divine victory is central to the New Testament witness and the faith of the Church."[24]

In the exodus event, Yahweh delivered Israel from Pharaoh and from Egyptian bondage, thus setting them on their journey toward the promised land that flowed with milk and honey.[25] At Calvary, Christ delivered those who believe from bondage to sin, death, and the devil, thus setting them on their way to glory. Salvation is deliverance and rescue from bitter servitude to evil and its attendant afflictions for the sake of freely serving the Lord and enjoying the abundance of divine blessings as heirs of eternal glory and joy. Decisively, salvation *is* victory.

21. Also, see Arrington, *Foundations*, 164.

22. The classic study is Gustaf Aulén, *Christus Victor*. According to McGrath, *Christian Theology*, 354, this view of the atonement remained popular until it ran aground of Enlightenment thinkers' rejection of "belief in objective evil spirits or a personal devil." Obviously, Pentecostals do not share that Enlightenment bias.

23. Pecota, "Saving Work of Christ," 339. Cp. Bloesch, *Last Things*, 214, 215–16.

24. Hart, *Truth Aflame*, 364. I will say more on the topic of these evil powers in chapter 5. For the time being, note with Don Thorsen, *An Exploration of Christian Theology*, 151, that although we know few details about the origin of these spiritual beings, it seems clear that they are personal beings who abused their power of free will for sinful purposes.

25. Again, this is also understood in cosmic terms in the OT. It is Yahweh's defeat of the gods and idolatry—the use of plagues, miracles and signs, God splits the water, etc., are all part of the battle. So, there is more here that we could unpack and connect with the NT. OT scholar Peter Enns has some great resources on his blog "Yahweh, Creation, and the Cosmic Battle."

One notices that the exodus model, discussed in the previous section, and the *Christus Victor* atonement model, now under discussion, intersect with each other and overlap at points. Not surprisingly, the songs of Moses and of Israel and Miriam celebrate the Lord as a "Man of War" who has triumphed over his enemies, pointing to not only Pharaoh and the Egyptians but especially to the false gods of the day (Exod 15:1–21). Accordingly, as Israel's exodus was finally accomplished with the Passover sacrifice, so Christians believe that "Christ, our Passover, was sacrificed for us" (1 Cor 5:7). The atoning death of Jesus Christ forms the basis for deliverance from sin and death and for all the attendant blessings that follow.

The following first describes the general basis of atonement theology in the Scriptures. Then, it surveys several leading theories of the atonement that have been suggested as primary models by which to interpret the significance of Christ's atoning death. Finally, it suggests specifics for how Pentecostal soteriology utilizes the *Christus Victor* model as a resource. Before beginning, it is needful to note that the doctrine of the atonement is irreducible to a single explanatory theory. The atonement of Christ is an immense, boundless truth that defies exhaustive explication. Rather than trying to select a single theory as a comprehensive description, it is better to see each one as communicating various aspects of overall atonement truth. However, this plurality of atonement theories is not a hindrance to understanding but is, instead, an enormous boon. Diamonds are usually cut to be multifaceted, that is, with many angled flat surfaces, because this increases their ability to reflect light. Even so, the atonement's multifaceted nature better illumines the depths of meaning inherent in Christ's death.

At its heart, the atonement is about the forgiveness of sins through Christ's death on the cross. The term itself expresses the notion of divine forgiveness as a removal or covering over of human guilt and, consequently, a turning away of God's wrath.[26] In Hebrew, the concept of atonement is expressed with the root *kpr*. From this root comes the verb *kāpar*, "to atone" the most frequent word for atonement in the OT and the nouns *kappōret*, "mercy seat," and *kippurîm*, "atonement." Among the Greek terms employed by the Septuagint (pre-Christian Greek translation of Hebrew Scriptures) to express the concept of atonement, three significant words are used by the NT. In the Septuagint, *kappōret* usually is translated as *hilastērion* ("mercy seat"); *kāpar* occasionally is rendered as *hilaskomai* ("make atonement"); and *kippurîm* sometimes is translated as *hilasmos* ("sacrifice of atonement").

---

26. This section draws on the brief but excellent survey of the concept of atonement by Rodrigues, "Atonement."

These three Greek words, the most commonly used to describe atonement in NT Greek, occur twice each in the NT.

The English word emphasizes the idea of "at-one-ment" in expressing the reconciliatory aspect of Christ's death.[27] Thus, emphasis is on the result of the atonement. In this vein, atonement signifies the healing of the broken relationship between God and humanity that Christ's death accomplishes. One advantage of the English term is that it enables those who may hold various theories of the intricate meanings of Christ's death to, nonetheless, agree on the ultimate significance of the cross of Christ. Yet, the term is biblical in a descriptive sense. That is, atonement accurately describes the Bible's teaching on the consequent purpose of Christ's atoning death. The specific biblical terminology, especially in the original languages, directs believers into the deeper significance of the intrinsic nature of atonement in Jesus Christ.

The OT describes atonement primarily as a ritual activity (especially in Leviticus). The atonement concept assumes that the relationship between human beings and God is fractured but can be temporarily restored by religious rituals. The verb *kāpar* literally means "to cover." Therefore, atonement is envisioned as covering over sin and, thus, cleaning it up. OT atonement rituals rely on animal sacrifices mediated by priests and taking place in the tabernacle or, later, in the temple. Their main outcomes are expiation and purification. The ruptured relationship between God and human beings is caused by human iniquity or sin. Sin contaminates life and causes a negative divine reaction (God's righteous judgment and wrath). Atonement or removal of iniquity produces purification on the human side and appeasement or propitiation on the divine side. Thus, the broader meaning of atonement is forgiveness. In short, the OT atonement ritual illustrates what it means to say that human sins are covered or forgiven by God.

The NT concept of atonement assumes the OT concept but explicitly elaborates it from a christological perspective. Jesus Christ is the priest who executes atonement (vb. *hilaskomai*; Heb 2:17); he functions as the means or place of atonement (*hilastērion*; Rom 3:25); and consummates the sacrifice of atonement (*hilasmos*; 1 John 2:2; 4:10). In the NT, expiation or divine forgiveness of sins is provided by Christ through his death on the cross.

To draw all this together, the biblical doctrine of the atonement teaches that Christ's death accomplishes forgiveness and cleansing of human sin. The so-called "theories" of the atonement seek to understand how the atonement works and to enumerate implications for Christian identity

---

27. Harvey, "Atonement," 33–35, in his *Theological Terms*, 33.

PARADIGMATIC SOTERIOLOGY 73

and existence. Yet, it is imperative to bear in mind that the atonement is not a theory; "it is an event, an act of God in history, a sacrifice by which God's justice is satisfied, man's sins covered, perfect love fulfilled and set forth as a goal, and victory over sin and death proclaimed and achieved, once and for all time."[28] With that caveat in mind, let's look at the major theories of the atonement.

There are, of course, several theories of the atonement. Some rise and fall in popularity depending on historical currents and other theological commitments. Some views on the atonement, such as the Calvinist/Reformed view of limited atonement or the Wesleyan-Arminian view of general/universal atonement, have more to do with the scope and reach of the atonement than how it works. Three main theories of how Christ's atoning death functions in regard to salvation call for specific attention: the *Christus Victor* view, the satisfaction view, and the moral influence view. Let's look at each in order.

Christus Victor has already been described, so suffice it only to say further that it presents the atonement of Christ as a drama in which Christ defeats not only sin and death but all evil forces and spiritual powers opposed to God's will. Twentieth-century theologian Gustaf Aulén persuasively demonstrated that this was the primary view of the church up until the Middle Ages.[29] Accordingly, it sometimes is called the "classical" view of the atonement. As such, it not surprisingly overlaps with the early "ransom" view or "recapitulation" view proposed by the Christian apologist and church father Irenaeus (ca. 125–202). Essentially, Irenaeus viewed the atonement as a ransom paid by Christ, who through his obedience reversed the Adamic fall and won victory over evil in order that all things might be finally summed up in Jesus Christ.[30]

Objections to the *Christus Victor* view usually involve questions such as: "To whom does God pay a 'ransom'?" "Does it portray God as making some kind of 'deal' with the devil?" "Does personifying evil run the risk of minimizing human responsibility?" However, these kinds of questions stem from an over-literalizing of the model's underlying truth. I recall a similar response by Nicodemus to Jesus' teaching on the new birth (John 3:1–8). The central truth still stands that Christ's atonement defeated evil.

---

28. Martin, "Atonement," 70.
29. See Aulén, *Christus Victor*.
30. Kelly, *Early Christian Doctrines*, suggests that Irenaeus's adaptation of the Pauline theme of recapitulation provides "the clue to soteriology" in the patristic church, 375–77.

Second is the satisfaction theory formulated by Anselm of Canterbury (1033–1109).[31] It argues that the honor of a holy and righteous God has been offended by sin and must be satisfied. Proponents of this view often argue that the righteous demands of divine justice against sin must be met in order to remove the cause of offense, which incurs divine wrath and judgment. Accordingly, as the God-Man, or fully divine and fully human, Jesus' sacrifice for sins was uniquely, that is, solely, able to meet the demands of divine justice to open the way for forgiveness of sins. Understandably, due to general similarity, the satisfaction theory is often confused with the penal substitutionary or vicarious view of the atonement. The latter, however, focuses on Christ's paying for human sin as a substitute; that is, he stood in for sinful humans who deserved judgment and took it in our place on the cross.

Objections to the satisfaction theory of the atonement usually revolve around such questions as "Does it merely reflect the medieval feudal system of Europe with an inordinate emphasis on offense of honor and the necessity of satisfaction?" (Images come to mind of a code of honor in which an offended party demands satisfaction in a duel with a perceived offender.) More seriously, "Does it misrepresent God the Father as an angry deity with Christ the Son as a loving deity, and thus set two persons of the Trinity at odds in some sense?" The first question forgets the biblical tradition's recruitment of the power of culture for clarifying Christian truth. For example, Paul often used analogies from military life and sports to explain doctrine (e.g. 1 Cor 9:24; 2 Tim 4:7). The second question clearly ignores the emphasis in the satisfaction theory on a loving God sending his obedient Son as a sacrifice for sins (think John 3:16). Far from being opponents, God the Father and God the Son are full partners in human redemption.

Finally, the moral influence theory of the atonement is often identified with Peter Abélard (1079–1142).[32] He argued that God decisively demonstrated his sacrificial love for humanity in the life and death of Jesus Christ. Accordingly, God's love in Christ actively inspires humans to lay aside fear and hate in order for themselves to live lives of sacrificial love. Abélard denied any need to somehow satisfy divine justice or pay a penalty for sin. For him, Christ's death moves people in the direction of personal moral improvement, in emulation of God's love as demonstrated in Christ. Thus, Christ's atoning death is an act of God's love designed to evoke responsive love in humans. This view has often been associated with "liberal" Christians (those tending to discard traditional values in favor of exploring other options).

---

31. Gasper, "Anselm of Canterbury," 118, 125, 136.
32. Hogg, "Theologies of Salvation in the Middle Ages," 118–19.

Objections to the moral influence theory are usually expressed through questions such as: "Doesn't it reduce the death of Christ to a moral example and thus rob it of any real *salvific* content?" "Doesn't it portray Christ as a martyr for a good cause, however magnificent, and thus diminish commitment to his divinity and exclusivity?" I cannot help but think of American President Thomas Jefferson's well-known view of Christ as a great moral authority and teacher, but certainly not the crucified and risen Son of God or Savior. First, neither of these objections apply unless the moral influence theory is viewed as the sole explanation of Christ's atonement. Second, although some proponents of the moral influence view may indeed view it as the sole explanation of Christ's atonement, that extreme position is not at all necessary for affirming its value in part. Third, it would be a mistake to reject any validity to this view on the grounds that it has been misused by certain groups. After all, Scripture presents Christ's suffering on the cross as an example for Christian living (e.g., 1 Pet 2:21).

Clearly, there is a problem with each of these theories of the atonement if they are presented in a reductionist manner. Christ's atoning death certainly defeated the powers of evil, and yet it is so much more than winning a wrestling match against wicked cosmic opponents. Christ's death, most certainly, is a payment for human sin through which a just and righteous God forgives guilty sinners. Yet, it is definitely more than a kind of *quid pro quo* transaction that makes God feel better about how he has been treated and helps people get over a guilt trip. Again, certainly God's love in Christ, including his death on the cross, challenges and inspires us all to live in love as we follow Christ's example. The hideous death of Christ on the cross, moreover, was not merely so everyone could deal a bit better with stuff. Jesus Christ is so much more than an ethical exemplar; he is the Savior of the world!

It is best to view the various theories of the atonement and their variations in an integrative manner. People often have a tendency to analyze rather than synthesize. When we analyze, we break something into different parts in order to examine them separately. Of course, there is a place for analysis. But after we analyze, sometimes we need to synthesize or combine constituent elements into a single or unified entity. That is what chemistry understands so well. For example, when sodium is combined with chlorine it produces sodium chloride—otherwise known as salt, a necessary staple of the human diet.

So then, why emphasize the importance of *Christus Victor*, or the classical view of the atonement, for Pentecostal soteriology? I could say that the *Christus Victor* theory is the *one* which needs reclaiming. Conservative evangelicals tend to emphasize penal substitutionary aspects of the satisfaction theory, while liberal Protestants tend to emphasize ethical versions of the moral influence theory. So then, let us reclaim *Christus Victor*. I am not arguing for simply *reclaiming* the *Christus Victor*/classical view but for *recognizing* its already existing resonance with Pentecostals.

Long before I ever heard/read the Latin term *Christus Victor,* I heard my dad and other Pentecostal leaders and ministers preach and teach that Jesus defeated the devil on the cross and won the victory for us in this world and in the next. Thus, Pentecostals used to love asking one another, "Have you got the victory?" And they used to love responding, "I've got the victory!" *Christus Victor* strikes a chord in the hearts and spirits of Pentecostal believers. It plays a familiar tune we know. We intuitively recognize that we share in the emotions and beliefs of the early Christians regarding the cosmic defeat of oppressive, damnable powers.

I suggest that there are at least four contributors to a Pentecostal sense of resonance with the classical view. First, *Christus Victor* clearly taps into the power of a primary biblical portrait of salvation—the exodus experience of ancient Israel—with its emphasis on deliverance, freedom, and victory. Pentecostals' biblicism affirms this aspect heartily. Second, at least in the early, formative days of the movement, and still so globally, many Pentecostals hail from the margins of society, often among the disenfranchised; so *Christus Victor* offers hope and optimism in the face of overwhelming circumstances. Third, again like Scripture and the early church—and like Pentecostals themselves—*Christus Victor* takes seriously the "spirit world" or spiritual realm of angels and demons, of principalities and powers, and, especially, of God and the devil. Fourth, rather than being an abstract theory, *Christus Victor* is narrative based—a testimony—that resonates strongly with Pentecostal spirituality. When my son Josh gifted me with a new trilby, I immediately saw that it was a great-looking hat. I still tried it on to see if it fit well and felt right. It did. For Pentecostals, *Christus Victor* is more than a great-looking theory; it fits well and feels right.

As seen at the beginning of this larger subsection, many biblical scholars and systematic theologians of a Pentecostal persuasion tout the value of *Christus Victor*. Interestingly enough, some Pentecostals tend to view scholarship as a compromising process. Perhaps, sometimes, it has been so. However, that is not necessarily the case. Regarding the atonement, it is quite to the contrary. Pentecostal scholarship has helped contemporary Pentecostals to "ask for the old paths, where the good way *is,* and walk in it" (Jer 6:16a). Reclaiming the deliverance, freedom, and victory of Christ's atonement is a good case in point.

This chapter has sought to discern models of salvation that distinctively coalesce in Pentecostal understandings of salvation. Paradigmatic models serving as primary indicators of distinctive Pentecostal soteriological emphases include the exodus of Israel, especially as manifested in the ministries of Jesus and of the apostles, and *Christus Victor* atonement theology. Again, these models are not exclusive of others—especially not of forensic justification or therapeutic regeneration/sanctification models. However, neither can a model of salvation as *deliverance, freedom,* and *victory* be excluded and still own any legitimate claim to represent authentic Pentecostal soteriology. In an age when so many are lowering the bar of their spiritual expectations, Pentecostals insist that the nature of salvation itself confronts death, hell, and the grave head-on and overcomes them all. Believers can live accordingly.

4

Soteriological Ethos

(Salvation Identity)

"Ethos" is one of those words that gets a lot of play, but its place on the team is not always put into precise perspective. Generally, ethos describes the definitive, typical elements of a culture, era, or community as demonstrated in its beliefs and values as well as in its goals and purposes. Rhetoric (since Aristotle, 384–322 BC) often uses ethos as a persuasive device (along with pathos and logos). I am not using it in that sense here. Rather, I wish to get at the heart of who Pentecostals are in regards to salvation. Chapter 3 of the present volume presented Pentecostal soteriology in terms of deliverance through the salvation models of ancient Israel's exodus from Egyptian bondage and in light of *Christus Victor* atonement theology. My previous volume *Essentials of Pentecostal Theology* asked, "What does salvation-as-deliverance mean for Pentecostal identity and ministry?"[1] In that volume, I offered a few brief observations. Now, the present chapter unpacks and expands on those comments for a somewhat fuller understanding of salvation-as-deliverance in respect to Pentecostal soteriological identity.

---

1. Richie, *Essentials*, 150.

AN ANTAGONISTIC ELEMENT

Salvation has an *antagonistic element*. Life is a battle, often an intense conflict involving sustained struggle. Evil is real. Actual survival—here and hereafter—is on the line. On their missionary/church planting journeys, Paul and Barnabas strengthened and exhorted the saints by teaching them that "We must through many tribulations enter the kingdom of God" (Acts 14:22). Years later, an aged Paul reminded young Timothy that "all who live godly in Christ Jesus shall suffer persecution" (2 Tim 3:12). Before Paul, Jesus identified his disciples as those who continued with him in his trials, and he promised them a kingdom for it (Luke 22:28–30). Centuries prior, the psalmist also described the righteous as those who endure many afflictions having the promise of the Lord's deliverance (34:19).

Indeed, Psalm 34 stresses the Lord's delivering activity on behalf of his troubled servants (vv. 4, 6, 17, 19). Commenting on verse 19, Augustine suggested that the troubles of the righteous in this life, which are followed by complete peace forever, ought to be considered in comparison to the troubles of the wicked, which extend into eternity and are increased rather than removed.[2] It appears that "the afflictions of the righteous" is not merely an admission that righteous people have problems the same as others, so much as an admonition that the righteous encounter opposition—antagonism—*because* they are righteous, directed toward them from the unrighteous (Ps 34:21).[3] Along this line, Jesus shockingly declares that he did not come to bring peace on earth but a sword (Matt 10:34). Nevertheless, the overall context of Psalm 34 includes "all times" (v. 1) or both aspects of affliction, the pain and suffering of life in this fallen world and the opposition that comes against those who honestly endeavor to be faithful followers of Jesus Christ in a wicked world.

There is a disconcerting tendency to view salvation almost exclusively in terms of an afterlife. For many people, it seems that salvation is mostly a question of "Where do people go when they die?" or, even more pressingly, "Where will I go when I die?" Obviously, those are important questions, and Christianity addresses them forthrightly. As has already been seen, and will be seen again in this volume, Pentecostals have strong beliefs in this area. We believe in eternal life for the righteous and eternal punishment for the wicked.

However, what about those people who are asking another set of questions, such as: "How am I going to take care of my family?" "How am I going

2. Augustin, *Expositions on the Psalms*, 8:77–78.
3. Lange, *Psalms*, 237.

to pay the bills?" "How am I going to deal with the pressures of my job?" and so on. These folks are not so much asking "Where are we going someday?" as "How do we make it through today?" Frankly, they may be forgiven for suspecting that Christianity, as it is often presented, is not very relevant for life in the here and now. However, that would be untrue. Pentecostals believe Christianity is good not only for eternity but for the daily struggles of life in this world. In reality, that's part of what salvation is about too.

Several years ago (in 2000), I traveled to Israel and Egypt. I had been there before, but this trip was different. We did not go to the usual tourist attractions. Organizers Paul Walker and Michael Baker led a small group of fourteen pastors and church leaders on a journey across deserts and mountains that was definitely off the beaten path.[4] It was a serious time of introspection. Once, when we were camping on the Sinai Peninsula with a group of Bedouins, our indigenous guide called attention to their practical economy. They had nothing they could not use and everything they had they used. I could not resist inquiring about whether our Bedouin hosts believed in God; and yes, they did. We were given to understand that they considered faith in God essential for their day-to-day existence. Pentecostals understand.

I grew up Pentecostal in an Appalachian coal mining family. I heard more than my share of preaching about heaven and hell, but many of the testimonies from people in the pews were about how God answered prayer and helped with the "trials and tribulations" of difficult life situations. For these mountain folks, salvation was about more than going to heaven someday. It was about more than not going to hell someday. It was about dealing with the battles and struggles of life in this world, too.[5]

Wherever one resides in this world, the reality of evil is all too evident. There is sickness and suffering. There is death. For example, as I write these words, the world, especially the United States, is deep in the throes of the dreadful COVID-19 pandemic. Over and over again, I have heard people say they have never seen anything like it. I have had friends—good friends, close friends—die from this dreadful virus. My immediate and extended

---

4. At the time, Paul Walker was the General Overseer of the Church of God (Cleveland, TN). Mike Baker is currently serving as the President of Pentecostal Theological Seminary (Cleveland, TN).

5. Accordingly, I sense that many Pentecostals would concur with Wesleyan theologian Don Thorsen, *Exploration of Christian Theology*, 403, about the problem of becoming "mesmerized and distracted by speculation about the afterlife" to the point of losing sight of "the importance of salvation here and now." They might even shout "Amen!" to his statement on the same page that "God sent Jesus to provide salvation, and the Holy Spirit to be forever present and empowering on our behalf, in this life and in the eternal life to come."

family has been impacted as well. Where is God in all of this suffering? How do we deal with the overwhelming fear it spawns? How does a theologian explain a pandemic? How does a pastor comfort a congregation during a pandemic? How does a chaplain or counselor console the bereaved hit by a pandemic? These are hard questions with no easy answers. We certainly cannot offer facile or superficial responses that ignore the complexities involved.

Yet, it is precisely at points like these that faith makes a difference. We believe in a loving God who sent his Son to save and deliver us from sin and all it entails and to give us the Holy Spirit to guide, comfort, and strengthen us on the journey to glory. Believers endure—indeed, expect—antagonism in this life. Yet an assurance that God loves us, that Jesus came for us, and that the Holy Spirit is always with us here and now, not just someday and somewhere, gives us what we need to make it through it all. We trust God to hear our prayers and to help us. We expect the Lord to deliver us. Unequivocally, deliverance is what the God who saves does.

Unfortunately, antagonism is not limited to the hardships of life. It is more direct, more explicit, too. For example, early Christians often faced persecution and martyrdom. On a wall in my home hangs a print portraying ancient Christians in the Roman coliseum.[6] Some were being thrown to the lions. Others were being burned alive. Sadly, it is not just an artist's imagination at work. These horrific events occurred. Indicatively, throughout the centuries, Christians have often been persecuted for their faith. Atheistic regimes have in fact attempted to stamp out the very name of Christ. In the early days of the Pentecostal movement, worshipers were harassed and buildings were burned. My own uncle Gridley Richie told me about hearing a rifle bullet whiz over his head as he stood outside a rural church where he had been conducting revival services. Locals had been heard boasting that they were going to scare off those "holy rollers" and "tongue talkers."[7] Needless to say, it did not work.

One Sunday evening in the early 1980s, I came out of a church service in which I had preached to discover all four of the tires on my car slashed. Fortunately for me, one of the brothers in that local church owned a gas station/garage. He immediately put four new tires on my car. I counted it a kind of blessing, since I had needed new tires anyway. About a year later, a man approached me on the street of a nearby town and confessed to the deed. He explained that my ministry had enraged him. Thank God, he had since repented of his angry act. He asked me to forgive him, and I did.

---

6. "Christian Martyrs' Last Prayer," by Jean-Léon Gérôme, 1863.

7. These are pejorative terms once commonly used to describe Pentecostals.

Nevertheless, I admit that the incident imparted to me a sharpened sense of antagonism in the life of faith.

In the United States, in spite of its vaunted ideal of religious freedom, opposition to Christians occurs. Rising antireligious and anti-Christian sentiment is not limited to any particular denomination, but evangelicals frequently bear the brunt of much of it.[8] Believers are everywhere vilified. Some unbelievers find Christianity a convenient scapegoat for their complaints. It has become popular to the point of faddishness to blame believers for just about everything wrong in the nation and in the world. It is quickly becoming quite conceivable that power-hungry hate groups in the United States will soon orchestrate organized persecution of Christians.

Tertullian (c. 155–c. 240), the "father of Latin Christianity" and "father of Western theology," said of the martyrs that "the blood of Christians is seed."[9] This statement belies a theology in which believers expect opposition to occur but not to overcome them. It reminds me of biblical incidents in which the devout were thrown into a fiery furnace or a den of lions but experienced glorious deliverances (Dan 3:1–30; 6:1–28). Yet as Scripture makes clear (Heb 11:35b–38), and as martyrdom itself implies, a glorious deliverance, or an eventual victory, may come at tremendous cost. Pentecostal soteriology expects antagonism. In a sense, it embraces the oppositional nature of the Christian life as it embarks in conversion on the faith journey. Those who accuse Pentecostals of triumphalism should take into account their oppositional assessment of life along with their enduring optimism inspired by a resilient faith.[10] The Christian's life is a battle, a struggle; but for all that, it is a life of deliverance and of victory. That is in large part what it means to be saved.

As for identifying the underlying nature of the antagonistic element in salvation, Jesus' paradigmatic declaration regarding the establishment of his church is in a context of conflict with spiritual forces—the gates of Hades (Matt 16:18). The offensive assault of Satan's domain cannot conquer the church or stop its advance.[11] Yet there is an inevitability to the conflict. At its root, the conflict is spiritual in nature; and it is evil. A protracted

---

8. Jackson, "Evangelicals Are Discriminated Against."

9. Tertullian, *Apology*, 55. Aulén, *Faith of the Christian Church*, 70, argues that the Christian faith's efforts to hold fast to the reality of divine revelation with emphasis on the opposition encountered in history results in an outlook with a "dramatic character." For Aulén, this oppositional drama defined by the act of God in Christ is not peripheral but is the essence of Christianity—a truth particularly evident in the doctrine of salvation, 65–66, 72–73, 161.

10. Richie, "Is Pentecostalism Just Another American Success Story?"

11. Blomberg, *Matthew*, 253.

and at times intense clash between Christ's followers and diabolical forces is unavoidable. In essence, a believer's inheritance includes persecution (Mark 10:30). Sadly, there are those who are best described as "enemies of the cross" (Phil 3:18). They are implacable foes for all who rely on the cross for their salvation.

Bob Seger's song "Against the Wind" was inspired by his experience in high school as a cross-country runner.[12] He applies it to moving forward against life's pressures. Most of us can likely identify. In the spiritual life, the theme of progress against resistance is, if anything, even more applicable. In the fourth century, Pseudo-Macarius, a Syrian monk, compared the Christian life to a hard-won chariot race.[13] Anyone who has ever seen the movie *Ben-Hur*, especially the 1959 version, can imagine how intense the competition/opposition could become. Think salvation. Often conversion involves personal struggle. Living out conversion in daily life certainly involves ongoing struggle.

Christianity is not a bland religion. It is not passive. It does not lack strength and initiative. I am always shocked when anyone presents Christians in milquetoast language. There is nothing feeble or timid about Christianity. In reality, true Christians are heroic! How can we forget that Christianity conquered the mighty Roman Empire? Have we forgotten that the Vikings struck terror into the hearts of Europe's inhabitants but then bowed before the cross of Christ? Any version of Christianity that does not have a double portion of the fighting spirit is unworthy of the title. As C. S. Lewis put it, "Christianity is a fighting religion."[14] As with Gideon, the angel of the Lord declares to the believer, "The Lord *is* with you, O valiant warrior" (Judg 6:12 NASB). In this world, Christians are often outnumbered and surrounded. As valiant warriors, they win the victory against evil through faith in Jesus Christ (1 John 5:4–5).

---

12. For more information, see "Against the Wind" (Bob Seger Song), https://en.wikipedia.org/wiki/Against_the_Wind_(Bob_Seger_song) (Retrieved 8/22/2020).

13. Pseudo-Macarius, *Pseudo-Macarius*, 42.

14. Lewis, *Mere Christianity*, 31. Of course, I am talking not about physical violence. This relates the Christian life as a struggle. It portrays a realistic picture of what the Christian life is all about. The imagery of war and struggle are pertinent to our times. Yet, a very militant strain of so-called Christian nationalism tries to justify storming the Capitol. See NPR contributor Gjelton, "Faith Leaders Nearly Unanimous in Condemning Assault on the Capitol." At the same time, we cannot throw away the image of struggle; it is a biblical image. Paradoxically, we must ask important questions: How do we work for change peacefully? How do we work through our struggle?

COSMIC CONTEXT

Salvation has a *cosmic context*. Individual believers and communities of faith are integral parts of a larger, panoramic, even universal-sized scale of events and issues in which their own fates play a significant role in the ultimate outcome. One of my favorite Bible stories is the Lord's dramatic correction of the Syrian view that the God of Israel was only a god of the hills but not of the valleys (1 Kgs 20:28–30). In other words, they viewed Yahweh as a localized—and therefore, limited—deity. They paid dearly for that theological error. Centuries later, the greatest of the Hebrew prophets would relay this reminder from the Lord to Israel that their worship structures could not contain their God: "Heaven *is* My throne, And earth *is* My footstool. Where *is* the house that you will build Me? And where *is* the place of My rest?" (Isa 66:1). The NT describes Jesus Christ as the "Savior of the world" (John 4:42; 1 John 4:14).

Strikingly, the last book of the Bible portrays cosmic conflict. The entire universe, the cosmos itself—not just the earth or all those that reside on this planet—is involved in protracted confrontation between good and evil. Whatever else interpreters may debate regarding the precise meaning of Revelation 12:1–17, clearly it graphically depicts conflict between good and evil involving heaven and earth.[15] Similarly, Paul viewed Christians as bold warriors locked in an intractable battle "against principalities, against powers, against the rulers of the darkness of this age, against spiritual *hosts* of wickedness in the heavenly *places*" (Eph 6:12).

Pauline angelology (doctrine of angels) is consistent with OT descriptions of heavenly "sons of God" (Job 1:6; 2:1; 38:7; cp. Gen 6:2, 4; Ps 89:6). These celestial beings appear to function as a kind of divine council or cabinet (1 Kgs 22:19; Jer 23:18, 22; Ps 89:5–7). These "holy ones" (Ps 89:5, 7) serve as messengers who do God's bidding. However, not all of them are good (1 Kgs 22:20–23). Satan was among them and perhaps served as leader of a sizeable contingent.[16]

Paul's letter to the Ephesians highlights the powers in the heavenlies, both good and evil, in purposes of redemptive history (1:10; 3:10; 6:12). Arthur Patzia asserts that Ephesians "presents a cosmic picture of God's saving activity and the role of Christ. It gives increasing attention to the

---

15. Chris Thomas, *Apocalypse*, describes Revelation 12:1—14:20 as "redemptive history in cosmic context," adding that it tells "the story of God's people in cosmic perspective," 351–52.

16. Alden, *Job*, 53–54.

principalities and powers and their defeat by God."[17] He concedes that the same is true of Colossians (cp. 1:16, 20; 2:10, 15):

> The central message of the Book of Colossians is that Christ has defeated these evil powers through his death on the cross. Consequently, they no longer have control or authority over humankind; believers share in that victory by virtue of their faith in Christ and by virtue of their union with his death and resurrection in baptism.[18]

In Ephesians and Colossians "all forms of life—whether on earth or in the far regions of the cosmos—know about God's eternal plan and purpose."[19] This Pauline cosmology informs and undergirds a Pentecostal approach to the cosmic context of soteriology.

Some liberal theologians "demythologize" the cosmologies of Ephesians and Colossians by denying that they refer to actual cosmic intelligences. They reject what they see as an archaic and indefensible worldview. Principalities and powers are revised to refer to politico-economic structures of society.[20] Pentecostal views on scriptural inspiration and authority do not permit that questionable strategy.[21] Rather, Pentecostals agree with the fourth century's Ambrosiaster, commentator and interpreter of Paul, that Paul describes angelic spirits of varying degrees of authority and that this calls for believers to "forsake their allegiance to the devil's tyranny."[22] As Origen (c. 184–c. 253) puts it when commenting on Ephesians 6:12, these signify "the vanquishing and overcoming of demonic spiritual powers."[23] Certainly, there is a cosmic context for Christian redemption.

---

17. Patzia, *Ephesians, Colossians, Philemon*, 125.

18. Patzia, *Ephesians, Colossians, Philemon*, 216. Moltmann, *Coming of God*, reminds of Oscar Cullman's dramatic image of a decisive battle in a war, or D-day, having already occurred though the fighting continues for a while, 11–12. Similarly, Karl Barth said the devil is already in checkmate but does not know it yet and so goes on playing, Moltmann, *Coming of God*, 342. I suspect he knows it all right but refuses to resign nevertheless.

19. Patzia, *Ephesians, Colossians, Philemon*, 216.

20. Patzia, *Ephesians, Colossians, Philemon*, 216.

21. Really this rejection appears to me to be nothing other than a willingness to sacrifice the integrity of Scripture on the altar of an *a priori* bias against the supranatural. The best scholarship among non-Pentecostals agrees that Pauline cosmology of angels, good and bad, and other spirit beings, should be taken as both literal and central to his thought. E.g., Ladd, *Theology of the New Testament*, 400–403.

22. Oden and Edwards, eds., *Galatians, Ephesians, Philippians*, 150–51.

23. Oden and Edwards, eds., *Galatians, Ephesians, Philippians*, 209.

So then, what does a cosmic context for redemption mean for a Pentecostal doctrine of salvation? In getting at that question, I offer a threefold response for consideration. The first two, I express in the form of negations; but the last one, as an affirmation. First, salvation is not just about the conversion of individual human beings. Second, salvation is not at all about the conversion of spiritual beings. Third, salvation is ultimately about the historical demonstration of the goodness and wisdom of God's eternal counsel and purposes. Let us look at these three statements in order.

First, I propose that salvation is not just about the conversion of individual human beings. Since the entire first chapter of this volume is dedicated to the richness and significance of conversionary redemptive experiences, I hope readers will not jump to the conclusion that I am now in any way undermining the unspeakable importance of conversion for individual believers. Most pastors have probably used the "starfish story" as a sermon illustration. An old man observed a little boy picking up starfish that were stranded on a beach after a storm and then tossing them back into the water. The boy explained that he was rescuing starfish from the heat of the sun before it killed them. The man noted that there were thousands of stranded starfish and that the boy would never be able to save them all. He then asked, "What difference are you making?" As the little fellow threw another starfish into the water, he replied, "I made a difference for that one!"

Christian salvation is about the conversion of human beings. Personal salvation certainly is important to me. Knowing that my sins are forgiven and that I have eternal life is of all matters most important for me. I trust it is for you too, dear reader. I cannot think of anything more important than the salvation of my loved ones, my family, and my friends. My wife, Sue, has said many times that, although pancreatic cancer took her father's life at an early age, she is, nevertheless, forever grateful that his two-year journey of struggle eventually led to his conversion to Jesus Christ. His personal salvation is paramount in her mind. Apparently, the great apostle to the Gentiles felt the same way about his Israelite family and fellow citizens (Rom 9:1–3). I do not at all intend to diminish the importance of individual conversion.

Rather, when I propose that salvation is not just about the conversion of individual human beings, I place a great deal of weight on the common English adverb *just*. Salvation is not *only* about individual conversion. To clarify yet further, salvation is not solely or exclusively about individual conversion. Without taking anything away from individual conversion, I wish to avoid limiting salvation to a matter of whether this one or that one accepts Christ as his or her personal savior.

Yet, affirming the cosmic significance of salvation does not reduce the vital role of an individual believer in God's plan of redemption. Actually, it is quite the reverse. Each individual convert is a major player in the divine drama of redemption that impacts every being in heaven and on earth. Amazing! When someone becomes a Christian, they enter into active participation in the greatest story ever told, including all its adventure, excitement, and immense outcome, literally, for all creation.

Second, I propose that salvation is not at all about the conversion of spiritual beings. Universalism, the belief that all beings, corporeal and incorporeal, will eventually be saved has been around at least since Origen and, more recently, has resurfaced in Karl Barth.[24] However, it has been consistently rejected by mainstream Christian theological tradition.[25] I agree. The reality of accountability for eternity is simply too strong. The teaching of our Lord alone is ample evidence on hell (Matt 5:22, 29, 30; 10:28; 18:9; 23:15, 33). The Apostle Peter makes it plain that eternal judgment and damnation includes the rebellious and wicked of the heavenlies (2 Pet 2:4). No, the cosmic context of redemption does not mean that "fallen angels," if we will, are redeemable. They are not.

The role of angelic hosts is something other than receiving or rejecting personal salvation. What is clear is that angels are interested in the experience of redemption and its unfolding as it moves toward its culmination. Peter says that "angels desire to look into" gospel reports and preaching (1 Pet 1:12). The word for "desire" (*epithymeō*) indicates intense craving. This issue of salvation is no light matter for the heavenlies. The gospel is serious business on a cosmic scale.

Possibly angels are interested in the gospel's salvation proclamation, because they delight in the things of God and that which glorifies God. It is conceivable that although angels do not experience gospel salvation that they, nevertheless, rejoice for those who do.[26] It is not hard to imagine the angels of God with such approbative attitudes. After all, rejoicing occurs in heaven over a repentant sinner (Luke 15:7, 10), and the angels of God worship the incarnate Christ (Heb 1:6). Angelic interest in human salvation could involve vicarious appreciation.

---

24. In the third century Origen speculated about the possibility of *apokatastasis* or universal restoration of all rational beings but did not advance it as dogma; Thomas P. Scheck, "Origen of Alexandria," 32–33. In the twentieth century Barth taught that Christ is both the electing God and the elected man and that all who receive the gift of salvation are elected in Christ accordingly. Since there are no limitations on "the friendliness of God" or "the friendliness of Jesus Christ," some version of universalism is, arguably, logically implied. Cp. Greggs, "Karl Barth," especially 312–14.

25. Oden, *Life in the Spirit*, 375.

26. Schreiner, *1, 2 Peter, Jude*, 75–76.

However, there are at least two further considerations to note concerning angelic interest. First, doxological aspects or sympathetic interests in gospel salvation do not explain the role of rebellious celestial beings. One would naturally expect these fallen creatures to be sullen. Second, there is an even more profound explanation for the significance of redemption in Christ as relative to the angelic hosts. My third proposal encapsulates the example of Christ both to humanity and to angels.

Accordingly, I propose, thirdly, that ultimately salvation is about the historical demonstration of the goodness and wisdom of God's eternal counsel and purpose. This historical demonstration centers first on the person and work of Jesus Christ and then on the establishment and continuation of his church. Jesus is, in nature and in authority, far above all principalities and powers (Eph 1:21). Indeed, the powers of heaven and of earth were created by him, and through him, and for him (Col 1:16). Jesus is head over all such authorities or rulers (2:10). Although believers' engagement in spiritual warfare with evil principalities is quite intense (Eph 6:12), they are assured that Christ has already openly defeated rebellious powers in the heavenlies (Col 2:15). Abundantly evident is that Christian soteriology and cosmology begin and end with the preeminence of the Lord Jesus Christ.[27] Paul's letter to Ephesus most clearly articulates a cosmic ecclesiology. It begins, once again, with Christ exalted to be the head over all things to the church (1:22; cp. Col 1:18). Then, it is the church that makes known God's manifold or multifaceted wisdom to the principalities and powers (3:10). Finally, it is specifically through the church that Christ glorifies God to all generations (3:21). Accordingly, the church's role is inseparably linked to its relationship with Jesus Christ.

Ephesians 3:10 is a key text for discussion of salvation as the historical demonstration of the goodness and wisdom of God's eternal counsel and purpose. In the fourth century, Marius Victorinus commented on Ephesians 3:10 that "The powers and principalities in heaven are learning the wisdom of God through a human mediator."[28] Heaven learns from humanity about God's wisdom. To elaborate, human redemption is the means God is using to instruct the population of heaven regarding his own good judgment.

The Virgin Mary once said to an angel "How can this be, since I do not know a man?" (Matt 1:34) Now some may be tempted to say "How can this be, since we know mankind?" In other words, how can fallen, sinful human

---

27. Cp. Patzia, *Ephesians, Colossians, Philemon*, 27. Thorsen, *Exploration of Christian Theology*, 182, points out that believers' attitude toward spiritual warfare is rooted in an understanding of Jesus' own "spiritual warfare," and that their level of openness to these realities may affect the focus of one's prayer life (cp. 194).

28. Oden and Edwards, eds., *Galatians, Ephesians, Philippians*, 150.

beings be the means by which the holy and righteous God demonstrates his own goodness to heaven? Nevertheless, that is precisely it. God's dealings with lost humanity prove his compassion and mercy, his kindness and righteousness—in short, the wisdom of all his ways—once and for all. The goodness of God's character and the soundness of God's judgment are laid bare for every eye to see in his redemption of a lost world of sinners. English poet John Milton wished to "justify the ways of God to men"; but Scripture goes even farther—it justifies the ways of God to men *and* to angels.[29]

A natural question would be "Why would God choose to do it this way?" Here, we remember David's humble admission: "Such knowledge is too wonderful for me; It is high, I cannot attain it" (Ps 139:6). One translation says, "It is *too* high" (NASB). The Hebrew *śā·ḡaḇ* indicates knowledge that is inaccessible, because it so high as to be out of reach. Now we may cry out with Paul, "Oh, the depth of the riches both of the wisdom and knowledge of God! How unsearchable are His judgments and His ways past finding out!" (Rom 11:33). And yet . . . the whole point of Ephesians 3:10 (and v. 11) is that God has chosen to make his wisdom known through his eternal purpose as it has been accomplished in Christ Jesus our Lord.

Accordingly, I am going to "step out of the boat," so to speak, in offering a few reflections. First, God always works according to his own character and nature. It is impossible for God to do otherwise. So, redeeming lost humanity was the right thing—in a sense, the only thing—for our holy and loving God to do. It is who he is. Again, that is precisely the point. God's redemption of lost humanity is not some contrived means of proving a point. It is just who he is. Otherwise, it would not prove anything at all. Redemption reveals God's true nature. Second, the omnipotent God does not rule by sheer force. God's kingdom is a moral government. In other words, God rules according to right rather than might. God, not *in spite* of being God but *because* of being God, willingly and wisely manifests his eternal purpose and wisdom for all to forever behold. He does it, unmistakably, through saving lost sinners when they put their faith in Jesus Christ.

Again, why? Specifically, why Christ? Why did God send his Son to be our Savior? I am sympathetic to the Anselmian line of reasoning asserting that God became man, because only man could save man but only God was qualified so God became man.[30] Our investigation into the cosmic context of the doctrine of salvation expands this assertion farther. One way to

---

29. Plavcan, "Mortal Reason and Divine Infinity."

30. We mentioned Anselm's ideas earlier (chapter 3). The hypostatic union, the doctrine that divine and human natures were combined in the single person of Christ, as it became known, was important in Athanasius's struggle to establish Nicene Christianity (fourth century) and directly related to his soteriology.

express it would be that the Anselmian rationale elucidates the *human* side for the necessity of Christ's incarnation. The *angelic* side, however, calls for elucidation as well. It is revealed in the relationship of the Second Person of the Triune Godhead to the principalities and powers in the heavenlies.

Jesus is in nature and authority far above all principalities and powers (Eph 1:21). They were created by him, and through him, and for him (Col 1:16). He is head over all such authorities or rulers (2:10). God did not send a seaman to do the admiral's job. He sent the person with the highest possible rank in relation to all heavenly authorities or rulers. He sent the one and only person who had authority among all heavenly authorities to redeem humanity. Heaven's hosts recognize and respect God's wisdom as manifested in the redemption of lost humanity through faith in Jesus Christ.

To be more specific, authorities and rulers in the heavenlies can see the wisdom of God's redeeming work in Christ as it is manifested through *the church*. For contemporary commentator Arthur Patzia, Ephesians 3:10 indicates that "the church has a cosmic function in the plan of God."[31] Paul delineates the climactic nature of this cosmic element as depicted in Ephesians via the unfolding of God's plan as it moves to himself (3:3), then to all humankind (3:9), and finally to the heavenlies (3:10). The "grand purpose of the church" is that through its agency "the manifold wisdom of God should be made known to the rulers and authorities in the heavenly realms."[32] Accordingly, the "church is a living testimony to the redemptive and unifying power of God on earth (3:9) as well as to all heavenly beings (3:10)."[33] Obviously, soteriology (doctrine of salvation) and ecclesiology (doctrine of the church) come together.

Several questions come to mind regarding the intersection of soteriology and ecclesiology in a cosmic context disclosing the goodness and wisdom of God's eternal counsel and purpose. For example, in what way does the church's worship manifest God's eternal counsel and purpose in the heavenlies? Again, in what sense does the church's mission manifest God's eternal counsel and purpose in the heavenlies? I suggest that God's compassion, goodness, and kindness are on display via the church's worship and witness. However, why is the *church* emphatically highlighted as the medium for manifesting God's goodness? It seems reasonable enough on the surface to simply reply that the church represents all those redeemed by Christ. But why not say that a lost sinner getting saved accomplishes that high and holy purpose? After all, clearly heaven puts a premium on the

---

31. Patzia, *Ephesians, Colossians, Philemon*, 214.
32. Patzia, *Ephesians, Colossians, Philemon*, 215.
33. Patzia, *Ephesians, Colossians, Philemon*, 218.

conversion of a single sinner (Luke 15:10). Yet according to Scripture, God's wisdom is specifically "made known by the church" (Eph 3:10). Could it be that there is something significant about the communal or corporate nature of the church?

It is easy to think of the church—or local churches—as more or less a collection or gathering of so many saved individuals. However, the existence and nature of the church confirms the adage that "the whole is more than the sum of its parts." The German language, with wonderful creativity, uses *gestalt*, a word basically meaning "form or shape," to insist that natural systems and their properties should be viewed as wholes rather than as a loose collection of parts. English borrows from the Greek *holos*, meaning "all, whole, entire," in describing this principle as *holism*. It is antonymic of words like "reductionism" and, especially, "atomism."

We can only be the church together. One saint does not a church make. Even a local gathering of saints can only be the church *at* Jerusalem or *at* Antioch or *at* Corinth or *at* someplace (Acts 8:1; 13:1; 1 Cor 1:2). To be sure, it is no small matter for a local church to be the church's presence *at* someplace; but it is not the *church*. It takes all believers together to constitute the church. It is the church that "makes known the manifold wisdom of God" in Jesus Christ to the principalities and powers in the heavenlies (Eph 3:10).

Therefore, let us remember that salvation has a cosmic context in which God's wisdom is manifested by the church to the principalities and powers in the heavenlies according to God's eternal purpose accomplished in Jesus Christ. Again and again, salvation is shown to be so much more than often assumed. The great American preacher and theologian Jonathan Edwards (1703–1758) wrote about "the grand design of God in all divine operations."[34] He was describing God's plan of redemption in Jesus Christ. Well said, sir! Everything in heaven and on earth is related to God's "grand design" in redemption.

AN IMPOSSIBLE SCENARIO

Salvation has an *impossible scenario*. Hopeless against insurmountable odds, helpless in the face of inconceivable opposition, inadequate to the point of absurdity, people are unable to accomplish the effects necessary for their own existence and flourishing. Disaster, destruction, is inevitable—and usually, imminent. The book of Esther serves as a dramatic portrait of divine salvation within an impossible scenario. The course of events in the book of Esther is set by seasons of fasting, which in the Jewish tradition

---

34. See Richie, "'Grand Design of God in All Divine Operations.'"

are associated with seeking God for aid in times of calamity and trouble (Esth 4:3, 16; cp. 9:31). This book especially demonstrates a setting in which human ability is completely incapable of resolving a desperate situation. Early and rabbinic Jewish interpretations agree that Esther is about God's deliverance of the people of Israel.[35] It is the story of a devout woman's role in the deliverance of the Jews from the murderous plan of Haman in the Persian Empire during the reign of Xerxes (485–464 BC). In the OT, Esther resembles the stories of Ruth and Deborah, two other women whom God used for accomplishing his plan. Most of all, it is the story of how the Jewish people survived a planned pogrom that would have meant their total annihilation. Of course, God was sovereign over it all.[36]

In Esther, the Jews occupy a special place in the divine purpose. In spite of pogroms and attempts to destroy them, God's providence preserves—that is, saves and delivers—the Hebrew nation.[37] The book of Esther dramatically illustrates salvation as deliverance in the face of insurmountable odds in the setting of an impossible scenario. The narrative nature of the book of Esther well suits Pentecostal hermeneutics. As noted in chapter 2, narrative theology strongly resonates with Pentecostals. Narrative informs not only the Pentecostal story and testimony but also Pentecostal theology and spirituality.[38] Implications are numerous in the story of Esther for a Pentecostal theology of salvation. For present purposes, we focus on one aspect: dealing with an impossible scenario.

The antagonistic element in salvation means that adversity and opposition are inevitable. Its cosmic context means that the consequences are far reaching. Both themes flow into the impossible scenario which confronts believers. The book of Esther presents one long, impossible scenario that continues to build into an incredible climax: foiling Haman's intended but unsuccessful annihilation of the Jews. A counterpart, the book of Daniel, presents a series of impossible scenarios: a potentially fatal situation about dietary observance (chapter 1), threatened execution over interpreting the king's dream (chapter 2), an attempted execution in the fiery furnace over refusing to worship the king's image (chapter 3), and a plot to kill Daniel in a den of lions (chapter 6). It is likely that most of us encounter numerous situations in life that are impossible for us to overcome on our own, but

---

35. Wolcott, "Writings."
36. Breneman, *Ezra, Nehemiah, Esther*, 277–78.
37. Breneman, *Ezra, Nehemiah, Esther*, 296–97.
38. While Pentecostals uniquely embrace and employ narrative, story, and testimony, McGrath argues in *Born to Wonder*, 89–91, that narration is essential to the human being's quest for meaning. Telling stories completes "This is what *happened*" with "this is what it *means*," 89 (original italics).

these may be thought of as several examples of one continuous attack from the enemy of our souls.

The phrase "win-win" is popular today, but an impossible scenario is more of a "lose-lose." There appears to be no way to win. If Esther does not help Mordecai and the Jews, it appears that they will certainly perish. If she does try to help, she will likely perish herself and the Jews may still perish anyway. Likewise, if Daniel and the other young Hebrew men worship the king's image their identity is destroyed. If they do not worship the image, they will presumably burn in the furnace of fire. One is "caught between a rock and a hard place," as the saying goes. There appears to be no way out.

In such impossible scenarios, a problem occurs in the *present* but has *permanent* consequences. It may be hard for many to imagine that a development or incident at work or school, or even at home, has eternal significance. Nonetheless, it is true. Our own eternal well-being, not to mention our witness to everyone around us, is wrapped up in the packaging of everyday words and deeds. It is crucial for a believer to realize that his/her own life experiences have huge significance far beyond their moment of occurrence or immediate consequence.

There is both an *overt* and a *covert* design in these crises—but the covert is the more significant. Usually, it is quite clear that one's own well-being is on the line. Perhaps, one's financial well-being is at stake, or it could be one's dreams for the future are threatened. Perhaps a relationship is strained or could become shattered. In extreme cases, one's physical life may be at risk. Each life circumstance is about more than comfort or money or advancement or love or pleasure or some such thing. Really, it is essentially about faithfulness and loyalty. The Christian life is about faithfully living out one's loyalty to the Lord Jesus Christ in spite of challenges to that ultimate commitment.

The crisis has the nature of a *dilemma*. Technically, a dilemma occurs in a situation when a difficult choice between undesirable alternatives is forced. For a devoted follower of Jesus, the dilemma will involve pressure to compromise commitment to Christ through making a wrong choice. How does one know which choice is wrong? It will be the one that does not honor Christ. Conversely, it may satisfy someone in authority; it may be pleasing to ourselves or others; but it will not honor Christ. An impossible scenario, in this sense, will intensify to the point of apparently being irresolvable, placing unbearable tensions between one's survival and one's commitment to Christ.

The pressures of the impossible scenario create a crisis of *faith* and *trust*. What will happen to me? Will God take care of me? Will I be hurt? Will I die? Esther faced the real possibility of immediate death if her presence and intercession with the king were unwelcome. With encouragement from Mordecai, and after a season of fasting, she finally declared resignedly, "If I perish, I perish" (4:16); and she plunged ahead (cp. Gen 43:14; Dan 3:18). There is a state of resignation in the spiritual life that is a place of absolute trust. This state of resignation does not assume calamity cannot or will not occur. Rather, it places oneself completely at the disposal of the Lord, no matter what comes or goes. It trusts God absolutely.

However, Esther's resignation to God's will exceeds saintly examples of absolute trust. She reminds us of Christ, willing to die for others yet, when confronted with the harshness of death itself, able to overcome and follow through because of personal yieldedness to God's redemptive will (Luke 22:42). Queen Esther may, thus, be described as a kind of Christ figure. That is, she is a type of Christ. Esther symbolizes and exemplifies the ideal of sacrificial love that is the defining characteristic of the coming messiah, the Lord Jesus Christ. Like Isaac, whose willingness to die for his father, and who was as good as dead, became an example of resurrection life (Heb 11:19), so Esther's victory in the face of almost certain death makes her an example of resurrection victory, of new life, and of fresh hope.

Those who are *faithful* in the face of overwhelming circumstances always *overcome*. Esther overcame, and so did Daniel and his friends. From the perspective of soteriology, the point of an impossible scenario is that no one can save him/herself, nor anyone else. In all reality, each of us is in a predicament. This predicament is more than difficult. It is more than embarrassing, more than unpleasant. It is desperation in the face of damnation. We are lost in sin and cannot do anything about it. The book of Esther is testimony to God's providential care in this life and beyond. As shall be seen, the book of Esther is part of an oft-repeated pattern.

Esther is not an exception. Israel was cornered at the Red Sea. They had nowhere to go and they could do nothing. They were desperate for survival in the wilderness. There was no way Israel could defeat the inhabitants of Canaan. Israel in Canaan was no match for invading Philistines. The followers of Yahweh could not withstand the rabid devotees of Baal. The pattern continues. Most of all, when Jesus died on the cross and was buried in the tomb, it surely seemed that the only way to describe the resulting scenario was with the word *impossible*! It was impossible to the nth degree.

Yet the impossible scenario of Jesus' death and burial was, in hindsight, the prelude, the setup, for salvation. Jesus arose! Amazingly, that is the other part of the pattern. The Red Sea parts. Manna comes down. The sun stands still. The walls fall. David kills Goliath. Dagon falls down flat. Fire consumes Elijah's offering. The rain comes. And Jesus arose! Jesus arose from the dead. No one should be surprised. It is what God had been doing all along, and the postlude is amazing. When faced with an impossible scenario, over and over again, it becomes clear that with God nothing is impossible (Luke 1:37; 18:27).

Salvation is impossible. Sinners cannot save themselves. There is no one. Isaiah saw it. There was no man to be counselor or to give an answer (49:28). No man could be intercessor (59:16). No man could save man. It was impossible. So, the Lord's own arm, the Lord's own ability and power, brought salvation (65:3; 59:16; cp. Ps 98:1). The salvation that is impossible for humanity, God accomplishes in Jesus Christ.

Terrorist attacks in Paris on the night of Friday the 13th in November 2015, perpetrated by gunmen and suicide bombers, hit a concert hall, a major stadium, restaurants, and bars almost simultaneously. They left 130 fatalities in their wake with hundreds more wounded. The following Monday evening my wife and I were scheduled to be part of an interfaith gathering in our hometown of Knoxville, Tennessee. The meeting had been planned for months; but in one night, the agenda was completely redirected. I was serving on the discussion panel for the group that evening among Jews, Christians, and Muslims who wept openly and waited for answers.

In my presentation, I addressed the darkness and despair that I think everyone in the room felt in the wake of this horrible attack. I insisted that without faith in God, despair would drown us all. Then I became more specific. I suggested that when Jesus died on the cross and was buried in the tomb, he entered darkness and despair, and embraced them. He took death and everything it stands for into himself. Then in his resurrection, Jesus overcame death and all the darkness and despair it brings. Although everything I say or do as a Christian in such settings is meant to be a witness, I was not "preaching" at them. I wanted to share from my faith that anytime anything seems impossibly hopeless that Jesus Christ turns it around. Jesus turns death into life, darkness into light, and despair into hope.

Accordingly, Pentecostal theology includes recognition of the impossible scenario of salvation. It also punctuates that it is at the point of impossibility that a savior is needed. That is precisely where our Savior and Lord Jesus Christ comes in for us. He does for us that which we cannot do for ourselves. Furthermore, not just here or there or in this or that: Jesus does all things well (Mark 7:37). In a word, our Lord is *omnicompetent*. Ultimately, he has surpassed all rivals in his fight on our behalf; he is our *champion*.

AN OMNICOMPETENT CHAMPION

Most of all, then, salvation has an *omnicompetent champion*. The all-powerful, all-wise, all-good God dramatically and totally defeats all the forces of evil. God completely rescues and abundantly blesses those who believe, those who put their trust in God and obey God's will. Isaiah 19:20 provides a framework for understanding the significance of the category of "champion" for the doctrine of salvation: "It will become a sign and a witness to the Lord of hosts in the land of Egypt; for they will cry to the Lord because of oppressors, and He will send them a Savior and a Champion, and He will deliver them" (NASB). This prophetic declaration occurs in a context of divine prediction that Egypt—the notorious oppressor of the Israelites—will one day turn to Yahweh, the God of Israel (19:16–25). The turning of Egypt to God evidences God's presence and activity. OT scholar John Oswalt explains that the language of Isaiah 19:20 is reminiscent of the book of Judges.[39] Just as Israel cried out to the Lord for deliverance from oppressors and the Lord heard and "sent his champions" in response, so will Egypt cry out and the Lord will do so again.[40] I might add, it will not be one more "savior and champion"—it is *the* "Savior and Champion."

Lee Roy Martin, a leading Pentecostal OT scholar, points out that a dominant theme in Judges is the problem of adequate leadership, especially an ever-worsening pattern of moral and spiritual decline among the judges.[41] Sharp theological contrast exists between the successfulness of the conquest and faithfulness of Israel depicted in the book of Joshua with the incompleteness of the conquest and Israel's unfaithfulness in Judges as a prelude to pre-monarchic disarray in 1 Samuel.[42] Israel's judges/deliverers/leaders—their charismatic "champions"—often fell woefully short. The book of Judges makes evident that only the Lord in his sovereign power and covenant faithfulness can really deliver or save Israel.[43] In short, only Yahweh is Israel's divine champion (cp. Jer 20:11). Pentecostal congregations have often been attracted to charismatic magnetic leaders. Yet, Pentecostal theology insistently affirms that God is the only absolute deliverer or savior, and therefore, the omnicompetent champion.

Historically, some suggest that the Isaianic reference to the Lord's savior and champion for Egypt could be a cryptic allusion to Alexander the

---

39. Oswalt, *Isaiah*, 379.
40. Oswalt, *Isaiah*, 379.
41. Martin, *Unheard Voice of God*, 74–75, 92.
42. Martin, *Unheard Voice of God*, 104.
43. Martin, *Unheard Voice of God*, 153–57, 159.

Great, whom the Egyptians welcomed as a deliverer. Theologically, it is clear that "Messiah is the antitype ultimately intended."[44] In other words, we may identify the final fulfillment of this prophecy regarding a "Savior and Champion" sent by the God of Israel to deliver and rescue this Gentile nation as none other than the Lord Jesus Christ. Interpreting Isaiah 19:20 against the background of an Israel-Egypt connection, with the example of the Judges in mind and while affirming the messianic nature of the text, enables several theological observations.

First, observe that while on the surface it appears that the Lord was fighting for Israel against Egypt, in reality, the Lord was fighting *for* both groups; that is, for all peoples, *against* the spiritual wickedness and sin that threatens to destroy them and damn them. Even when the Lord was delivering Israel from Egypt, the divine plan with its redemptive purpose extended to Egypt as well. In fact, it embraces all humanity (John 3:16). On the one hand, Israel, as a kind of microcosm of humanity, encapsulates in miniature form the characteristics and qualities of the larger human community. God used biblical Israel to teach the world about the nature of human sin and of divine redemption (1 Cor 10:6). On the other hand, Egypt, Israel's adversary and archfoe, itself needs redemption. When Yahweh fought against idolatry and oppression in Egypt, he was fighting for their eventual deliverance and salvation. The omnicompetent champion, as I put it, is not merely the champion of a certain group or people. He desires to deliver all people.

Nevertheless, the Lord's universal concern no less pits him against the powers of evil, against the idolatry and oppression, of a fallen, sinful world. Biblical Egypt serves as a kind of archetype of idolatry, immorality, and oppression. Ancient Egyptian religion oddly mixed pantheism and animal worship. The Egyptians were polytheists (worshipers of many gods/goddesses) who believed certain animals embodied various deities. Ptah, the Creator, the god of Memphis, was at the head of the pantheon, then Amon, the god of Thebes. Amon, like most of the other gods, was eventually identified with Ra, the sun-god of Heliopolis. This idolatry and immorality came—and must always come—under the judgment of the one true and living God. Yet, incredibly, this pagan, polytheistic people was not beyond the range of God's compassionate concern. Neither is any other people or person.

Pentecostal soteriology emphasizes the universality of salvation. In other words, Pentecostals affirm a doctrine of general or universal redemption. These terms do not suggest that everyone will be saved. *Universality is not universalism.* The Lord desires—and therefore makes provision through Christ Jesus—for every human being to be saved (1 Tim 2:4–5). Yet, only

---

44. Jamieson et al., *Commentary on the Whole Bible*, 1:452.

those who respond in faith and repentance are actually saved (1 Tim 4:10; 2 Pet 3:9). Howbeit, the Lord works—even fights—on behalf of the world's Egyptians, too. Israel illustrates redemption for everyone but redemption is not limited to Israel. A Hebrew prophet named Jonah discovered the truth of God's inclusive kindness, we might say "the hard way" (Jonah 4). Hopefully, contemporary Pentecostals will not have to relearn his lesson.

In light of the preceding, we might understandably inquire about the character and nature of God. "What is God really like?" Common responses would probably include: God is loving and merciful; God is holy and righteous; God is good; God is all-knowing and wise; God is all-powerful; God is eternal; and, God is lawmaker and judge. What is your mental "image" of God? Do you primarily picture God as Creator? Savior? Healer? Absolute King or Sovereign Ruler? Lord and Master? Do you mostly think of God as your Friend? Your Father? Of course, all these common responses are correct. It's not so much either/or as both/and when it comes to God. The infinite and almighty God is larger than human descriptions and perceptions.

God as "Champion" includes an idea that God is "Defender" or "Protector." God resists the attacks of evil made on humanity. God keeps or makes safe from danger and harm. The worst danger is eternal and spiritual, but also temporal and natural harm is a matter of concern to people and to their God. Usually, these overlap anyway. God defends the weak and protects the vulnerable. At some level or time that includes everybody. God is the Great Fighter. After the defeat of Egypt and Pharaoh, Moses and Israel sang that "The Lord is a man of war" (Exod 15:3). Isaiah also described the Lord as "a man of war" (42:13). That makes modern folks nervous. I understand. It is because they compare God's warfare to human warfare, but there is more to it than that.

An ancient heretic named Marcion (85–c. 160) was offended by the battles (and other matters) in the OT. But he (and others since) missed the underlying reality. Although the OT portrays the Lord as the Champion or Defender and Protector of Israel in battles against surrounding nations, such as Egypt, we have seen that he was, in actuality, fighting for deliverance and freedom from sin and death for both nations. The OT battles were not about Israel versus the Egyptians or Canaanites or Philistines or Assyrians. The great rabbi Gamaliel warned that Israel itself was in danger of fighting against God at times (Acts 5:33–39). The Lord fights against evil. He fights for souls. He fights on our behalf. He fights for all of us. The Lord is the omnicompetent champion who fights to save humanity and the cosmos from the destructive forces of evil.

Second, observe that the lesson of history, both scriptural and otherwise, is that all human champions are inadequate to save; only the sovereign

SOTERIOLOGICAL ETHOS   99

Lord saves; further, the Lord compassionately and patiently grants mercy but never ceases to demand faithfulness and righteousness. There are at least three reasons that humans, by definition, are incapable of being their own or anyone else's savior and champion. Human beings are *fallen*, *frail*, and *finite*. Fallenness describes human sinfulness. Frailty describes human infirmity and weakness. Finitude describes human limitations and boundaries.

As stated, fallenness describes human sinfulness. Theologians talk about "original sin," the continuing impact of the first human sin on the rest of the race, and "actual sin," specific acts of disobedience committed by individuals against God's will.[45] If one has an infection in his/her body, then he/she will usually have various symptoms such as fever, chills, or fatigue. Even so, adultery, murder, thefts, and other evils are symptomatic of the evil that resides in human hearts (Mark 7:21; Jer 17:9). The connotation of "fall" is descriptive of an idea that God created humans for a higher purpose from which they descended—or rather, plummeted—as a consequence of their primal and deliberate choice to reject God's imperative and undertake their subsequent rebellious action. Humans, therefore, lost their way. They are no longer what they were created to be. In addition to the just judgment their Creator imposes on them, for their ungrateful betrayal of his goodness and love, they have become deficient in every way. They abused their free will; now it is in bondage to sin. They abused their powers of reason; now their minds are darkened. They abused God's gift of holy affections; now their disposition is toward illicit desire and ungodly lust. They allowed their physical nature to rule their spirit; now their flesh constantly rages against them. They lifted themselves up in arrogant pride; now they have plunged into utter despair. Fallen human beings are the quintessential example of tragedy, and they are certainly in no shape to save themselves nor anyone else. Quite to the contrary, human beings desperately need saving. To be more specific, people need the Savior.

As stated, frailty describes human infirmity and weakness. It is probably impossible today to even begin to imagine the glorious condition and state of pre-fall persons. Psalm 8 grants a peek. It reveals that God made a deliberate choice to place humankind at the center of a vast universe.[46] God's creation of humankind with the *imago Dei* (image of God) makes men and women unique among all creaturely beings (Gen 1:26–27). Originally,

---

45. Rybarczyk, "Pentecostal Perspective on Salvation," 77. Bloesch, *Essentials of Evangelical Theology*, 109–14, demonstrates that a biblical view of sin runs counter to the idealist optimism of the modern mindset. However, he rightly affirms "an optimism based on grace" in sharp distinction from "an optimism based on human resources" per much of post-Enlightenment theology, 114.

46. Broyles, *Psalms*, 72.

humans must have been quite Godlike. As such, they enjoyed an intimate communion with God and shared in God's dominion over the created order. In his sermon on Psalm 8:4, John Wesley characterized the demise of humanity when he predicated that man was created to "know, and love, and enjoy, and serve his great Creator to all eternity," but through sin "became lower than even the beasts that perish."[47] Created to walk with God, sin brought humans to a level lower than animals! Their former glory gone, humankind became but a shell of their former selves.

Philip Melanchthon (1497–1560), Martin Luther's famous protégé and an influential theologian in his own right, explains that "the deterioration of human strength through sin" results in "man's inability to free himself from sin and death" and limits "the works that man is able to do in such a state of weakness."[48] In their original state humans, had "a free, unimpeded will," but because of sin "God withdrew from them and man's natural powers became very weak."[49] Melanchthon graphically describes humanity's post-fall state as the "great ruin of human powers" in which "man's will and heart are wretchedly imprisoned, impaired, and ruined."[50] Essentially, this monumental weakness means that natural man does not have the spiritual or moral hardiness to successfully withstand the onslaught of sin. Again, people need the Savior and Champion that only God can send.

As stated, finitude describes human limitations and boundaries. When the psalmist says the Lord knows our "frame" (*yetsrēnû*), that is, our form or shape (103:14), it signifies that which constitutes humanity's boundaries or limitations. Human nature exists within form—with *shape*; it has demarcated arrangement in space. Human beings are restricted within space. The psalmist is saying a great deal more than "God understands my constitution." Perhaps it could be better put thus: "God understands that I am constituted." Not just that I *have* a frame—of course that—but more so, that I *am* framed. I exist within a frame. The sum of it is simple enough: the Lord knows humans are finite rather than infinite. Indeed, although the text refers to that frame as "dust," or the material/physical part of the person, finitude is not limited to bodily existence. The psalmist is not merely saying, "Dust is what people are made of." Rather, he is saying something more like, "People are made." Therefore, finitude properly describes the spiritual/

---

47. John Wesley, "What is Man?," 2:225–230, in *Wesley's Works*, 2:229–30.

48. Melanchthon, *Christian Doctrine*, 51. Here and below I relate Melanchthon's actual words with apologies for his gender exclusive terminology. I have no doubt that his descriptions apply equally to women as well as men.

49. Melanchthon, *Christian Doctrine*, 52.

50. Melanchthon, *Christian Doctrine*, 52.

immaterial part of creaturely existence as well.[51] All creatures, including humans, are finite. Only God is infinite. Therefore, only God can be the Savior and Champion who is needed so desperately by a lost world.

To be clear, human finitude is not a consequence of the fall but an inevitable fact of human creatureliness. In this sense, it is distinct from human fallenness and frailty. Further, it is not in itself a negative. Humans before the fall were finite and after glorification, will still be finite. They necessarily have ontological boundaries and limitations inherent in their very existence as well as in their range of abilities. Humans have never been nor ever will be omni-anything. Only God is omni. That is, only God is omnipotent, omniscient, and omnipresent. Obviously, only God is the omnicompetent champion who saves, delivers, and heals. The one who redeems creatures and creation must be greater than those creatures and that creation. Only the Creator fits the bill.[52]

Psalm 147:5 declares, "Great is our Lord and mighty in power; His understanding is infinite." Literally, God's knowledge cannot be numbered, cannot be measured. This conveys the absence of all limitation as well as the fullness of all perfection. There is nothing beyond the compass of God's understanding. His understanding embraces everything there is to know. Theologically, this perfection applies to all divine attributes. The truth that God is infinite in his being and in all his perfections pervades Scripture. It could not be otherwise if God is unoriginated, exalted above all limits of time, space, and creaturehood, and dependent only on God's self. In a sense, infinity is what it means to be God: boundless perfection. It is not so for mere mortals. Therefore, Psalm 146:3–6 exhorts us to not trust in humans for help, because they are bounded by time; rather, hope in the Lord who made heaven and earth, and who reigns forever (v. 10). As Edwards insisted, God is infinitely above all creatures and infinitely good.[53] The Lord is our Savior and Champion.

Third, observe that ultimate and absolute victory over spiritual wickedness and sin is accomplished through the crucifixion, resurrection, and ascension of Jesus Christ, with Pentecost as divine affirmation and

---

51. See Richie, "Pragmatism, Power, and Politics."

52. In Christian theology "eternity" can describe either a mode of existence not subject to time or a peculiar attribute of God. The former addresses the general idea of immortality, that is, of endless duration, while the latter is more strictly theological and is, by very definition, unique to divinity. Similarly, "infinity" refers to the quality of limitlessness or endlessness in terms of space, extent, or size, and is, therefore, predicated only of divinity. Thus, even in their enjoyment of immortality, humans will continue to be finite creatures.

53. See Marsden, "Challenging the Presumptions of the Age," 102.

confirmation.[54] There is a once and for all nature to Christ's redeeming work (Rom 6:10; Heb 7:27; Jude 3). It is terminal and eternal. Crucifixion represents voluntary submission to ultimate humiliation. Resurrection represents not only the defeat of death but validation of Christ and the significance of his cross. Ascension represents victory not only in this world but the full and final conquest of evil powers at the cosmic level by the ultimate authority of the Savior and Champion.[55] Speaking prophetically of this validation and victory, Psalm 110:1 declares, "The Lord said to my Lord, 'Sit at My right hand, Till I make Your enemies Your footstool,'" and elucidates their fulfillment in the crucified, risen, and exalted Lord Jesus Christ.

Philippians 2:5–11 dramatically depicts Christ's humiliation and exaltation. The way to exaltation is not prideful rebellion against divine authority. It is humiliation, or self-emptying and self-sacrifice, that leads to exaltation. Therefore, Christ has a name above every name. He is exalted over everyone. And everyone, including those "in heaven," "on earth," and "under the earth"—all beings everywhere—will pay homage to Christ as Lord. Christ will be acknowledged as supreme master and ruler of everyone everywhere forever. The name of Jesus will be worshiped in every conceivable habitation of personal beings.[56] As stated above, this does not mean that evil angels or demonic entities will be saved. These rebels will not confess Christ as Lord unto *salvation*; rather they will confess Christ as Lord in *submission*.

On April 9, 1942, Major General Edward P. King Jr. surrendered at Bataan, Philippines. Consequently, 78,000 troops (66,000 Filipinos and 12,000 Americans), the largest contingent of US soldiers ever to surrender, were taken captive by the Japanese. In the eschatological scene depicted in Philippians 2:10–11 (cp. Isa 45:23), the most momentous surrender ever will occur as evil is finally forever vanquished. Satan will surrender! All Satan's armies will relent, and they will acknowledge Jesus Christ as Lord. In so doing, they will admit the goodness and wisdom of God's eternal counsel and purpose. Both the psalmist David and the apostle Paul saw that ultimately God will be justified (Ps 51:4; Rom 3:4). God will be fully and forever vindicated in Christ (cp. 1 Tim 3:16).[57]

---

54. Rybarczyk, "Pentecostal Perspective on Salvation," contends, "Jesus is the solution to sin's shame, guilt, infection, and death," 77.

55. Bloesch, *Essentials of Evangelical Theology*, 31–32, does not go far enough when he asserts: "The resurrection of Jesus Christ signifies the supreme act of the sovereignty of God, and his heavenly ascension connotes his elevation over the whole world." I propose that Christ at the right hand of God signifies his "elevation" over all the cosmos.

56. Melick, *Philippians, Colossians, Philemon*, 107–8.

57. I sympathize with Lewis's complaint about God being "in the dock" or on trial before "modern man," *Collected Works of C. S. Lewis*, 464–65. And yet, truth be told, it

In associative concurrence with the preceding scenario of victory through Christ's death, resurrection, and ascension, Pentecost testifies to the identity and ministry of Jesus Christ as the one sent by God to be the Savior and Champion of all who will believe. Significantly, God's messianic affirmation and confirmation at the public event of Jesus' baptism in water by John occurred as the Holy Spirit descended (Matt 3:13–17; Mark 1:9–11; Luke 3:21–23). Even so, Pentecost climaxes Jesus' public ministry with affirmation and confirmation by the Holy Spirit's public descent upon his church (Acts 2:1–4, 33). This public witness of the Holy Spirit to Jesus Christ in the church continues to occur again and again wherever devout believers will receive it (8:14–17; 10:44–48; 19:1–7). Whenever the Holy Spirit falls on the church of Jesus Christ, his triumph is both publicly proclaimed and experientially extended.

In this chapter, I have endeavored to get at the heart of who Pentecostals are in regards to salvation. I contended that, *for Pentecostals, salvation has an antagonistic element in a cosmic context with an impossible scenario requiring an omnicompetent champion.* Then I unpacked and expanded on that contention in order to explicate a somewhat fuller understanding of salvation-as-deliverance in respect to Pentecostal soteriological identity. The next chapter further focuses on Pentecostal understandings of the oppositional nature of salvation and, accordingly, of the Christian life, by giving attention to one of Pentecostals' most emphatic, and at times, most controversial, doctrines: the reality and nature of spiritual warfare.

---

has always been God who willingly put himself "in the dock" or "on trial."

5

Oppositional Soteriology

(Spiritual Warfare in Salvation)

Pentecostals believe that the devil and his demons are actual entities malevolently bent on destroying them, and ultimately, through sin and death, on damning them, as part of evil's arrogant rebellion against the holy and righteous God. Pentecostals further believe that they are totally unable to rescue themselves or to win victory. Fortunately, Pentecostals believe, the good news of the gospel is that the benevolent and loving God has graciously accomplished their deliverance through their crucified and risen Lord and Savior Jesus Christ and through the gift of the Holy Spirit. In this context, Pentecostals believe that God empowers them by the Holy Spirit for divine mission and service, until the destined consummation of God's purpose in the triumphant return of his Son Jesus Christ.

THE DEVIL AND DEMONS

Beginning in 2007 and for several years, I served as a Pentecostal Representative on the Commission of the Churches on International Affairs.[1] One morning at breakfast during a CCIA meeting, I had an eye-opening

---

1. The CCIA is an NGO (nongovernmental organization) that works with the United Nations in conjunction with the World Council of Churches on issues involving intersections of religious, social, and political concern on an international scale.

conversation about the devil with a fellow commissioner. We had worked together on the commission for some years in different parts of the world. He knew my Pentecostal identity. I knew his Anglican commitments as an accomplished theologian and that he was from Sri Lanka, a country with a strong Buddhist and Hindu background. We were (and remained) on friendly terms. As he shared with me about the oppression and violence going on in his part of the world, I made a general remark about the devil's work. My allusion to the devil precipitated a strong disagreement.

My friend argued that the devil is not a real personal being but a symbol of the evil residing in human hearts. He further averred that I and other Pentecostals were taking an easy way out by projecting blame for sin onto some cosmic mythical figure while excusing human beings.[2] We went back and forth for a while with him basically repeating the same charge and with me constantly referring back to the biblical witness. We never resolved the issue by the time we were called to our work, but I have long remembered the discussion. For me, it illustrates the mindset of many today regarding the devil and demons.[3]

I still insist that the biblical witness cannot be dismissed regarding its teaching about the devil and demons. The same Bible that witnesses of Christ also warns against the devil and evil spirits (Matt 4:1–11).[4] In my mind, the "easy way out" here is accepting the comforting truth of Scripture about God but avoiding its discomfiting truth about the devil. Pentecostals cannot be so selective. Accordingly, Pentecostals view the devil and his demons as actual entities. In other words, they are real personal beings of a spiritual nature.[5] Unlike many schools of thought today, Pentecostal theology does not dilute the NT in order to explain away the presence of the devil

---

2. Actually, this theme has deep roots in historic Christianity. E.g., in the third century, Origen presented salvation as "spiritual combat" beginning at baptism and continuing throughout the Christian life; Scheck, "Origen of Alexandria," 22–23. Bloesch argues in *Last Things*, 52, that "the fundamental biblical opposition" is "between God and the devil, Christ and Satan, the Holy Spirit and the Unholy."

3. Harvey, "Satan," 216, *Theological Terms*, observes that liberal Protestants abandoned the concept of Satan as a personal demonic being "as a relic of a prescientific mentality." Note that this view is a departure from historic Christian belief and that its direction is determined by an uncritical appropriation of science rather than by the authority of Holy Scripture.

4. E.g., who was Jesus talking to during the temptation in the wilderness (Matt 4:1–11)? Himself? No one? What really happened? Anything? Nothing? That is absurd.

5. Bloesch argues in *Last Things*, 52, that real evil and actual temptation require personality, and that impersonal evil is, in fact, impossible.

and demons. They are not merely symbols of the reality of evil. They are *real* and they are *evil*.[6]

However, there is another side to it. Admittedly television comedian Flip Wilson's Geraldine character was uproariously hilarious when "she" quipped "The devil made me do it!" In real life, there is nothing funny about people avoiding responsibility for their actions. Pentecostal demonology does not do that. Pentecostals firmly defend human free will and, consequently, human moral accountability. The devil cannot force anyone to do anything. He uses deception and lies to manipulate people into making bad choices (Gen 3:13; 2 Cor 11:3; Rev 12:9). If Pentecostals do not believe God's grace is irresistible, then they certainly do not believe diabolical temptation is irresistible either. In other words, human choice is involved in either case. Like Adam and Eve, everyone makes choices regarding good and evil, and, also like them, everyone answers for those choices accordingly. There is no denying that the human heart certainly is "deceitful above all things" and "desperately wicked," but the Lord searches and tests hearts and minds before judging the actions that arise out of them (Jer 17:9–10).

Assuredly, human existence is dramatically impacted by evil beings malevolently bent on destroying human lives on earth and, ultimately through sin and death, damning as many as possible for eternity. Their malevolence is all part of evil's arrogant rebellion against the holy and righteous God. Furthermore, people are totally unable to rescue themselves or to win victory. Yet the good news of the gospel is that the benevolent and loving God has graciously accomplished deliverance through the crucified and risen Lord and Savior Jesus Christ. Additionally, God empowers the redeemed by the Holy Spirit for divine mission and service, until the destined consummation of God's purpose in the triumphant return of his Son Jesus Christ. The evils and perils of the last days (2 Tim 3:1) are countered and overcome by the power of the last days' outpouring of the Holy Spirit (Acts 2:17).

In at least one area, Pentecostal demonology (doctrine of the existence and nature of the devil and demons) calls for careful qualification. Are Pentecostals dualists? If not philosophically, are they nevertheless functional dualists? Resoundingly, no. Pentecostals are not dualists. Warrington rightly suggests that concerns over an implicit cosmic dualism in Pentecostal spirituality and theology arise from a lack of understanding about what Pentecostals actually believe regarding the devil and demons.[7] Pentecostals do not

6. Contrariwise, Bradnick, *Evil, Spirits, and Possession*, appears to be a clear departure from traditional Pentecostal theology regarding demonology.

7. Warrington, *Encounter*, 293–94. Aulén, *Faith of the Christian Church*, 201–6, has a provocative discussion of the "legitimacy and limitation of dualism" from the standpoint of general Christian theology and the problem of evil (theodicy).

believe there are two more or less equal and opposite powers or principles, that is, good and evil, light and darkness, God and the devil, instigating the conflictual nature of existence. God the Creator is infinitely superior to the devil, a created being. The devil is a fallen angel, who has rebelled against God but will be, indeed has already been, inevitably and incontrovertibly defeated by Jesus Christ (Gal 1:4; Eph 2:2; Col 1:13).

Pentecostals predicate their demonology on the conviction that the career of the devil and his demonic cohorts is an inferior aberration from the divinely ordained order of existence of its original godly purpose (Isa 14:12). The devil is a *rebel*, not a *rival*.[8] In other words, the devil wickedly resists God's established order of righteousness; the devil is not real competition with God for superiority.[9] Satan craves worship but concedes to God (Matt 4:8–11; cp. 2 Thess 2:1–12). In the first installment of the blockbuster *The Avengers* fantasy series, the rebel Asgardian, Loki, demanded to be worshiped as a god. The mighty Hulk responded by easily beating Loki into abject submission. As he turns away in obvious disdain, Hulk snarls, "puny god."[10] That puts it pretty well. As "the god of this age" (2 Cor 4:4; cp. John 12:31), the devil is a "puny god"—small and weak, minor and petty; finally, in the grand scheme of eternity, insignificant. Yet for all that, spiritual warfare in this present age can be intense.[11]

Theologically speaking, how are we to understand the reality of spiritual beings and spiritual warfare? Put another way, is there a credible and defensible theology behind belief in the existence of spirit beings and spiritual warfare? Does belief in demons, or for that matter, angels, fall into the category of a religious version of extraterrestrials and flying saucers? Is it some superstitious carryover from premodern peoples? I do not think so. There is a credible and defensible theology behind belief in the existence of spirit beings and spiritual warfare.[12] Scripture is the basis of Christian belief

---

8. As Thorsen, *Exploration of Christian Theology*, 120, puts it: "Satan was an angelic creature who apparently rebelled against God and continues to lead spiritual opposition to God's purposes in the world."

9. As Lewis, *Mere Christianity*, 36, bluntly puts it, the "universe is at war," but this is not "a war between independent powers"; rather, "it is a civil war, a rebellion," but "we are living in a part of the universe occupied by the rebel."

10. For helpful context, see Peter Sanderson, "The Avengers: fictional superhero team," revised and updated by J. E. Luebering, *Britannica*: https://www.britannica.com/topic/the-Avengers-superhero-team.

11. Bloesch, *Last Things*, 54–55, rightly bemoans the tendency of leading theologians such as Karl Barth, Oscar Cullman, and Dietrich Bonhoeffer to underplay "the continuing warfare between Christ and the devil."

12. E.g., OT scholar Peter Enns offers a strong apologetic for the "cosmic battle motif" which undergirds the concept of spiritual warfare in "Yahweh, Creation, and

in the spirit world, and biblical references to spirit beings and their actions are innumerable.[13]

However, some see even the Bible as slight evidence for the spirit realm. For them, there is little to no difference between traditional Jewish and Christian belief in angels and demons and in pagan Greek and Roman beliefs in gods and goddesses in their respective mythologies. More than half a century ago, Rudolf Bultmann urged modern readers of the NT to demythologize unacceptable aspects of the first century worldview in order to get at the kernel of truth embedded in that naïve perspective.[14] Demythologizing mostly meant stripping away the husks of "myths" such as angels and spirits and anything supernatural—including the resurrection of Jesus.[15] Due to their high views of scriptural inspiration and authority, Pentecostals reject demythologization in biblical interpretation. Rather, the program of Bultmann and other demythologizers exposes their own philosophical skepticism, unduly influenced by an unsustainable post-Enlightenment bias against immaterial reality.[16] So then, what is an example of a credible theology of the existence of spirit beings and spiritual warfare that is true to Scripture and relevant for today?

Genesis 3 describes the tragic separation of humanity from the enjoyment of unfettered fellowship with their Creator God. The sinful attempt to be "like God" resulted in loss of the blessing of being "with God."[17] Human alienation from God's presence serves as an indicator of a rift in reality itself,

---

the Cosmic Battle."

13. Bloesch, *Last Things*, 47–48, points out that both sacred tradition and scriptural witness affirm the existence of both the visible (humans, animals, etc.) and the invisible (angels and demons) worlds.

14. Bultmann, *Jesus Christ and Mythology*.

15. Smith, *Thinking in Tongues*, chapter 4, "Science, Spirit, and a Pentecostal Ontology," esp. 89–98, ably demonstrates that "naturalism" and "supernaturalism" are problematic terms but not easily disposable either. Avoiding dualism, on the supernaturalist side, and reductionism, on the naturalist side, is challenging. Smith opts for an "enchanted" or, better, "en-Spirited" view of nature as open to and primed for extraordinary divine acts from within rather than from without, 103–5.

16. The Enlightenment was an eighteenth-century movement that elevated reason as the highest authority. Some Enlightenment thinkers rejected religion altogether; others subjected religion to rationalist criteria, discounting categories of divine revelation and authority. See Clark, Lints, and Smith, *101 Key Terms in Philosophy and Their Importance for Theology* (Kindle locations 460–77). Unfortunately, the cutting criticism of Southern, *Western Society and the Church in the Middle Ages*, regarding problems of societal biases in the churches that "The truth is that they could not be overcome because they were invisible to contemporaries," 15, is not limited to the Middle Ages.

17. Sailhamer, *Pentateuch as Narrative*, 100, 102.

that is, of a crack, a split, a break in the nature of reality (cp. Isa 59:2).[18] When the universe was whole, the spiritual and physical would have been seamlessly unified. The Lord God walked in the garden in direct, intimate fellowship with his creatures Adam and Eve. Yet, sin drove them from God's presence and expelled them from the place of union, driving a wedge between their worlds. A barrier was put in place between humanity and divinity, between the natural and the spiritual.[19]

Origen sadly opines of humanity's fall that the opening of the "eyes of sense" was accompanied by the closing of the "eyes of the mind," so that they no longer "enjoyed the delight of beholding God and his paradise."[20] In sum, their spiritual vision became impaired (as with other senses), until it could no longer sense the divine or the world of spiritual reality as had once been the case. Pseudo-Dionysius (late fifth/early sixth century) comments that "the power to know and to see God, to receive the greatest gifts of his light, to contemplate the divine splendor in primordial power" were affected by the human fall into sin.[21] Allowing for the mystical and contemplative context of these comments, an idea of a literal breach between the divine and the human remains.

Accordingly, those who desire and seek a relationship with God now walk or live by faith rather than by sight (2 Cor 5:7). Faith maintains an assurance of an unseen reality (Heb 11:1). Thus, Wesley described faith and its experience as spiritual senses comparable to the physical senses.[22] Faith asserts that one day, that is in the eschaton, unity, or really more than that, union between the divine and the human and between the spiritual and the physical, will be fully restored as so powerfully portrayed in Revelation 21 and 22. God will be "with" his people in a world made new (21:3). And

18. Ironically, atheist philosopher Ludwig Feuerbach (1804–1872) proposed that religion is an illusionary projection of the divine which alienates humans from each other. See "Feuerbach, Ludwig," in Clark, Lints, and Smith; *101 Key Terms in Philosophy and Their Importance for Theology* (Kindle locations 712–20). Unable to deny humanity's chronic and acute sense of alienation, rather than acknowledge its source in separation from God, he oddly turns it on God and blames belief in God for it. However, as Paul Tillich, *Systematic Theology*, contends, humanity's "estrangement" and "aloneness" stem from turning away from the true ground of being (unbelief in God) and turning toward self and self's world as a false center (*hubris*), 44, 47, 49, 71–72. Thus, separation from God further alienates us from one another and from our true selves.

19. Although our focus is in a different direction, Bloesch, *Last Things*, 161, 163, 165, argues that the traditional doctrine of the communion of the saints also bridges this barrier, even across the boundaries of death itself.

20. Oden and Louth, eds., *Genesis 1–11*, 80–81.

21. Oden and Louth, eds., *Genesis 1–11*, 102.

22. Oden, *John Wesley's Scriptural Christianity*, summarizes Wesley on experience, 84–91.

what does Scripture say? They will "see his face" (22:4). In theology this eventual seeing of God is known as "the beatific vision" and is considered "the ultimate destiny of the redeemed."[23] Beholding the beauty of God's glory has long been the hope of the saints (Ps 24:4; Matt 5:8). The following characteristic old hymn reflects this hope:

> I'm looking now across the river
> Where my faith will end in sight
> Just a few more days I wait in labor
> Then I will take my heavenly flight.[24]

Yet, between the primeval fall and the eschatological restoration there are times when the world of spiritual beings intrudes into the material world. Rather than the so-called "intrusion" being unwelcome or uninvited, it is usually more a matter of being unexpected. Perhaps unaware is an even better description. The narrative of Elisha and his young aid is a case in point. When Elisha prayed, the young man's eyes were opened to see into the spiritual realm where horses and chariots of fire were all around (2 Kgs 6:17). This scene is reminiscent of the ascent of Elijah in a chariot of fire drawn by horses of fire which Elisha himself had witnessed (2 Kgs 2:11). The description of spirit beings (and conveyances!) as "fire" is doubtless telling, regarding their appearance and nature when beheld by physical eyes. For another example, at the Mount of Transfiguration, the disciples Peter, James, and John saw Christ's appearance changed before them as Moses and Elijah appeared and God's voice sounded (Matt 17:1–8). There are many comparable examples in the Bible (innumerable times the Lord appeared and spoke): The Lord and his angels appear to Abraham at Mamre (Gen 18:1–15); Jacob wrestles with God at Peniel (32:22–32); the Commander of the Lord's Army appears to Joshua (Josh 5:13–15); the angel Gabriel appears to Mary (Luke 1:26–33); and an angel freed Peter from prison (Acts 12:5–11).

Scholars call God's sovereign choice to manifest the divine person to human senses a "theophany." However, intersections between the spiritual and, for lack of better terms, natural or material worlds, exceed theophanic encounters.[25] Jacob's dream at Bethel grants remarkable insight into inter-

---

23. Harvey, "Beatific Vision," 68–69, *Theological Terms*, 39.

24. "Beulah Land" is a well-known gospel hymn by Edgar Page Stites (1836–1921) with music by John R. Sweny (1837–1899). See Cyber Hymnal at https://web.archive.org/web/20140202231041/http://www.hymntime.com/tch/htm/b/e/u/beulah2.htm.

25. J. Wesley Stamps, "Ephesians," 1019–86, in Arrington and Stronstad, eds., *Full Life Bible Commentary*, 1082, explains that Paul's use of "heavenly realms" in Ephesians has to do with "the unseen spiritual sphere in contrast to the material dimension of life

action between the spiritual and physical worlds (Gen 28:10–22). Jacob's dream or, perhaps more specifically, Jacob's interpretation of a ladder between heaven and earth with angels ascending and descending upon it portrays a connective link between the heavenly/spiritual and earthly/physical. The connective link, so to speak, may be especially strong in a sacred space.[26] In addition to formation of a theology of worship emphasizing reciprocal encounter that arises rather directly out of this liturgical precedent, affirmation of intentional engagement between the divine/spiritual and the human/physical occurs.

In a somewhat different vein, Paul describes being caught up or transported to paradise where indescribable or unutterable revelations were given (2 Cor 12:1–7). Paul's description of ascent to a heavenly realm identifies the person who ascended, and the time and circumstances of the ascent as well as its destination.[27] Obviously, Paul recounts a datable encounter beyond the present world of space and time that transcended physical awareness. Indications include, among other things, that there do indeed exist actual heavenly and earthly dimensions of reality and that it is possible under certain circumstances for interaction between them to occur. Clearly, these "certain circumstances" begin and end with God's sovereign purpose. They do not depend on human machination or attempts at manipulation of the spiritual dimensions of cosmic reality.

The account, therefore, of a backslidden Saul consulting a witch, or really, a medium, is dark and tragic (1 Sam 28:3–25). Biblical scholarship debates what happened that dark and dreadful night. A straightforward reading of the text itself without interposition of conflicting assumptions suggests a possibility of a mediated encounter between a living human being and one who had died.[28] This would be in flagrant violation of biblical prohibitions (Exod 22:18; Lev 19:31; 20:6, 27; Deut 18:1–11). However, that a medium was actually successful, or even that God granted some special dispensation, is a controversial diversion, not necessary to the present

---

that is visible." Note his use of "sphere" and "dimension" as descriptors for the alternate realities under discussion. "Worlds" works as along as limitations are kept in mind. For example, today when speaking of the "Majority World," the "Developed World," the "Industrialized World," or as was once popular, the "Third World," it is clear that these describe, geographically and economically speaking, a part of a shared "world" of life on this planet.

26. Mathews, *Genesis 11:27–50:26*, 452–53. Cp. Bloesch, *Last Things*, 59–61, "An Excursus on Angelology."

27. Harris, *Second Epistle to the Corinthians*, 833.

28. Bergen, *1, 2 Samuel*, 266–67.

purpose. What is necessary is to note *something* assuredly happened. Something *transpired*.

To be clear, this section suggests the reality of distinct spiritual and physical realms that are not, at least not entirely, impassable. This suggestion aligns well with a theological interpretation of the biblical account of the implications of the fall of humanity for the fragmentation of a previously whole cosmos. Perhaps we might describe the cosmos as it presently exists in terms of a multidimensional universe? If so, then might we also describe it as, in some sense, permeable or porous in nature or structure?[29]

In Ernest Hemingway's "The Snows of Kilimanjaro," the character Harry dies tragically and painfully, but then he transitions so smoothly into another dimension that neither he nor the reader quite realizes at first what has happened. The hardest part about the whole experience was the *dying*, not the *death*. Death takes away his pain and burden, transporting him to the place of his dreams.[30] Through this literary device, Hemingway taps into a common assumption that death serves as a transition into another realm of existence. Scripture indicates that interdimensional encounters or experiences occur not only in *death* but in *life*. Again, the purpose of this section is to affirm the biblical and theological credibility of belief in the reality of spirit beings and the spiritual world for the sake of informed discussion regarding their role in spiritual warfare, with its soteriological implications.

SPIRITUAL WARFARE

Pentecostalism has been credited with bringing about a remarkable renewal of interest in "spiritual warfare."[31] Spiritual warfare understands that the Christian life involves ongoing conflict between good and evil, the kingdom of God and the kingdom of Satan, and that malevolent beings bent on human ill must be withstood and overcome in faith, obedience, and prayer, facilitating all through the knowledge of God's sovereignty. The basic premise of spiritual warfare is certainly biblically correct (2 Cor 10:3–6; Eph 6:10–18). Jesus, doubtless, thought of the church as existing in an intractable conflict with the "gates of hades"—though assuring the church's victory in the defeat of evil (Matt 16:18).[32] The premise of spiritual warfare is theologically correct

---

29. Reid, "Heaven," suggests that "cultures that traditionally have a more immediate sense of the closeness of 'the other world,' might have much to teach other Christians (particularly in the West)," 372.

30. Hemingway, "Snows of Kilimanjaro," 55–56.

31. Gilbert, "Spiritual Warfare," 847.

32. Bloesch, *Last Things*, 32, offers an important reminder that "As soldiers of Christ

too. As Aulén indicates, there is an emphatically "militant" nature to faith and to prayer as it seeks to surrender all to God's will and to stand against all that is contrary to God's will.[33]

However, perhaps nowhere else is Pentecostal openness to the Spirit world more prone to error or abuse. Intricately developed and highly speculative demonologies and strategies for dealing with them are by nature susceptible to excesses.[34] Moderation is in order. Gilbert's advice is well taken: focus should always be on the reality of God, rather than on the demonic; inordinate power must not be attributed to demons, but neither should they be dismissed as harmless; and, the ethical dimensions of spiritual struggles and the allegiances they entail are best addressed only "with the supernatural help of the Holy Spirit."[35] Let's look at a famous example.

C. S. Lewis was an Anglican rather than a Pentecostal. However, he displayed Pentecostal sympathies, including an appreciation for the significance of speaking in tongues.[36] More to the point, he had an exceptional understanding of spiritual warfare. His *Screwtape Letters* has become a classic on the topic.[37] Utilizing the format of a fictional satire, Lewis imagines a scenario in which a senior demon named Screwtape writes a series of letters offering advice to his nephew Wormwood, a novice demon assigned the task of securing the damnation of a British man known only as "the Patient." The devil is called "Our Father Below" and God is simply referred to as "the Enemy." The brilliance of this work is that it presents the battle plan of spiritual warfare from the demonic point of view, rather than from that of humans or from that of the divine. This dark perspective is most enlightening.

Lewis primarily addresses issues of temptation and resistance to temptation. Screwtape focuses on undermining the influence of God's Word in the Patient's life and on promoting abandonment of God altogether. Screwtape advises Wormwood to take full advantage of flaws in human nature in accomplishing his damnable purposes. When the Patient converts to Christ, Wormwood wants to lure him into extravagant sin, but Screwtape advises, instead, a more gradual, subtle method. Primarily, it entails promoting human complacency that consequentially impacts various areas of daily life. If possible, Wormwood is to keep the Patient from prayer altogether; if he

we can battle by the side of our Lord and in the power of his Spirit, but only he—Jesus Christ—is the real conqueror and victor."

33. Aulén, *Christian Faith*, 402–6.

34. Kraft, "Spiritual Warfare," 1095–96. Elaborate demonologies and so-called "mapping strategies" are more typical of charismatics than of classical Pentecostals.

35. Gilbert, "Spiritual Warfare," 850.

36. See Richie, "Transposition and Tongues."

37. Lewis, *Screwtape Letters*.

does pray, Wormwood must prevent his prayers from becoming serious or being sustained regularly. Fortunately, the demons, though united against God and against humanity, also bicker among themselves. Eventually, the Patient dies and goes to heaven, resulting in the demons furiously turning on one another. A happy ending if ever there was one!

Lewis later confessed that *Screwtape Letters* was so difficult to write that he resolved not to do anything else like it (although he did eventually briefly revisit Screwtape nearly twenty years later). It has been described as the book Lewis least enjoyed writing.[38] Apparently, he experienced nearly intolerable spiritual opposition and oppression while writing—or spiritual warfare, as Pentecostals are prone to call it. Thankfully, this work has been a boon to many readers for generations since. What can Pentecostals take from *Screwtape Letters* in terms of spiritual warfare?[39] More specifically, what does Pentecostal soteriology have to do with Screwtape and spiritual warfare?

Certain observations are in order. These apply equally no matter the specific manifestation or incident of spiritual warfare. First, spiritual warfare is about undermining one's salvation or the salvation of family or friends. In the event that spiritual warfare cannot actually undermine someone's salvation, it attempts to, at the least, tarnish someone's salvation testimony. Second, spiritual warfare may manifest itself in psychological or physical forms but occurs primarily in the spiritual realm. It originates with spiritual beings, and it is energized by spiritual forces. Third, spiritual warfare is temporal rather than eternal. It occurs in the realm of time but cannot reach into God's eternal destiny for his people. Fourth, spiritual warfare applies pressure to believers in purposeful challenge to their fidelity or loyalty to Jesus Christ. Its main aim is to damage our relationship with our Lord. Finally, there is a foundational consideration that bitterly flavors all else: Satan's adversarial identity. Let's look at each of these observations in order.

First, the diabolical agenda of spiritual warfare determines to undermine one's salvation or the salvation of family or friends. At the least, it attempts to tarnish someone's salvation testimony. However, too often some use spiritual warfare as an excuse for anything negative that happens in their lives. In my first pastorate, a church member once told me that the devil had given him a flat tire. It would have been comical, except he was quite serious. I eventually discovered that he had run over a nail. Spiritual warfare should not be used to describe every little inconvenience

38. Clark, "Which Book Did C. S. Lewis Least Enjoy Writing?"

39. However, one must not blame it all on the devil and his minions. According to Lewis, *Mere Christianity*, 44, "fallen man is not an imperfect creature who needs improvement: he is a rebel who must lay down his arms." Spiritual warfare runs deep.

in life. That trivializes it. It also comes across as "flaky" or "kooky." Spiritual warfare is serious business, a battle for the souls of women and men and girls and boys. That puts it in perspective. The thief comes to steal, kill, and destroy; but Jesus came to give abundant life (John 10:10). Their two agendas are diametrically opposed.

Set in the context of Jesus' self-identification as the Good Shepherd (John 10:1–18), in John 10:10, "Christ puts Himself in contrast with the meaner criminal" who he describes as "the thief."[40] It is not hard to imagine in this parabolic statement an apt description of the devil's selfish and destructive exploitation of God's flock. Jesus, however, secures the safety of the flock and sustains its life above and beyond every necessity. If one were to picture a vicious predator, say a lion or bear or a pack of wolves, attacking a defenseless flock of sheep, snarling and slashing with fangs and claws in wanton slaughter, that would be an apt description of demonic activity against believers. Next, imagine a picture of a devoted shepherd courageously fighting off these vicious predators, even at the cost of his own life. Thus, a portrait of spiritual warfare emerges that reveals the character and nature of the main combatants. Significantly, "the good shepherd" Jesus is "the provider of salvation and care."[41]

Second, spiritual warfare may manifest itself in psychological or physical forms but occurs primarily in the spiritual and moral realms. Not every psychological or physical problem is demonic in nature, although a spiritual component may be present.[42] In any case, spiritual warfare itself originates with spiritual beings and is energized by spiritual forces. Temptation is its primary tool; defeat and discouragement its objectives. Temptation seeks to lure people into sin. Why does God allow the devil to tempt Christians? For the same reason that he allowed the devil to tempt Christ: *temptation is a time of testing*. God has long used various forms of testing to prove and to develop the faith of the saints (1 Pet 1:7).[43] Even our Lord was tempted by the devil (Matt 4:1–11), and the servant is not above his/her master (10:24). Also like our Lord, and through his atoning blood and our testimony of faith in him, we can overcome the devil, including temptation (Rev 12:11). Jesus overcame by standing on God's Word. So can his disciples. Prayer is key to victory (Luke 22:40). When anyone successfully endures temptation, then, they are accepted and approved (*dokimos*) by God (Jas 1:12). They pass the test! As a seminary professor, I often administer tests to students. Needless

---

40. Vincent, *Word Studies in the NT*, 190.
41. Benny C. Aker, "John," 66.
42. Thomas, *Devil, Disease and Deliverance*, is quite helpful on this topic.
43. Jamieson et al., *Commentary on the Whole Bible*, 1:28.

to say, students do not enjoy tests. Tests, however, are necessary to evaluate and to develop students to their maximum ability. See the connection?

Note that temptation cannot be entirely blamed on the devil. Humans' own inordinate desires are a source of temptation—and, if one succumbs, of sin itself and its consequence, loss of the life of God (Jas 1:14–15). Personal accountability is unavoidable. Yet, the devil is at work in temptation, using whatever weapon he can to entice people to rebel against God. In Christ's case, the devil could not lay hold of anything. There was no inordinate desire in him, not anywhere in his being or nature, that could be used against him (John 14:30). Neither should believers give the devil any opportunity (Eph 4:27). Unfortunately, all too often, the devil does get a grip on an inordinate desire or misplaced passion in our hearts, then he uses these to entice and entangle.

Accordingly, sanctification, especially in the sense of mortification, that is, in crucifying—putting to death with Christ—the fleshly nature's inordinate desires and immoral passions (Gal 5:24), is essential for effectiveness in spiritual warfare. When believers submit to God and resist the devil, he will—he must—flee (Jas 4:7). It is called "warfare" for a reason. Victory over the devil and over temptation and sin is its brave goal. Like Winston Churchill, Pentecostals (in battle against an enemy worse even than the Nazis) believe in "victory at all costs, victory in spite of all terror, victory however long and hard the road may be; for without victory, there is no survival."[44] If this is true in the natural, how much more in the spiritual?

Third, spiritual warfare is temporal rather than eternal. It occurs in the realm of time but cannot reach into God's eternal destiny for his people. I agree with Hollis Gause, both that the binding of Satan in Revelation 20:1–3 is one of the most dramatic events in the Apocalypse and that it is, nevertheless, not the most important one (which is reserved for the climactic manifestation of divine glory).[45] I further agree that the "release of Satan from the bottomless pit and his subsequent attempt to continue his revolt will demonstrate his incurable rebelliousness."[46] Universalism is untrue. Satan will neither quit nor repent. Even more importantly, the manner of the Lord's triumph over Satan will show the glory of God as well as his wisdom and patience.[47] Gause's allusion to patience turns attention to pressures of the passing of time in the matter of conflict with evil.

---

44. From Prime Minister Winston Churchill's "Blood, Toil, Tears and Sweat" speech before British Parliament, May 13, 1940. https://www.nationalchurchillmuseum.org/blood-toil-tears-and-sweat.html.

45. Gause, *Revelation*, 250.

46. Gause, *Revelation*, 257.

47. Gause, *Revelation*, 257.

Many may typically understand the English noun *patience* merely as describing a capacity to wait in line without getting annoyed or to sit through heavy traffic without getting upset. Actually, it derives from an adjective "patient," going back to the Latin participle of *pati* meaning "to suffer." No wonder the King James Version used "longsuffering" for patience. Patience includes thoughts of bearing pains or trials without complaint, manifesting forbearance under provocation or strain, of not being hasty or impetuous, and of being steadfast despite adversity or difficulty. Therefore, one who is patient is able or willing to bear with challenges, to use the adverb form, "patiently."[48]

In terms of spiritual warfare, patience points to the appropriate attitude of believers in this present age, while moving inexorably toward the ultimate and permanent defeat of Satan and all his demons. This action will precede the climax of history as it begins to transition into eternity, where everyone and everything will be subject unto God as "all in all" (1 Cor 15:28). Evil will not last forever! We may indeed suffer with Christ presently—but not permanently; and present sufferings will not be worth comparing to eternal glory (Rom 8:17–18). Let us be patient as God is patient. Patience is essential to endurance, and endurance is essential to final salvation (Matt 10:22; 24:13). Those who do not quit, will not lose.

Fourth, spiritual warfare applies pressure to believers in purposeful challenge to their fidelity or loyalty to Jesus Christ. Its main aim is to damage our relationship with our Lord. The church at Ephesus provides a case study regarding loyalty (Rev 2:1–7). John Christopher Thomas notes that this church is "clearly commended for its tenacious loyalty during difficult circumstances."[49] Nevertheless, they are reproved for leaving their "first love" (v. 4). In this context the reproof entails not a diminishment of zeal but a compromise of "one's relationship with Jesus."[50] Essentially, those who all make the same claim of the name of Jesus no longer love him as they once did. Compare this startling insight with the dragon's (Satan's) war on those who are "loyal to the commands of God and have the witness of Jesus," and a diabolical concern to subvert Christian loyalty looms clear (Rev 12:17).[51] Indeed, "a sense of fidelity" (faithfulness, loyalty) may well describe a requisite standard for purity (Rev 14:4–5).[52]

---

48. *Merriam-Webster's Collegiate Dictionary.*
49. Thomas, *Apocalypse*, 115.
50. Thomas, *Apocalypse*, 117.
51. Thomas, *Apocalypse*, 380.
52. Thomas, *Apocalypse*, 425.

Why does Satan so desire to subvert the believers' loyalty to Jesus Christ? Surely it is because believers can do nothing of themselves but only in union with Christ (John 15:1–17). Satan's strategy to hinder the fruitfulness of believers and to lead them in the direction of damnation rests entirely on undermining their relationship with Jesus. Since Christ Jesus cannot be unfaithful (2 Tim 2:13), Satan seeks to undermine the believers' side of the relationship. Nothing damages a relationship like unfaithfulness (spiritual/moral infidelity!). If the devil can persuade a believer to betray Christ, whether outright like Judas Iscariot or through hypocrisy and insincerity, he can rob him/her of their vital source of strength. In that weakened state, he or she can be easily overcome and overthrown.

No matter what hardships believers endure and no matter what pressures believers encounter, they must not allow these to weaken their relationship with Jesus. Quite the contrary; hardships must become a source of strength. Just as weight lifters increase their physical strength by increasing the resistance placed on their muscles, so believers may approach the resistance of hades itself with a firm commitment to only grow stronger in Christ. God gives strengthening grace to those who are faithful Christian "soldiers," enduring hardship as they engage in spiritual warfare (2 Tim 2:1–3). Once believers recognize that spiritual warfare is a tool of the devil to undermine their relationship with their Lord and Savior, and determine within themselves, like young Daniel of old (Dan 1:8), to be faithful in the midst of an idolatrous and immoral world, then they become indefatigable and unstoppable.

Finally, but really first in a sense, is a foundational consideration of implacable adversity. The devil is foremost "the adversary" (1 Pet 5:8). *Satan* in Hebrew literally signifies "adversary." Satan is an antagonist or opponent who opposes God and seeks to frustrate his plans and to lead his people into rebellion. Satan hates God with relentless hostility. Therefore, he hates God's people, too. Satan's hatred against humanity in general as those created in God's image is intensified even further against those who are born again and adopted into God's family as his children. Satan's anger and hatred are expressed in his adversity to all God's purposes for his people. Any blessing, any benefit that God desires to graciously grant unto his people, Satan opposes with all his might. Fortunately, his might is limited; God's is not. As Satan discovered and Job confessed, God's purpose cannot be effectively thwarted (Job 1:6–2:10; 42:2 NASB).

Regarding the eventual fate of Satan and those who follow his rebellious lead, as indicated in Revelation 20:9, Thomas observes that "all opponents and opposition to God, his Lamb, his Spirit, and his people have no future but judgment and eternal punishment"—and this is most certainly the case "regardless of the strength they may currently exhibit."[53] Believers will have the blessed privilege of observing "the end of the cosmic battle."[54] Commenting on Revelation 21:1, Thomas adds, "evil will have no place in the new creation."[55] The adversary will be fully and finally defeated. Evil's inevitable defeat is the sure and certain outcome of salvation history. But what does Satan's assured defeat mean for believers engaged in heated spiritual warfare today?

First, it does not mean that the battle is not real. The struggle between believers and the diabolical realm can be, and often is, intense. Whether through temptations or trials, the conflict is harsh and hurtful. Second, Christ's victory, and therefore the victory of his church, is already assured. There can be only one ending to this story: Christ wins! In fact, Christ has already won the war; he is just finishing up now. Third, though Christ's victory and Satan's defeat are already assured, the victory or defeat of individual believers is yet determined. The place of a particular believer after the final battle depends on his/her keeping faith with Jesus Christ. Yet, the already established outcome provides believers with all the grace sufficient to successfully, that is, to victoriously, fight the "good fight" and finish well (1 Tim 6:12; 2 Tim 4:7). Thus, a hymn that was popular a generation or two ago exhorts Christians to "Keep on the firing line," because "You must fight, be brave against all evil, Never run, nor even lag behind; If you would win for God and the right, Just keep on the firing line."[56]

POWER ENCOUNTERS

Up to this point, this chapter has discussed Pentecostals' belief that the life of faith involves ongoing spiritual power encounters between good and evil. Such encounters may take personal and/or individual and social and/or institutional forms with attendant consequences. The ultimate demonstration of God's triumphant power in the resurrection of Jesus Christ and its unparalleled manifestation at Pentecost in the outpouring of the Holy Spirit empowers and equips believers for victorious service, affirmatively in Christian mission, and antagonistically against all evil in whatever form it takes. Whether spiritual or physical, individual or social, all evil is overcome through active faith in Jesus by the power of Spirit. In addition to personal

---

53. Thomas, *Apocalypse*, 612.
54. Thomas, *Apocalypse*, 613. See Enns, "Yahweh, Creation, and the Cosmic Battle."
55. Thomas, *Apocalypse*, 620.
56. Otis L. McCoy, "Keep on the Firing Line," in *Church Hymnal*, 212–13.

salvation and flourishing, the power of the Holy Spirit sustains resistance to oppression of other kinds, including economic and racial.

Christ's resurrection declares the identity of the Son of God and demonstrates God's power by the Spirit (Rom 1:4; Acts 4:33). Moreover, Christ's ascension forms an inseparable whole with his resurrection as the basis of victory (Eph 1:19–23). Ephesians 4:7–10 intrigues here. Couched in a larger discussion of Christian unity, ministry, and maturity (vv. 1–16), it explains Christ's provision of gifts of grace (*charismata*) and his unique position as the gift giver. As Stamps puts it, "Christ gives grace gifts as the ascended and exalted Lord Jesus."[57] Here the ascended Christ is the conqueror who plunders the enemy and distributes spoils to his people (per Ps 68:18; cp. Col 2:15). Christ's ascension, therefore, includes a splendid victory celebration.[58] Redemption's decisive victory has already been won, and the enjoyment of its benefits by the redeemed has already begun. Therefore, believers wage spiritual warfare as those who are already victors in Christ.

Parenthetically, Paul asks readers to consider that Christ's ascent was preceded by a descent, which then made his ascent all the more remarkable (Eph 4:9). Interpreters since the Protestant Reformation, apparently with a persistent anti-supernaturalism bias, have interpreted this verse as an oblique allusion to Christ's incarnation. However, the early church originally interpreted it as Christ's descent into hades, the region of departed spirits, in a dramatic confrontation with evil.[59] It is known in Latin as the *descendit ad inferos* because of a clause in the Apostles' Creed.[60] Luther conceded that it probably meant that Christ descended into Satan's citadel and conquered him and his demonic legions, but Calvin flatly rejected that idea.[61] Contemporary Wesleyans send mixed signals on Christ's literal descent into hades,

---

57. Stamps, "Ephesians," 1061.

58. Aulén, *Faith of the Christian Church*, 241–47, labors mightily to demonstrate that Christ's atoning death on the cross, his resurrection to life, and his ascension/exaltation to glory are all of a whole; and he may thus be named *Kyrios-Christus* (Acts 2:36), while nonetheless insisting that it is in his ascension/exaltation that Christ is set free from earthly limitations, belongs to the divine life, and exercises his dominion (*regnum Christi*).

59. Stamps, "Ephesians," 1062.

60. Pentecostals' noncreedal identity does not necessarily mean rejection of the truth statements of a particular creed, so much as an insistence on the authority of Holy Scripture rather than human tradition. For more on this topic, see Tony Richie, "Value of Creeds."

61. Harvey, "Descent into Hell (Hades)," 68–69, *Theological Terms*, 69. However, there are different versions of the creed, some including it, some not, and of the Latin as well.

OPPOSITIONAL SOTERIOLOGY   121

sometimes affirming and sometimes not—and to varying degrees.[62] Over the years in congregational contexts, I have heard Pentecostal preachers connect Ephesians 4:9 with 1 Peter 3:18–20 and 4:6, and, sometimes, with Revelation 1:18, in affirmation of Christ's literal descent into and conquest of hell/hades. Although not explicitly rejecting it outright, Stamps bows to a majority of Protestant interpretations and suggests an incarnational interpretation of Ephesians 4:9 that fits well with the overall context of Ephesians.[63] Arrington affirms Christ's actual descent into Hades, arguing that as the first stage of his exaltation, it demonstrates Christ's victory and reminds that his lordship extends into all realms.[64] I agree.

Personally, I tend to favor early patristic interpretations of Scripture as much as possible. After all, they were closest to the age of the apostles and the original source of Scripture.[65] I also favor early Pentecostal interpretative instincts as much as possible. The spiritual and theological trajectory of the Pentecostal movement was set in motion by these pioneers and trailblazers. Furthermore, I favor a view that seems to fit best with the overall NT depiction of graphic confrontation with the powers and principalities.[66] Is all that language merely figurative or did something really happen? I am inclined to believe something really happened. Those three inclinations together add up to an openness to *descendit ad inferos*, or to be more specific, *Descensus Christi ad Inferos*, "Christ's descent into Hell."[67]

If that is correct, it dramatizes Christ's victory over the devil and the demonic in such a way as to incentivize spiritual warfare combatants immensely. A face-to-face, head-on "showdown," so to speak, serves as a positive model for believers today. Of course, even if not, Christ's victory as portrayed in his resurrection and ascension is no less decisive. In any case, Jesus' "past experience with death and continuous experience with life made him a captor and a victor over death and his companion Hades," indicating that Jesus' mastery over both is clear and, accordingly, that "there is no need

---

62. Heather Hahn, "Did Jesus descend into hell or to the dead?," discusses this topic from a United Methodist Church perspective.

63. Stamps, "Ephesians," 1062.

64. Arrington, *Christian Doctrine*, 2:84, 86.

65. This places me in line with evangelicals and Pentecostals who, as Louth puts it, "are rediscovering the history of the Holy Spirit" through patristic resources that have been largely missing from this tradition since the days of Luther and Calvin, and, especially, with Wesley. See Oden and Louth, eds., in *Genesis 1–11*, xx.

66. I agree with O'Brien, *Ephesians*, 468–69, on this point.

67. Sometimes it is called "the harrowing of hell" or "Christ's harrowing of hell."

to fear death and Hades because Jesus holds the keys!"[68] Christ's absolute authority, in fact, grants his disciples victory over the realm of evil.

Further, consider the surpassing and incomparable greatness of the Holy Spirit in battle against evil spirits. While there are myriad spirits, good and evil, there is only one Holy Spirit, one Spirit of the Lord God. The Holy Spirit is superior to all other spirits, exceeding them in ability and power and in every way. As God, the Holy Spirit is without equal, matchless among the spirits. First John 4:4 puts it plainly: "You are of God, little children, and have overcome them, because He who is in you is greater than he who is in the world." Clearly, this victory "has occurred in the past but its effects are still felt."[69] First John 4:1–6 contrasts the Spirit of God with all the spirits which are not of God. The Spirit of God confesses the incarnation of Jesus Christ, but the spirits working in false prophets, the spirit of Antichrist, do not; God's Spirit speaks from God, but the world's spirits speak from the world; thus, believers can distinguish between God's Spirit, the Spirit of truth, and the spirit of error. Emphatically however, it is verse 4 that sums up the Holy Spirit's divine superiority with the comparative adjective "greater" (from *megas*), asserting that the Spirit who indwells believers is more, that is, greater, larger, stronger than all opposing spirits. Jesus uses this same comparative adjective to describe his incomparable love (John 15:13). Just as the love of Christ is greater than any other love, so the Holy Spirit is greater than Satan. Hilary of Arles (c. 401–449), commenting on 1 John 4:4 said, "God's power to save us is always much greater than the devil's power to do harm."[70] Amen!

In a similar vein, but with an interesting twist, Pentecostal NT scholar Robert Berg adds that "God's sufficiency supersedes the believers' perception of insufficiency."[71] The interesting twist is the sad fact that deceivers and false spirits often put on a show of sufficiency, of strength, that convinces the foolish. Believers may need reminding that the power of God's indwelling Spirit is "greater" than that of the spirits who dwell in the world. This wonderful superlative describes an immeasurable and advantageous difference with God's Spirit both in quantity (infinity) and in kind (divinity). Those in whom God's Spirit dwells "have overcome" (from *nikaō*), that is, conquered, prevailed, triumphed, over evil spirits and their false prophets. Among other things, this means that the power of the Holy Spirit enables believers to win the victory in spiritual warfare.

68. Thomas, *Apocalypse*, 104–5.
69. Thomas, *1 John, 2 John, 3 John*, 207.
70. Oden and Bray, eds., in *James, 1–2 Peter, 1–3 John, Jude*, 211.
71. Berg, "1–3 John," 1510–11.

Believers who rely on the power of the Holy Spirit for overcoming the devil and his demons in the trenches of spiritual warfare are following the example of Christ. He testifies that during his incarnation, his ministry of deliverance and exorcism was accomplished by the Spirit of God in demonstrative proof of the initiation of God's victorious kingdom (Matt 12:28).[72] Indeed, Jesus' exorcisms remind that believers share in Jesus' victory over principalities and powers (Luke 8:26–39; Acts 19:13–20).[73] The question emerges: how do believers avail themselves of the Spirit's power in spiritual warfare? Obviously, again as with the Lord Jesus, being full of the Spirit empowers one to confront the devil effectively (Luke 4:1–2). The Holy Spirit works through the life of a Spirit-filled believer to confront and to overcome evil. Furthermore, Paul teaches on the necessity and nature of the "weapons of spiritual warfare" (2 Cor 10:4). These include the "sword of the Spirit" (Eph 6:17) and "praying in the Spirit" (6:18). What are these weapons of the Spirit, and how do they work in spiritual warfare? Ephesians 6:10–20 sets the context for a response.

Incontrovertibly, Ephesians 6:10–20 is crucial to the Pentecostal theology of spiritual warfare. Stamps argues that this passage sums up the central message of the entire epistle to the Ephesians and that "it relates to God's plan of redemption and the cosmic reconciliation that is the goal of Christ's death-resurrection-exaltation."[74] It builds on the premise that this world is "a war zone that is under attack and being challenged by God's enemy—Satan and his network of evil powers."[75] The reality of spiritual warfare occurs on a cosmic front (the "vertical battle" between God and Satan) and on an earthly front (the "horizontal battle" between believers and evil spirits).[76] Christ has won the decisive victory already, but believers must be prepared to fight until Christ comes again to consummate his victory.[77] Therefore, Paul's militaristic imagery in Ephesians 6:10–20 of a soldier ready for battle goes beyond figurative speech in depicting the reality of the believers' readiness for spiritual warfare.

O'Brien agrees that Paul's concluding appeal in Ephesians 6:10–20 "catches up many of the theological and ethical concerns of the letter," and

72. Warrington, "Synoptic Gospels," 86 (cp. 101–2).

73. Arrington, "Luke," 436.

74. Stamps, "Ephesians," 1080.

75. Stamps, "Ephesians," 1080.

76. Stamps, "Ephesians," 1080.

77. Stamps, "Ephesians," 1080–81. As Indonesian Pentecostal pastor and church leader Niko Njotorahardjo says in *Messenger of the Third Pentecost*, 103, "life as a soldier is not just about doing spiritual warfare, but to also come out as a winner over personal issues, the temptation of the devil, and over many challenges in our lives."

that Paul "describes in cosmic terms believers' responsibilities as they live in the world," using the "sustained imagery of a spiritual battle" that "depicts the Christian life as a struggle against supernatural evil forces."[78] Obviously, neither Stamps nor O'Brien consider spiritual warfare an aberrational or marginal theme but as significant, even principal, importance in Christian faith and life. O'Brien's thematic summation is well worth quoting in full:

> Paul's cogent point here is that the Christian life as a whole is a profound spiritual warfare of cosmic proportions in which the *ultimate* opposition to the advance of the gospel and moral integrity springs from evil, supernatural powers under the control of the god of this world.[79]

Chrysostom (347–407) makes the astounding assertion that the believers' current spiritual warfare against the demonic "puts an end to the previous war against God," and that as "we are making war with the devil, we are making peace with God."[80] He adds that the good news is that the victory is already won.[81] Biblically speaking, fallen humanity exists in a state of warfare against God and God's will (Rom 8:7; Eph 2:15–16; Jas 4:4). Accordingly, those who make peace with God do not then exit the war but rather change sides. Elijah's stirring challenge goes out to everyone to make a decision about whom to serve and whom to fight (1 Kgs 18:21). Salvation depends on the only appropriate response: surrendering to God as Lord and Savior and engaging the real enemy in battle.

Accordingly, Ephesians 6:10–20 portrays the status of the Christian soldier in the spiritual conflict. Without going into a detailed and lengthy exegesis, a short general exposition serves to outline several salient features.

- Imperative of relying on the Lord as the source of strength and power (v. 10)
- Injunction to put on the whole or full armor of God in order to stand against the devil (v. 11)
- Explanation of the identity of spiritual warfare's opposing combatants (v. 12)
- Repetition of the command to take up the whole armor of God in order to resist or stand when evil is present (v. 13)

---

78. O'Brien, *Ephesians*, 490.
79. O'Brien, *Ephesians*, 466. Italics are original.
80. Oden and Edwards, eds., in *Galatians, Ephesians, Philippians*, 211.
81. Oden and Edwards, eds., in *Galatians, Ephesians, Philippians*, 211.

- Yet another repetition of the command to stand, with a specific and extensive description of the armor imagery: belt of truth, breastplate of righteousness, feet "fitted" with the sandals of the gospel of peace, shield of faith, helmet of salvation, and sword of the Spirit or word of God (vv. 14–17)
- Climactic importance of prayer, especially praying in the Spirit but including all forms of prayer (v. 18)
- Circumstantial application to Paul's personal ministry (vv. 19–20)

Thus, Ephesians 6:10–20 portrays the Christian soldier as occupying "ground" or "territory" that has been won but must be maintained in the present age against constant assaults. As early church bishop and theologian Cyprian (c. 200–258) put it, "There is a strong conflict to be waged against the devil. Therefore, we should stand bravely so that we may be able to conquer."[82] The Christian equipped and prepared for battle need not fear. Quite to the contrary. As Tertullian (c. 155–240) boldly told Christians in an earlier age, rather than being frightened by their enemies, they "ought to be feared by evils spirits," because they have "received power over evil spirits."[83] Yet victory is not automatic—that is, it does not occur by itself without the believers' conscious and intentional involvement.

Paul's description of the armor and weapons of the Christian soldier indicates attributes and actions essential for defeating the devil and the demonic. Victory requires dedicated commitment to and personal appropriation of truth, righteousness, peace, faith, salvation, and, of course, God's Word and prayer. Conclusively, spiritual warfare involves an ongoing conflict between good and evil, indicating that malevolent beings bent on human ill must be withstood and overcome in faith, obedience, and prayer. Only accordingly may believers win victory in the trenches of spiritual warfare. Hence, Paul associates two "weapons" specifically with the Holy Spirit: the "sword of the Spirit" (Ephesians 6:17) and "praying in the Spirit" (6:18). What are these weapons of the Spirit and how do they work in spiritual warfare?

The "sword of the Spirit" represents the word of God as a weapon against evil powers.[84] When the devil tempted Jesus, he repeatedly, and effectively, responded with God's Word (Matt 4:1–11). The truth defeats the deceiver. However, it was not the mere citing or quoting of memorized texts nor merely confessing the word of faith like some magical spell that won the

---

82. Bercot, "Satan," *Dictionary of Early Christian Beliefs*, 594.
83. Bercot, "Angels," *Dictionary of Early Christian Beliefs*, 19.
84. Turner, "Spirit as the Spirit of prophecy in Ephesians," 193.

victory for Jesus. It was speaking the word out of a living relationship with God.[85] When the devil quoted Scripture, it was empty of any power. When Jesus quoted Scripture, it became the sword of the Spirit. It is the same for believers. A living relationship with the true God arms believers with "a two-edged sword" (Heb 4:12). When believers read God's Word, meditate on it, and pray over it, when they apply it to their lives through their obedience in humble faith, then it becomes a sharp blade drawn from the sheath of their heart to thrust into the devil.

What about praying in the Spirit? To be precise, Ephesians 6:10–20 does not identify prayer as one of the pieces of armor or weapons at all, but Paul gives prayer more attention in terms of space and climactic positioning than any of the specified weapons. Prayer is the necessary element that makes everything else effective.[86] In a sense, prayer *is* spiritual warfare (Dan 10:12–14). All authentic prayer is inspired and energized by the Holy Spirit. Yet, Paul apparently points to praying in other tongues as having a specialized role in spiritual warfare (cp. 1 Cor 14:1–5 and 14–19; Jude 17–22).[87] For Pentecostals, it makes perfect sense that reaching beyond this world into the mysteries of the spiritual realm to do battle requires prayer that transcends human understanding and infirmities (Rom 8:26–27). A Pentecostal theology of spiritual warfare regards Scripture as more than a source of doctrinal information or emotional inspiration. It also regards prayer as more than petitionary in nature. Believers engage in the ultimate conflict between good and evil through participation in the Word of God and in prayer to God.

Various revivalist cultural influences aside, the occasional intensity of Pentecostal preaching and prayer among other things may be, to an extent, understood in this light.[88] Pentecostals are doing battle, and battle is usually

---

85. Shelton, "Matthew," 146.

86. O'Brien, *Ephesians*, 483.

87. Stamps, "Ephesians," 1084.

88. Brown, *Spirit of Protestantism*, 208–11, offers a series of observations which help provide context for my following discussion. There is a basic tension between "order and ardor" that often gets expressed as tension between the individual and the community and/or between freedom and order. The first is best addressed through defining the individual self as "self-in-community" and the latter as seeking "freedom within order." The role of the Holy Spirit is critical to achieving the proper relationship between order and ardor. Brown wisely warns that order can be "stagnant" and "loveless" but also that ardor can be "erratic" and "irresponsible," 211. If Pentecostals agree with him that many "have often demonstrated a well-developed capacity for obstructing the Spirit's working," then perhaps they should also agree that "the Spirit will have the healthiest opportunity for creative endeavor" where it is remembered that the Spirit gives those in leadership their powers and can withdraw them as well, 211.

noisy and messy. Unlike the false prophets of Baal, Pentecostals understand that God is not impressed with or moved by frenzy and volume (1 Kgs 18:28; 19:12).[89] Yet, the increasingly muted nature of contemporary Pentecostal prayer and preaching, probably due to overconcern for decorum, signifies a cooling of passion accompanied by a waning of power.[90] Doing battle can be intense. While they have their place in daily discipleship and intimate communion with God, neat devotionals and quiet times do not always match the fervor of warfare. Going into battle sometimes requires prayer and praise "with voices loud and high" (2 Chr 20:19). Scripture exhorts God's combatants to "clap your hands" and "Shout unto God with the voice of triumph" (Ps 47:1).

True enough, Pentecostal vigor can devolve into mere emotional vehemence; but more often, authentic spiritual engagement is best expressed through impassioned tones arising out of the inner depths of one's being. Here, Pentecostals may borrow Jesus' words about the ministry style of the hard-edged, rough-hewn desert preacher John the Baptist, in answering refined critics and detractors who prefer a more genteel approach (Luke 7:24–30). Pentecostal worship, especially including spiritual warfare, cannot be conducted according to parlor etiquette. It is by nature fiery and can at times be fierce. Real Pentecostals are not primarily interested in being cool and popular or smooth and polished. Pentecostals want victory!

Finally, we should note resonance of Pentecostal salvation-as-deliverance theology and spiritual warfare's place in salvation with non-Western, Global South, Majority World Christians.[91] An African Yoruba chieftain once told me that he feared and resented Pentecostals more than any other Christians for this very reason. According to him, Yoruba belief in a complex cosmology of spirit entities makes its adherents vulnerable to Pentecostal beliefs and practices addressing those same realities from a Christian perspective. However, he defiantly argued that he viewed the result as more of a syncretistic mix than a clearly Christian religion. ("Even when they become Christian, they are still Yoruba!") Nevertheless, research indicates that Pentecostal emphases on the Holy Spirit's power as experienced in Spirit baptism, speaking in tongues, spiritual gifts, and so on, have transformed notions of power among many traditional Africans, including Nigerians, residing in

---

89. As the Israelite religion stood in stark contrast with the frenzies of Canaanite Baal worship (1 Kgs 18:28; 19:12), so the Christian religion stands in stark contrast with the religious ecstasies of ancient Greek Dionysus worship. For Pentecostals, spiritual/religious experience does not entail loss of volitional control or committing mindless acts.

90. Cp. Martin, *Praying People*, 27.

91. E.g., Muzorewa, *African Theology*, 85–86.

the heartland of Yoruba religious devotion. This is a repetitive phenomenon throughout the Global South. *Christians* in these areas often retain an enspirited worldview reminiscent of an indigenous tradition but transformed by *Pentecostals* into an intentional biblical perspective. (One could say: "These Christians are not still Yoruba after all; rather, they are Pentecostal!")

In closing, recall that the focus of this chapter has been soteriological considerations of the Pentecostal belief that the devil and his demons are actual entities malevolently bent on destroying them and damning them. This chapter has presented this spiritual warfare, as it is popularly described, as part of evil's arrogant rebellion against the holy and righteous God, and has maintained the inability of believers to rescue themselves or win victory. Despite this background, Pentecostals believe the good news of the gospel is that the benevolent and loving God has graciously accomplished their deliverance through the death-resurrection-ascension of the Lord and Savior Jesus Christ. Further, Pentecostals believe that God empowers them by the Holy Spirit for divine mission and service until the destined consummation of God's purpose in the triumphant return of his Son Jesus Christ. Accordingly, a distinctive and persistent element in Pentecostal theology views soteriology as consisting largely of spiritual and moral conflict with the objective of present and permanent victory over evil. The next chapter discusses the ultimate objective of incentivizing and energizing believers: *eternity*.

6

Eschatological Soteriology

(Salvation's Eye on Eternity)

A Pentecostal view of salvation-as-deliverance is both otherworldly and this-worldly. This life is fixed on and framed by the life to come—by eternity, by heaven and hell and beyond—and not the other way around (Matt 12:32; Luke 18:30; Rev 20:11–15). Actually, the relationship between this world and the world to come can be more than a bit complex. Do Christians have ethical and social responsibilities toward the present age? If so, to what extent? Is there danger of becoming so "heavenly minded" that one is no "earthly good"? If so, what is an acceptable resolution? A further pressing question is, "Which is the primary focus of Christian salvation, this world or the next, the present age or eternity?" A not-so-simple, not-so-straightforward answer might be that it is impossible to separate completely the importance of the present from the importance of eternity (or vice versa).

Yet Jesus taught that gaining the whole world and losing one's soul would be obviously of no benefit, that the human soul is of incomparable value in contrast to the best this world has to offer (Matt 16:26; Mark 8:36; Luke 9:25).[1] As illustrious Pentecostal scholar Stanley Horton, referencing Philippians 1:6, says, "the whole Bible focuses on the future, a future that is assured by the very nature of God himself."[2] Accordingly, this chapter looks

---

1. Arrington, "Luke," 442.
2. Horton, "Last Things," 597. Moltmann, *Coming of God*, notes that Karl Barth and Peter Althaus sought to eliminate futurism from eschatology, viewing eschatology as

at personal salvation from the perspective of *eternity*. As a matter of course, it addresses Pentecostal theology regarding otherworldliness—heaven and hell and related matters, and Christ's coming again, all with a view toward their soteriological significance.

OTHERWORLDLINESS AS ESCHATOLOGICAL ORIENTATION

Being "otherworldly" usually signifies orientation toward preparing for another world. Being "this-worldly" signifies preoccupation with the present world age and its order of existence. Pentecostals have viewed life in the present world as primarily an opportunity for getting ready for heaven (and avoiding hell). In such a mindset, redemption involves *an eschatological orientation* of transformation, exchanging the usual love and preoccupation of this temporal world order and its values for the abiding realities of the age to come.[3] "Worldliness," therefore, is an obstacle, or perhaps better put a rival, for the saints who wish to spend eternity with the Lord (1 Thess 4:17b). Precisely what constitutes "worldliness"?

Lamar Vest has served as Presiding Bishop of the Church of God (Cleveland, TN), Chairman of the National Association of Evangelicals, President of the American Bible Society, President of Pentecostal Theological Seminary, and in many other leadership roles. Nevertheless, Vest has expressed suspicion regarding his movement's traditional definitions of "worldliness."[4] All too often, "worldliness" has been synonymous with the violation of a strict dress code and hard-and-fast (and, often, harsh) rules about almost every aspect of daily conduct. NT teachings (e.g., Rom 12:2; 1 John 2:15–17) on living distinctly from this present world order have been applied rigorously but indiscriminately. Sincerely, for holiness-minded Pentecostals, the question is not whether worldliness is wrong. It is wrong. But we must ask, what is "worldliness"?

---

eternity's entrance into the present; but later both were forced to reconsider the importance of the future in Christian eschatology, 13–19. Kelly's study of patristic teaching, *Early Christian Doctrines*, notes that the Christian hope and doctrine of last things has always had a tension between "a twofold emphasis" on the completeness of present salvation and its consummation in the eschatological future, 459. Kelly insists that this tension, characteristic of the NT itself, "must always remain" as "a feature of the eschatology of authentic Christianity," 462.

3. As both Origen (third century) and Theodoret of Cyr (fifth century) argued from Romans 12:2, in Oden and Bray, eds., *Romans*, 308–9.

4. Vest, *Reflections on the Journey*, 150, 152.

Pentecostal theologian Steven Jack Land clarifies this well. The world as God's creation is good, but the "interlocking systems and structures arrayed in rebellion against Christ the King" are not—nevertheless, the mission of redemption "is here and now in *this* created, fallen, redeemed, and being-consummated world."[5] A righteous stance against worldliness does not entail rejection of God's created world. God created it good (Gen 1:4, 10, 12, 18, 21, 25, 31). "Good" in the creation account of Genesis 1 (*tôb*) indicates that which is attractive, desirable, and pleasing, that which is beneficial, useful, and valuable. It is the very opposite of anything evil. The ancient Gnostic heresy, influenced by certain strands of classical Greek philosophy, that the material or physical is inherently evil, is not biblical. Neither, although Pentecostals at the popular level have sometimes been "fuzzy" on this error, is any teaching that the "flesh" is substantively evil. What the Bible warns believers against is the works or acts of the fallen fleshly nature in contrast to the fruit produced in the human life by the agency of the Holy Spirit (Gal 5:16–26).

Second, alignment of systemic evil against the righteous reign of God in Christ is the epitome of worldliness. Babel/Babylon serves as the epitome of the essential nature of worldly rebellion against God (Gen 11:1–9; Rev 17:1–19:3). It is no small wonder that F. Scott Fitzgerald's short story "Babylon Revisited" depicts tragic struggling and suffering due to a lifestyle of decadence, with its inevitable consequences.[6] In Scripture, Babylon is characterized by proud and stubborn self-will and self-exaltation, rather than by loyalty to God's will and reverent worship of God. It is and will be judged by God accordingly. The world's economic, political, religious, and social systems' rebellion against God is sinful and, thus, to be avoided by devout believers. Inarguably, any attempt to govern life apart from God or against God's will is worldliness. Worldliness may be expressed through one's attitude, actions, and yes, even appearance; but the core problem with worldliness is a systemic culture of arrogant rebellion against a holy and righteous God. Whether in the ancient Roman Empire or in contemporary America, or anywhere else, a Christian's first and deepest loyalty and real citizenship is not to this world's kingdoms but to the heavenly kingdom of the Lord Jesus Christ (Phil 3:20).

Third, the redemptive mission of the church occurs in the context of this sinful world order. To go further, the church's mission is not only *in* this world but *for* this world. An "in the world but not of the world" attitude is common among many Pentecostals. As seen above, Land describes

---

5. Land, "Pentecostal Spirituality," 486.
6. Fitzgerald, "Babylon Revisited."

this world as "created, fallen, redeemed, and being-consummated." We have already addressed the world as God's good creation; however, note further that as Creator, the earth and everything in it, including all the world and its inhabitants, rightfully belong to God (Ps 24:1; 1 Cor 10:26, 28).[7] Accordingly, God has authority over this world and responsibility for this world. Yet, it has fallen into sin. Chapter 1 of this volume talked about the Genesis account of human beings falling into sin, thus becoming distorted, twisted, and lost. In a sense, the systems of this fallen world represent humanity's alternative "creation" set against God's good creation. This is a world of their own making. In vain attempts to be their own god they have "created" their own world. And it is a wicked world destined for divine judgment (Isa 13:11; Matt 13:38). It is not surprising that the Bible concludes with an emphasis on "God's exercise of judgment over the world through his Christ."[8] Presently, believers must exercise constant vigilance against the world's corrosive and intrusive grip.

Emphatically, wickedness does not get the last word. It does not even get to have next to the last word. God's love sent Jesus to redeem and to save the world and the people of all its nations (John 3:16–17; Rev 1:5). Even now, the whole creation is bringing forth the birth of a new order of existence (Rom 8:22; cp. 8:19). The power of new life is already present in this old world. Therefore, the mission, the assignment and task, of the church is to proclaim the gospel in all the world and to make disciples of all nations until the end of this present age (Mark 16:15; Matt 28:19–20). This world is in transition. The old is passing away, and the new is coming into being (1 Cor 7:31; 2 Cor 3:7). It is in the process of becoming what God created it to be and will be finally completed and perfected accordingly in the eschaton (God's future for it). The same is true of believers themselves (2 Cor 5:17).

We have arrived at an important juncture. Christian salvation is *intrinsically eschatological.*[9] In its current "now-not yet" state, it is moving toward redemption's climactic and conclusive completion: the consummation. Yes, Pentecostal theology of salvation is both otherworldly and this-worldly, but

---

7. Thus, we can agree with Wright, *Salvation Belongs to Our God*, that "Biblical salvation belongs to God. It is not ours to achieve, to dispense or to manipulate," 194.

8. John A. McGuckin, "Book of Revelation and Orthodox Eschatology," 115.

9. In the first century, Jesus repeatedly corrected those who placed priority on the immediate, temporal manifestation of the kingdom of God (Luke 17:20–21; Acts 1:6–7). Is it not ironic that many of his disciples today appear to be more interested in a present, temporal manifestation of God's righteous reign than in Christ's coming again to establish that reign forever? Can we fault first-century Jews for conceiving of the messiah in political terms as one who would throw off the Roman yoke, if we ourselves conceive of Christ primarily in terms of confronting this world's "empire"? Have we so soon forgotten Jesus' words to Pilate in John 18:36?

life in this temporal age is fixed on and framed by life in the endless ages to come—by eternity. Believers are on a journey toward a divinely ordained destiny. The journey is important but penultimate. Like the "wilderness wanderings" of Israel on the way to Canaan, distractions only hinder progress toward the moment of entry into the promised land. Enjoyment of life in this world must never become an end in itself. It is not the endgame; it is only the opening. The opening is, however, important. In chess, it determines a player's endgame position. Similarly, a boxing enthusiast knows that the undercard, however exciting, is only a buildup to the main event. This world is a prelude to the next. Eternity is the main event! Hence, we put Pentecostal otherworldliness into perspective. This world is not our home. We seek a better city, a better country, indeed, a better world (Heb 11:13–16).

From this perspective, then, Russell Spittler's observation that otherworldliness appears to be a fading value among North American Pentecostals is deeply disturbing.[10] To be clear, I agree; yes, I applaud Pentecostal eschatologist Peter Althouse's affirmation of moving Pentecostal theology "from isolation to inclusion, from separation to ecumenism and from otherworldly preoccupation to transformation."[11] Yet, moving from one extreme to another—as in exchanging otherworldly preoccupation for this-worldly preoccupation—is not progress to my mind. Unfortunately, Brown's mid-twentieth century fears for Protestantism has applicable force for contemporary Pentecostals: "For in our day, the danger is not so much that Protestantism will shun culture too disdainfully as that it will embrace it too eagerly."[12] Economic and social advancement according to the standards of this world appear to be displacing otherworldliness as a leading value. More is at stake here than sectarian development or evolution. Salvation is at stake. If focus on the world to come is essential to Pentecostal soteriology,

10. Spittler, "Spirituality, Pentecostal and Charismatic," 1098. In my opinion, in the United States (at least) fading otherworldliness among Pentecostals appears to be taking on different forms with a similar *reorientation* at its root. On the right hand, so-called Christian nationalism equates God's reign with this world order via a political agenda of establishing a Christian nation. On the left hand, so-called Christian socialism equates God's reign with this world order via an economic agenda of social justice. In their own ways, both trade the everlasting kingdom of Jesus Christ for a terrestrial version. That is not to say that a nation founded on Christian principles or equality among its populace is bad, but they are poor substitutes for God's eternal righteous reign.

11. Althouse, *Spirit of the Last Days*, 197.

12. Brown, *Spirit of Protestantism*, 188. Brown advocates for a circumspect attitude toward this world's culture, aiming at positive appropriation but reminding that "culture is not simply an end in itself, and that when it sets itself defiantly against the God who gave it birth, it has already sowed the seeds of its own destruction," 194.

then diminishing that focus devalues the salvation of a lost and dying world in exchange for the trinkets of this present age. Obviously, this diminishment applies to materialists, but it may go further. Do Christians who make social justice and economic inequality (worthy causes though they be) the center of their mission, implicitly (at least) place the human condition in this world above their participation in the world to come?[13] The answer, admittedly, is complicated, but there is possible danger in going down this road.

Christians, including, and in some ways especially, Pentecostals, live in two worlds. Believers have responsibilities toward both worlds, but which world receives primary attention? Can these bilateral loyalties be adroitly balanced? As stated previously, Jesus' teaching that gaining the whole world and losing one's soul would be of no benefit, rather would be a tragic loss, and that the human soul is of incomparable value in contrast to what this world offers (Matt 16:26; Mark 8:36; Luke 9:25), places priority on eternity.[14] Clearly, salvation is on the line. Wesley's "practical eschatology" goes a long way toward holding these poles together through a theology of perfecting love.[15] Pentecostals likely could learn a lot from his example.

Spittler further notes that otherworldliness reflects the biblical teaching but is inappropriately applied if used to evade ethical responsibilities in the present age.[16] Scripture teaches that the love of the world is incompatible with the love of the Father (1 John 2:15–17). Not surprisingly, believers must overcome the world because it does not hear God's voice (4:4–6). Realistically, a complete break with the world is impossible (1 Cor 5:9–10). Nevertheless, a certain moral and spiritual distance or separation is necessary (2 Cor 6:14–7:1; cp. Isa 52:11). So, what is the appropriate stance of the church, including Pentecostal churches, regarding this world? Pauline theology of mission is helpful in responding to that important question.

Christians are called to be *ambassadors* to this world of God's reconciling work in Jesus Christ (2 Cor 5:12–21; Eph 6:20). To act as an ambassador, from *presbeuō*, means to act as an authorized representative of one sovereign or nation to another. Christians, therefore, represent God

---

13. Brown's chapter on "Holy Worldliness" in *Spirit of Protestantism* makes a great case for an integrated approach to life in this world with attendant responsibilities for believers, 197–208, esp. 197–200. Significantly, Brown closes the book with a short affirmation of the pilgrim identity and journey nature of Christian life, 222–26. I agree with him regarding the danger of becoming so focused on the destination that we neglect fellow sojourners, 225–26. However, there is also a danger of becoming so focused on the challenges of the journey that we neglect to keep the destination in sharp focus.

14. Arrington, "Luke," 442.

15. Van Buskirk, "John Wesley's Practical Eschatology."

16. Spittler, "Spirituality, Pentecostal and Charismatic," 1098.

and heaven to humanity and earth. It is critical that we never allow ourselves to forget which side we represent. American Colonial icon Benjamin Franklin (1706–1790) served as ambassador to France, living in that nation from 1776 to 1785.[17] He enjoyed France a great deal and was quite popular with the French populace. In his official role, his task was to garner support for his own fledgling nation. He was never a Frenchman. He was ever an American. It is so with the Christian who represents the kingdom of Jesus Christ in this world. Loyalties and priorities must be clear. To do otherwise would be to follow the sordid example of Judas Iscariot's betrayal.

IS HEAVEN AND HELL FIT FOR PUBLIC CONSUMPTION?

The subjects of heaven and hell certainly capture the attention of popular imagination. At the highbrow level, imaginative depictions of heaven and hell, as in the English poet John Milton's (1608–1674) *Paradise Lost* and the Italian poet Dante Alighieri's (c. 1265–1321) *Divine Comedy*, are among the all-time greatest works of literature. For more general consumption is the original television series *Star Trek*, with its probing episode "This Side of Paradise."[18] Recently, *Heaven Is for Real*, a Christian drama film describing a near-death experience (technically known as a NDE), was a box office hit.[19] Understandably, movie versions of hell tend to come mostly from the horror genre.[20] Enough said?

For all the popular utilization of heaven and hell, serious commitment to the doctrine is in substantial decline. Belief in "the sweet by and by," on the one hand, and, on the other, "hellfire and brimstone," is in marked decline in North America. Exceptions exist among fundamentalists and conservatives. Yet, even where it is formally accepted, it is often radically reinterpreted to lessen its literal force. Belief in everlasting bliss and, especially, in everlasting punishment, appear to be out of step with the contemporary mindset of most people, even many Christians.[21] Is it therefore advisable to include

17. Isaacson, *Benjamin Franklin*, devotes three chapters to Franklin's time in France.

18. *Star Trek*, Season 1, Episode 24, original airdate March 2, 1967.

19. The movie *Heaven Is for Real* is based on the *New York Times* best-selling book by Todd Burpo and Lynn Vincent of the same title.

20. See Bradshaw, "Most Disturbing Movie Visions of Hell."

21. Earl W. Kennedy, "Heaven and Hell," suggests that "the modern, scientifically informed mind has difficulty taking the biblical language of heaven strictly at face value," 371. However, surely Wolfhart Pannenberg, "Task of Christian Eschatology," is correct both in his assertion that the "truth of Christian doctrine cannot be maintained where Christian proclamation gives priority to adaptation to the secular mentality" and

a discussion of heaven and hell in a text on Pentecostal theology of salvation? I think it is. Faithfulness to Scripture requires it. Belief in justice also requires it.

The demands of justice obviously are not met in this life. People do, in fact, sometimes "get away with murder"—and other heinous acts. The sardonic comment that "no good deed goes unpunished" has enough truth in it to have bite. No, life is not fair. The best it has to offer is an imperfect, uneven approximation. Either the demands of justice are never met, or they are met in the world to come. Holy Scripture and the majority tradition of Christian theology for over two millennia affirm both: that the demands of justice will be met and that they will be finally and fully met beyond this present world order. Notwithstanding, heaven and hell are much more than convenient assurances that sooner or later everyone is "going to get what's coming to them."

Questions like "Where will I go when I die?" and "Where will I spend eternity?" are important questions.[22] Addressing them responsibly requires biblical and theological context. Pentecostal theology of heaven and hell should not be driven by speculative curiosity about the afterlife and eternity, but by Scripture and sound doctrine. Christian doctrines of heaven and hell are best understood against the backdrop of teaching on eternal reward and punishment.[23] In other words, teaching about heaven and hell is not "pulled out of the air" to neatly wrap things up, as it were; rather, heaven and hell are set within the framework of divine justice and just recompense.

The word translated "reward" in Jesus' teaching (e.g., Matthew 5:12) is *misthos*, a noun referring to the paid outcome of a particular work or action, that is, an equitable recompense. The English word *recompense* comes from the medieval Latin *recompensare* meaning "to reward, remunerate." *Re-* or "again," and *compensare*, signifies to "balance out," or literally to "weigh together."[24] A just recompense conveys impressions of an appropriate payment. The idea that deeds done in this life, whether good or bad, will receive just recompense, that is, reward or punishment, in the age to come is

---

in his insistence that this "applies especially to the Christian eschatological hope for a life beyond death," 1.

22. Moltmann, *Coming of God*, 49–57, insightfully discusses the impact of attitudes toward death for this life as well as the so-called "afterlife." Suffice to say that *suppressing* the reality of death *reduces* the quality of life.

23. McGrath, *Born to Wonder*, 79–80, asserts that one of the most important aspects of religion is its ability to provide a framework for meaning and significance in life and the afterlife, including expectations of "rewards for acting well and punishment for doing evil."

24. *Online Etymology Dictionary*, "Recompense."

continuous throughout Scripture and entirely consistent with the doctrines of salvation by grace and of the character of God's love.[25]

Thomas Oden, a founder and leader of paleo-orthodoxy, which emphasizes the continuing importance of patristic and biblical interpretation for contemporary Christian theology, affirms the role of good works for those justified by faith in Jesus.[26] Salvation by grace and justification by faith assume an active life of doing good works (Jas 2:14–26). Each of Jesus' beatitudes in the Sermon on the Mount is accompanied by a promised reward (Matt 5:1–11; cp. Matt 5:46; 6:1, 2, 4, 5, 6, 16, 18; 10:41–42; 16:27), climaxing with "great is your reward in heaven" (v. 12). Yet, as Jesus' response to a widow's small but sacrificial gift indicates, reward for good works is not simply a matter of mathematical equivalence (Matt 12:42–43). Even rewards for "services rendered" arise out of and are regulated by divine generosity, as in the parable of the laborers (20:1–16). Paul, the proponent of salvation by grace through faith par excellence, nonetheless, is preeminent in his teaching on heavenly reward for good works grounded in faith (Rom 2:6; 1 Cor 3:8; 2 Tim 4:7–8). Paul is always clear that although sin earns its wages no one can ever merit the gift of salvation (Rom 6:23).[27] Both Jesus and Paul affirm that there will be varying degrees or levels of reward or punishment based on the extent of understanding and quality of service (Luke 12:48; 1 Cor 3:12–15).[28]

Candidly, the *eternal* nature of eternal punishment is a problem for many people. One of the basic principles of civilized society is that punishment should be proportionate to the crime. How does everlasting torment fit the sins of finite human beings?[29] Unfortunately, history has had many monstrously evil people, such as Herod, Judas Iscariot, Nero, "Bloody" Mary Tudor, Ivan the Terrible, Adolf Hitler, Joseph Stalin, Pol Pot, Idi Amin, Ted Bundy, and Osama bin Laden. Yet, even if one begins to imagine that eternal

---

25. Gerig, "Reward."

26. Oden, *Life in the Spirit*, 153–56.

27. For believers who die young or convert late, the absence of good works does not invalidate their faith. Cp. Oden, *Life in the Spirit*, 155–56.

28. Cp. Bloesch, *Last Things*, 230.

29. Crisp, *Jonathan Edwards*, points out that the great American theologian of yesteryear Jonathan Edwards, a favorite of many evangelicals, suggested that a just response of eternal punishment for sin arises out of the infinite worth of the being sinned against—i.e., God, 132–33. Accordingly, a more appropriate question would be rather "How could sin against the eternal and infinite God be judged in any other manner except eternal punishment?" The answer? Either the sinner suffers infinite punishment or "a suitable vicarious substitute"—Jesus Christ—offers up "a merit of infinite value that may offset any infinite disvalue generated by human sin," 133.

torment may be appropriate for those who commit incomprehensible evil, how could it be fair for the sins of most (average) people?

Admittedly, everlasting torment is impossible to imagine. The human mind cannot begin to grasp the concept of eternity, much less eternal punishment. Everlasting punishment is one of those areas that it is best to trust to God's unsearchable ways and wisdom (Job 9:10; Rom 11:33). Yet, Bible readers withal are not left without some insight. It is clear that no one is consigned to everlasting hell because of one or two unfortunate choices, nor even for a lifelong pattern of bad behavior for that matter. John 3:16 must be the best-known verse in the Bible. It tells of God's saving love for a lost world through his Son. Verse 17 elaborates on the mission of Christ to save rather than to condemn. Moreover, succeeding verses (vv. 18–21) expose the corresponding side. Jesus makes several points painfully clear. First, people are condemned *because* they refuse to believe in the Son of God. Second, they choose to reject God's Son and the salvation he offers *because* they love darkness rather than light. Third, they love darkness rather than light *because* their deeds are evil. Fourth, those who practice evil hate the light and avoid it *because* it exposes them and their evil deeds. As Aker sadly assesses this passage, "Unbelief confirms one in the state of condemnation."[30]

People do not go to hell because they slipped and said a "cuss word" when they stubbed a toe, or because they became impatient in heavy traffic, or some such thing. First, anyone who goes to hell does so in spite of everything a loving God has done to save them from that horrible fate. Second, anyone who goes to hell does so because they confirm or establish themselves in a state of condemnation. That state of condemnation sentences people to hell as the only appropriate place remaining for them. Fortunately, there is a much better alternative available through Jesus Christ. Praise God!

HEAVEN OR HELL AS ALTERNATIVE OPTIONS

With the above context in mind, Pentecostal teaching on life after death or heaven and hell is not exceptional according to historically traditional concepts, probably due to continuing reliance on Scripture with a straightforward hermeneutic. Pentecostals think of death in a threefold manner: physical, spiritual, and eternal.[31] Physical death involves the separation of the

---

30. Aker, "John," 22.

31. Parts of the following draw on Duffield and Van Cleave, in *Foundations of Pentecostal Theology*, 514–19. A threefold view of death was the general consensus of classical Christianity until Friedrich Schleiermacher (1768–1834) and subsequent liberal Protestant theology separated spiritual death, redefined as a matter of religious

soul from the body with a transition from the visible world to the invisible world. Upon physical death, believers enter into paradise in heaven where they dwell in the presence of Christ (2 Cor 5:18; Phil 1:23). Unbelievers enter hades with its sufferings (Luke 16:22–23; Matt 10:28; Rev 20:13). Physical death is the result of sin and impacts all humanity, but its "sting," its painful wound, has been removed for believers through Christ (1 Cor 15:55–56). A Christian can, therefore, approach death with anticipation rather than trepidation (Phil 1:21).

Spiritual death describes separation from the life of God due to the sinful state (Gen 2:17; Eph 2:1). One who comes to Christ (converts) is made alive, passing from death to life in restored fellowship with God (1 John 3:14). Ultimately, eternal death is the fate of those who die in their sins, that is, those who are persistently unrepentant (Jas 5:20). Eternal death is final, irrevocable separation from God's presence and goodness (2 Thess 1:7–9). At the Great White Throne Judgment, the wicked dead will be cast into a lake of fire burning with sulfur (Rev 20:13–15). The punishment at this final judgment is abiding and permanent (Matt 18:8; 25:41, 46; Mark 3:29; Jude 7; Heb 6:2). There is neither relief nor release.

Chapter 2 of this volume affirms the centrality of the bodily resurrection for soteriology. The term "intermediate state" describes the condition of the soul between physical death and the resurrection. Unanimity does not exist on all points. However, the following is generally descriptive of many Pentecostals' views on the postmortem state. Upon death the wicked, who are already under a sentence of condemnation (John 3:18), immediately go to a place of suffering and torment called hades (Luke 16:22–31) to await final judgment in hell (Rev 20:13–15). Hades (*hadēs*) is a general term for the place of departed spirits, but hell (*gehenna*) more properly refers to the place of everlasting fire and punishment (Mark 9:43). The OT *sheol* is of complex origin and broad range but generally signifies the realm of the dead. Sheol can, therefore, describe not only hades or gehenna but also the grave or the pit (e.g., 1 Sam 22:6; Ps 6:6; 139:8; Isa 14:9).[32]

The punishments of hades and hell are retributive rather than restorative. There is neither annihilation nor liberation. Ecclesiastes's cryptic philosopher puts it well, "And if a tree falls to the south or to the north, In the place where the tree falls, there it shall lie" (11:3b). Specifically, hell's punishment is "everlasting" (*aiōnios*) or enduring forever, ages without end (Matt 25:46; 2 Thess 1:9). The intermediate state of the wicked may be thought of

---

consciousness, from physical death, redefined as the natural course of biology. See Schleiermacher, *Christian Faith*, esp. Section 75.1 and cp. Sections 75–77. Pentecostals have not generally followed the lead of liberal theology.

32. Gerleman, "Realm of the Dead," 1279.

as somewhat analogous to that of a convicted criminal residing in a local jail awaiting sentencing and subsequent transfer to a federal penitentiary, except the incarceration of the wicked is eternal. There is no parole or probation. One's final state is . . . *final*.

Upon death, however, the righteous enter into paradise (Luke 23:43). Many believe that the resurrected Christ transferred paradise, also called "Abraham's Bosom" (Luke 16:22–23), from sheol to heaven to be in the presence of the Lord (Eph 4:8; Ps 16:10–11). Indeed, upon death believers are present with the Lord (2 Cor 5:8; Phil 1:23). In the NT, the word *paradise* (*paradeisos*) occurs only three times (Luke 23:43; 2 Cor 12:4; Rev 2:7), though the concept itself is more common.[33] Paradise literally describes a delightful garden full of delicacies. In Scripture, it can refer to either the garden of Eden or the transcendent eternal place or to heaven. Paradise primarily signifies a place of blessedness and joy.[34] Accordingly, the intermediate state for believers is enjoyment of divine favor, a state of perfect happiness and blissfulness. Yet, the perfection and fullness must be carefully qualified—it is not complete. The believer's deepest longing will be completely satisfied only at the resurrection of the body (2 Cor 5:1–11).

The American rock group Kansas has had two one-million-selling hit singles with "Carry On Wayward Son" and "Dust in the Wind."[35] Interestingly, both address human fate. "Carry On Wayward Son" encourages with the assurance that "there will be peace when you are done." However, "Dust in the Wind," reminiscent of Genesis 3:19 and Ecclesiastes 3:20 and 12:7, bemoans the transitoriness of this present life, especially its materialism—a reality that cannot be ignored. As early as 700 BC, the prophet announces that one day the redeemed dead—literally those who dwell in the dust of the earth—will rise and sing in new life (Isa 26:19). Eight hundred years later, the apostle Paul explains that though humans have borne "the image of the man of dust" (Adam), believers will bear "the image of the heavenly Man" (Christ) (1 Cor 15:48–49). Therefore, a solid resurrection hope strengthens and sustains believers (Acts 23:6; 24:15; cp. 1 Pet 1:3).

The intermediate state occurs between life in this world and that of the age or world to come. That is, the intermediate state occurs *after* death and *before* resurrection. Therefore, it differs from life in this present age in that it is a disembodied state, but will be concluded by bodily resurrection. All the human dead, both righteous and wicked, will be raised to face their reward

---

33. Jeremias, *Paradeisos* (transliteration), 5:769.

34. Michael E. Peach, "Heaven."

35. See the history tab of the band's official website at https://www.kansasband.com/history/.

or punishment (John 5:28–29). The intermediate state is anticipatory in that inhabitants begin to experience the consequences of their earthly life, yet it is temporary in that it only lasts until final judgment and is then superseded by a permanent state of being. This earthly life, before physical death, is the prelude to eternity. Eternity is the climactic postlude to life on earth. The intermediate state is the interlude between this earthly life and eternity.

An intermediate state is necessary because of the obvious fact of history that human beings live and die at different times. Even so, everyone will enter eternity together. There will be no delay then (Rev 10:6). In the meanwhile, everyone, both the saints and the unrighteous, will wait until the consummation of earthly history (as we know it) for the "grand opening" of eternity. For the redeemed, the intermediate state doubtless includes the suspense of a pleasant and excited expectation of ultimate blessedness as a result of God's grace in Jesus Christ. For the wicked, the intermediate state doubtless includes the suspense of dread in fearful apprehension and reluctance at standing before God to receive the just due of their sinful acts. Indeed, should not consideration of one's future state impact his or her present life as well? Thus, this earthly life sets the trajectory for eternity, while the intermediate state sets the tone for eternity.

Pentecostals may be somewhat remarkable for continuing commitments to literal understandings of heaven and hell in an age when many have moved to metaphorical interpretations. Of course, Pentecostals understand that biblical language regarding heaven and hell includes metaphor and symbolism. How could it be otherwise? Do not heaven and hell necessarily defy description? Pentecostals, nonetheless, believe that the graphic imagery represents literal truth about eternal realities. Therefore, Pentecostals still affirm that a literal heaven and hell exist. More to the point, they still believe in life after death and that real people actually go to either a real heaven or a real hell. So then, what are a few salient implications of this theology for the doctrine of salvation?

Here we may receive an assist from Ken Boa's fascinating study of the intersection of theology and psychology regarding the problem of self-interest and self-love.[36] Human beings tend to be (often overly) concerned about their own well-being. At its worst, this self-centeredness tends toward the sin of selfishness. However, God is to be loved for himself, not merely for the benefits he gives. Expressly, authentic love does not love God merely to avoid hell or to attain heaven. Yet, when the Supreme Good (God) is loved above all other goods, one is "delivered from the devouring egoism which

---

36. Boa, *Augustine to Freud*, 186–87.

distorts self-love" without losing his or her desire for joy.[37] Accordingly, a healthy self-interest and self-love replaces sinful self-centeredness (selfishness). Within this context, it is entirely appropriate to desire and to seek the joy of being with God forever rather than suffering separation from God forever.

Accordingly, the desire to be with God in heaven appropriately serves as an *encouragement* in the Christian faith and life, while the desire not to be separated from God in hell appropriately serves as a *deterrent* against sinful living. In other words, a belief in heaven supports an enduring commitment to serve Christ, while a belief in hell discourages apostasy (backsliding). Thus, the biblical and theological teaching on heaven and hell serves a pastoral function.[38] In terms of soteriology, it establishes the goal for eternity and undergirds the temporal stance necessary for its eventual achievement. Who would not want to go to heaven? Who would want to go to hell? The answers seem self-evident to any sane mind.

CHRIST'S COMING AS ESCHATOLOGICAL READINESS

N. T. Wright argues that Paul's doctrine of justification includes emphasis on eschatology and on the Spirit.[39] I agree. Pentecostal theology's emphasis on a nexus of eschatology, pneumatology, and soteriology arises out of just this kind of emphasis, but with a Lukan starting point. The Pentecost Day outpouring of the Holy Spirit in Acts 2:1–4 is paradigmatic for Pentecostal belief and experience, but Peter's Pentecost Day sermon in Acts 2:14–36 adds requisite clarity.[40] The outpouring of the Holy Spirit accompanied by speaking in tongues signifies that the last days have dawned. Although not consummated or completed yet, the age of fulfillment has begun. Theologians call this an "inaugurated eschatology" (also referred to as "now-not yet" eschatology), because the last days have already begun but have yet to finish their course. What are the implications of this view of eschatology for soteriology?

---

37. Boa, *Augustine to Freud*, 187. The classic allegory by C. S. Lewis on human nature and the afterlife, *Great Divorce*, is well worth reading.

38. Admittedly, these are relative rather than absolute statements. Individuals are free to choose/refuse the encouragement or deterrent regarding their relationship with God and its impact on their own eternal well-being (Deut 30:19; Rev 22:17).

39. Wright, *Justification*, 189–90.

40. Arrington, "Acts," 544–45.

Arrington points out that the "purpose of the outpouring of the Spirit is to prepare God's people" for the coming Day of the Lord.[41] Furthermore, he asserts that the church exists in these "last days," between the two events of Pentecost and Christ's return, to proclaim the gospel in order that people may be saved before Jesus comes again.[42] This nexus of eschatology, pneumatology, soteriology, and missiology is critical for understanding Pentecostals and their theology. The task of this present section is not to explore the intricacies, or perhaps better, the twists and turns, of Pentecostal ideas about eschatology. Rather, it examines implications of this dynamic intersection for a Pentecostal doctrine of salvation. However, a brief survey of basic Pentecostal eschatology is necessary for an informed discussion.[43]

The contours of a typical Pentecostal eschatology can appear a bit convoluted for noninitiates. Traditional Pentecostals adhere to a premillennial eschatology, maintaining that the second coming of Christ precedes and prepares the way for a literal one-thousand-year reign of Christ on earth. For the most part, that has meant belief in a pre-tribulation "rapture" (catching away) of the church to meet the Lord in the air (1 Thess 4:16–17), followed by seven years of unprecedented tribulation on earth (Matt 24:21) before Christ's actual coming to earth (Heb 9:28) and the aforementioned millennium (Rev 20:1–6), followed by final judgment of the present age and establishment of the new creation (20:7–21:1). As noted above, Pentecostals believe in eternal life for the righteous and eternal death (separation from the life of God, not annihilation of existence) for the wicked (Matt 25:46).

Hollis Gause has offered a nuanced theology of *progressive revelation* suitable for the ethos of Pentecostal eschatology.[44] Progressive revelation describes an ongoing unfolding of divine disclosure throughout the biblical canon that retains a prophetic and predictive character without destroying its universal applicability, while pointing to its climactic fulfillment in the eschaton.[45] A theology of progressive revelation respects the diversity-in-development of the Holy Scriptures, without undercutting their overall advancement-in-continuity as with some versions of the system outlined above. In other words, progressive revelation resists compartmentalizing redemptive history and its culmination. Yet, significantly, it maintains commitment to the imminent return of Christ, so long as it is not confused

41. Arrington, "Acts," 545.
42. Arrington, "Acts," 545.
43. This survey draws on Richie, *Essentials*, 162–66.
44. Gause, *Revelation*, 18–21.
45. This idea of successive but closely related periods of time coming to their eventual fulfillment appears compatible with how Paul uses the term "dispensation" (Eph 1:10).

with immediacy. In other words, Christ may come at any time, but that does not mean he necessarily will come at the present time. This continuing commitment to eschatological imminence will be critical for the purpose of this study.

As indicated, Pentecostal eschatology is an integral component of a powerful triad, inseparably linked with empowering pneumatology and passionate commitment to mission and service. Suffice it to state that Pentecostal conviction that Spirit baptism is an empowerment for vocational service, especially for evangelism and witness in these last days, has generated a movement with unprecedented, almost unbelievable, missional effectiveness (Luke 24:49; Acts 1:8).[46] The exalted Lord is pouring out the Holy Spirit upon the church in order to enable her to win lost souls prior to his imminent return.

Nearly thirty years ago, I happened to be a bystander when an automobile accident occurred. A car was traveling a rural highway a bit too fast when the right front tire slipped off the shoulder. The driver instinctively jerked the steering wheel in the opposite direction. Unfortunately, she overcompensated and sent her vehicle careening in the other direction where it left the highway, becoming airborne and crashing into an old barn on my property, about twenty feet from where I was standing. Fortunately, the driver was unhurt; but she was one scared lady. She had every right; that accident easily could have been fatal.

It is my considered opinion that many Pentecostal believers today are overcompensating for past slips in the area of eschatology. Perhaps they are embarrassed by a history of rampant sensationalism and unbridled speculation. I do not blame them there. Perhaps, they are ashamed of shabby social ethics rooted in undisciplined eschatological fervor. Again, I do not blame them. I am sure, however, that it would be wrong to "throw the baby out with the bathwater." Evangelical theologian Michael Bird is correct that "the return of Jesus is not a dispensable part of the Christian faith."[47] Regardless of past mistakes, the content of what theologians believe and teach about the return of Jesus is of critical importance too.

It is critical that Pentecostal theology maintain its eschatological, pneumatological, and soteriological convergent emphases. Critical to this triad is a continuing commitment to the imminent return of Jesus Christ.[48] As Jesus' parable of the faithful and wise steward (Luke 12:41–48) indicates,

---

46. Riggs, *Spirit Himself*, 30–31, 80, 163, and Land, *Pentecostal Spirituality*, 168–69.

47. Bird, *Evangelical Theology*, 318.

48. To adapt an insight from Wolfhart Pannenberg, "Task of Christian Eschatology," "the expectation of a second coming of Christ is inseparable from the other issues of Christian eschatological hope," 13.

those who lose their expectant hope of their Lord's imminent return are vulnerable to temptation and judgment (cp. 2 Pet 3:3–4).[49] I ask, "Are we Pentecostals serving in faithful stewardship for our Lord until he comes again?" Pentecostals prefer to identify with the faithful and wise steward in Jesus' parable. However, those who say, "Our master delays his coming" (Luke 12:45) have more in common with the parable's unfaithful and foolish character. As early as 1964, Charles Conn, a denominational leader, after lauding early eschatological expectations, challenged the Church of God with what appear to have been prophetic words:

> But what have the years done, and what are they doing to us and our expectation of his return? . . . It is possible that this generation will have waited through the years and now will be complacent when he comes. . . . Though we have waited, we must even now make sure that we are ready to meet him when he comes.[50]

In my opinion, Pentecostals cannot afford to let go of the eschatological soteriology and pneumatology that has driven their sense of mission. The price for that abdication is too great.

Perhaps some American readers have been traveling along a rural highway, when they came across a large roadside sign with the words "Prepare to meet thy God!" emblazoned on it. If so, did it evoke a smile or a frown? Perhaps some readers have encountered a person carrying a large placard on a busy city street corner with "The end is near!" written on it in bold lettering. Even if you agree in principle, is it distasteful? Though probably well-intentioned, zealots can hit folks in the face with their doomsday prophecies. Healthy eschatology helps people to prepare without beating them over the head with it, as they say. Jesus taught that believers should always be ready for his coming (Matt 24:44; Luke 12:40). The word for *ready* (*hetoimos*), describes a state of complete preparation or a condition for immediate action. Pentecostals believe that obedience to Jesus' command requires constant vigilance regarding the state of one's soul.

As nearly everyone knows, there are myriad versions and visions of eschatology. The core of Pentecostal eschatology comes together around a concept of *eschatological readiness*. I could not agree more with Bird that "there is a deeply practical side to theology-as-eschatology since how we act

---

49. According to David Novak, "Law and Eschatology," Christianity emerged out of a Jewish environment of eschatological "hope for a radically transformed future," specifically hope for the days of the Messiah, hope for the resurrection of the dead, and hope for the coming world, 91.

50. Conn, "They Waited, But . . .," 27.

in the present is deeply impacted by what we think of the future."[51] Attention to one's personal salvation means always being ready for Jesus to come. Believers live daily in the light of Christ's coming again. Like Paul, we strive to have a conscience clear of offense before God (Acts 23:1; 24:16)—not in fear, but, with John, in the perfect love that grants boldness on the day of judgment (1 John 4:17–18).

The key word for Pentecostal eschatology is not *fear* but *hope*! Believers are encouraged and inspired by the blessed hope of Jesus' return (Titus 2:13). Indeed, we are saved by hope (Rom 8:24), and this saving hope strengthens and sustains throughout the vicissitudes of life (8:25). As NT commentator Van Johnson puts it, hope "defines Christian existence from the moment one comes to know Christ."[52] Hope (*elpis*), which looks forward to a future with Christ in confident expectation, has saving influence. Hopeful believers yearn for Christ's return. The hopeful heart cries, "Maranatha!" "O Lord, come!" (1 Cor 16:22).

This chapter looked at personal salvation from the perspective of *eternity*. It addressed Pentecostal theology regarding a tradition of otherworldliness, a belief in heaven and hell and a few related matters raised thereby, and a commitment to Christ's imminent coming again with a view toward their soteriological significance. In short, Pentecostals live out their faith in Jesus Christ in this world with an eye ever on eternity's horizon. A Pentecostal theology of salvation recognizes that both this present age and the age to come are important, but this life is fixed on and framed by the life to come—by eternity—not the other way around.

---

51. Bird, *Evangelical Theology*, 301.
52. Johnson, "Romans," 750.

7

Corporeal Soteriology

(Physical Healing in Salvation)

The term *divine healing* signifies bodily healing through divine intervention, usually in association with believing prayer. Christianity's long history of divine healing stretches back to the healing narratives of the Old and New Testaments, especially in the ministries of Jesus and of the apostles, and spans more than two millennia of Christian thought and practice. Yet, perhaps few would contest that the doctrine of divine healing took on its most insistent and persistent emphasis with the rise of contemporary Pentecostal movements. Harvard religion scholar Candy Gunther Brown rightly says, "Divine healing practices are an essential marker of Pentecostal and Charismatic Christianity as a global phenomenon."[1] Strictly speaking Pentecostals do not practice so-called "faith healing."[2] In other words, for Pentecostals, divine healing is not located in the recipient's faith. Pentecostal theology locates divine healing within its doctrine of salvation (soteriology) through its teaching that divine healing is provided in the atonement. Arguably, although controversial, this "corporeal" aspect of soteriology has

---

1. Brown, ed., *Global and Pentecostal Charismatic Healing*, 3. Later she adds that "Pentecostalism, healing practices, and globalization will all play important, indeed increasing, roles in shaping the twenty-first century world," 378.

2. Even Nancy Hardesty's critical *Faith Cure* acknowledges the theological complexity of Pentecostals' healing theology via its atonement-based soteriological underpinnings, 87.

contributed significantly to, perhaps even been a primary conductor of, the healing experience and practice among Pentecostals for more than a century. This chapter provides some context before it examines, clarifies, and at times, critiques the Pentecostal doctrine of divine healing, by proposing a nuanced theological understanding of divine healing drawing on its distinctive soteriological setting in the Pentecostal movement.

CHRISTIAN HISTORY OF DIVINE HEALING

Before directly discussing Pentecostal healing beliefs and practices, some background regarding divine healing in the historic Christian tradition will be helpful. Ronald Kydd's extensive *Healing through the Centuries* not only recounts the tradition of healing in Christianity for two millennia but also provides theological models that classify healing practice in various contexts.[3] Kydd is clear that Christian history and theology regarding divine healing arises out of the healing ministry of Jesus, with its continuation entrusted to the church. He lists six theological models attempting implementation of that healing commission: the confrontational model, the intercessory model, the reliquarial model, the incubation model, the revelation model, and the soteriological model.[4] Our primary interest is in the soteriological model, but a brief sketch of the other models will facilitate understanding for that process.

The confrontation model of divine healing was prominent in the early church (ante-Nicene Christianity, that is, prior to 325 AD) with representatives as diverse as Irenaeus, Tertullian, Cyprian, Origen, and Lactantius. It has been more recently represented by J. C. Blumhardt (nineteenth century) and John Wimber (twentieth century). This model tends to be more theologically sophisticated than other models. In this view, healing is integrated into God's overarching purpose and activity, not only in human affairs but in the entire universe, by sending his Son to earth to establish God's reign as a direct—and successful—challenge to evil. Divine healing and exorcism in this model are closely associated. Emphasis is on confrontation, victory, and liberty through Jesus Christ. Divine healing is considered a principal

---

3. While a helpful heuristic tool for present purposes, Kydd's model is not perfect. E.g., one could well describe all the models as "soteriological" in a general sense. Also, there is overlap between several models, especially between *Christus Victor* and soteriological, confrontational, and intercessory themes. Furthermore, the reliquarial model and the sacramental model are, if not identical, very close, since they both presume the sacramental nature of creation and, thus, the mediation of divine power through material objects.

4. Kydd, *Healing through the Centuries*, 16–17.

component of planting the kingdom of God in this world in anticipation of its full realization.⁵ This model resonates well with many Pentecostals, especially those who emphasize inaugurated or now-not yet eschatology (see chapter 6).

The intercessory model places great confidence in the prayers of the community of saints who have passed into God's presence and are thought to have special influence with God. This approach is tied to the veneration of the saints and is popular among Roman Catholics and Orthodox believers, but rejected by Protestants. The intercessory approach, or praying to departed saints for healing, became increasingly common from the second to the eighth centuries of Christianity, and continues to this day. In Montreal, Quebec in the twentieth century, healing attention grew up around a monk known as Brother André and St. Joseph's Oratory. Beginning in 1981 in rural Bosnia-Herzegovina, a series of visions related to the Virgin Mary, or Mary of Medjugorje, became widely publicized for reported occurrences of healing.⁶ Pentecostals are loath to deny the miraculous but, nevertheless, have serious reservations about the unbiblical, quasi-idolatrous nature of the intercessory model (per such passages as Rev 19:10 and 22:8–9).

The reliquarial model attaches healing power to the physical remains and to the various objects or relics associated with deceased saints. Again, Protestants reject the healing power of relics, but the veneration of relics has been popular with Roman Catholics and Orthodox churches for centuries. Prominent examples of healing movements from late antiquity occur as well as from eighteenth century Paris around the tomb of Francois de Paris.⁷ Veneration of relics appears to many Pentecostals as baseless, unbiblical superstition, not far removed from magical amulets. Admittedly, Pentecostals themselves employ "prayer cloths" (see below) based on biblical passages such as Matthew 9:20–22 and Acts 19:11–12. In contrast, Pentecostal uses of material objects are christologically based (not based on the supposed power of deceased saints) and are aids to faith or serve as a point of contact in prayer (sort of an extension of the laying on of hands).⁸ Incontrovertibly,

---

5. Kydd, *Healing through the Centuries*, 19.
6. Kydd, *Healing through the Centuries*, 61–62.
7. Kydd, *Healing through the Centuries*, 115–16.
8. For example, my father, Andrew Richie, recounted to me an incident from his boyhood. When he was less than twelve years old, his mother suffered from tuberculosis. She was listening on the radio to Oral Roberts preach when he instructed those with disease or illness to lift one hand toward God in heaven and place the other hand on the radio as a point of contact while he prayed for them. My grandmother followed directions and received her healing during that prayer. However, no one thought the radio had healing power.

there is no magical power attributed to the objects, rather healing power is attributed to Christ alone (Luke 6:19).

The incubation model represents something of a departure from the previous patterns and their assumptions of dramatic, immediate healings. Associated with Johann Christoph Blumhardt, it attempts to provide a positive, nurturing environment where healing can occur as a process over time. This led to the creation of residences or "healing homes" where patience and prayer combined to facilitate healing. Two healing ministry residences located in Switzerland, Männedorf and Yverdon-les-Baines, are well known.[9] This model exemplifies how loving care and believing prayer may work together. Pentecostals certainly are not opposed to this model but have generally relied more on the prayers of believers during corporate worship services (as in Matt 4:24; 8:16; 9:2, 32; 14:35; 17:16).

Another approach is the revelational model of divine healing.[10] Practitioners of this model believe that God gives them special knowledge, impossible for them to have otherwise known, regarding what needs are present, who is being healed, and/or what actions must be taken. The healing practitioner then acts accordingly, perhaps announcing the time of healing or giving a call to faith or simply praying according to the word of knowledge. William Branham (1909–1965), a preacher from Kentucky, and Kathryn Kuhlman (1907–1976), a female evangelist based out of Pittsburgh, were famous but complex examples of this approach. While this model has influenced Pentecostals, it is not generally representative of the movement's approach to healing ministry.[11] There is some biblical precedent for associating revelational insight with healing (e.g., Acts 14:9) and it assumes the operation of a charismatic gift (1 Cor 12:8). Yet this modality is relatively rare among Pentecostals (Branham and Kuhlman aside). It is best understood as an exceptional approach for certain gifted individuals rather than a paradigm for ministers. For Pentecostals, cautious reserve attends a model that places such emphasis on individual gifting and power. If so, it may appear too vulnerable to exploitative sensationalism for complete comfort. However, it would be unwise to completely discount it.

Finally, the soteriological model of healing, a theologically self-conscious approach, teaches that people can be healed through the same means by which they became Christians: the atoning work of Jesus Christ. Accordingly, the attack upon illness is located within soteriology, often with

---

9. Kydd, *Healing through the Centuries*, 142.

10. Kydd, *Healing through the Centuries*, 167.

11. I have seen my own uncle, Lewis Richie, now with the Lord, operate in this mode of ministry, which was common for him.

theological sophistication. The roots of the soteriological model of divine healing are traceable to mainstream American Christianity in the nineteenth century. Ultimately, the soteriological model of healing places emphasis on the authority of Scripture and on personal faith in Jesus Christ. Although healing in the atonement was advocated by Carrie Judd Montgomery, A. B. Simpson, A. J. Gordon, and other nineteenth-century luminaries, its best-known proponent was "the quintessential Pentecostal" Oral Roberts (1918–2009). A Choctaw American who had himself been healed of tuberculosis and stuttering, Roberts, with ordination in both the Pentecostal Holiness Church and the United Methodist Church, boldly represents the soteriological model of healing.[12] The soteriological model of divine healing typifies the core of Pentecostal healing theology. The formal Declaration of Faith of the Church of God (Cleveland, TN), my own denominational affiliation, unambiguously states that "Divine healing is provided for all in the atonement."[13]

Kydd concludes his extensive study of divine healing by advocating for both "a wide view" of healing and "a narrow view" of healing. A wide view includes diversity, accepts human agents, per the practice of medical science and professional healthcare, and recognizes social dynamics. A narrow view affirms direct divine intervention or miraculous healing. Both have their place. Kydd further suggests a place for mystery in divine healing and adds: "In the end, one must acknowledge that healing arises out of one's relationship with God. And that is enough."[14] Amen!

Especially in Pentecostal contexts, three additional healing approaches bear mentioning. The first involves so-called "positive confession theology."[15] Positive confession theology, also known as the "Word of Faith movement," derives from the teaching of E. W. Kenyon as popularized by Kenneth Hagin, Kenneth Copeland, Charles Capps, Frederick K. C. Price, and others.[16] In spite of claims to be biblical, it belies a clear metaphysical New Thought

---

12. Kydd, *Healing through the Centuries*, 199–201, 202–3. After extensive research, Hardesty, *Faith Cure*, concludes that an integration of medical means with prayer and faith is more effective for healing than either approach alone, 151–52.

13. See the Church of God web page: http://199.191.59.139/beliefs/declaration-of-faith/.

14. Kydd, *Healing through the Centuries*, 213–15, esp. 215.

15. Leonard Lovett, "Positive Confession Theology." To be clear, Pentecostals do still believe that words spoken in faith are impactful.

16. I might note that Word of Faith teaching on positive confession is an androcentric understanding of healing rather than a theocentric one. Pentecostals have always been theocentric. Arguably, the androcentric position makes positive confession a species of Pelagianism (a fifth-century heresy accenting human endeavor at the expense of divine activity).

philosophical bent. It basically teaches that those who have faith can confess selected quotes from Scripture to achieve, or really to create, their preferred reality. Accordingly, it is colloquially known as the "name it and claim it" movement or, due to its inevitable foci, the "health and wealth" gospel (or sometimes simply "the prosperity gospel"). Clearly out of sync with established Pentecostal theology, it has nevertheless made significant inroads at the lay and popular levels and even with some gullible clergy. Regarding healing, positive confession theology teaches that the act of speaking healing and health in faith inevitably and universally accomplishes healing. Pentecostal pastor and scholar Leonard Lovett rightly challenges positive confession theology for its distorted and selective use of Scripture and for redefining the focus of the gospel of Christ.[17] Pentecostal theology affirms financial and physical blessings but with emphasis on the soul's salvation (3 John 2).

An additional consideration is the role of the gifts of healing in Pentecostal faith and practice.[18] Pentecostals believe *charismata* enumerated in 1 Corinthians 12:8–10, including gifts of healing, continue to operate within the context of today's Christian worship and fellowship. The gifts of healing are specifically and repeatedly mentioned as part of the divine provision for healing (1 Cor 12:9, 28, 30). While Pentecostals tend to understand the gifts of healing as a special impartation of healing ability or power under the sovereign distribution of the Holy Spirit, it is of great importance to note two clarifiers. First, the context of the gifts of healing includes the overall biblical witness to the reality and continuity of divine healing. Therefore, the gifts of healing cannot be understood properly apart from the overall biblical context. Second, the gifts of healing are not an exception to (or "shortcut" around) divine healing as provided in the atonement but rather a particular manner of its implementation. Accordingly, we may still maintain our attention to the relationship of the doctrine of divine healing and soteriology.

Finally, and perhaps to the surprise of some, is the sacramental approach. Stirring testimonies of divine healing have been reported in conjunction with sacramental worship so that miraculous healings have come to be expected in connection with sacramental observance, especially the Lord's Supper or Communion.[19] The sacramental nature of Pentecostal healing includes both formal sacraments such as water baptism, communion, and foot washing, as well as less formal sacramental acts such as anointing

---

17. Lovett, "Positive Confession Theology," 993–94.
18. Francis Martin, "Healing, Gift of."
19. Tomberlin, *Pentecostal Sacraments*, 69–70, 81.

with oil and laying on of hands.[20] My own wife experienced this type of healing recently. Having been diagnosed with advanced (late stage 3) colon cancer, she had participated in several prayer encounters. However, the evening before her surgery, she and I took Holy Communion together. With tears of joy streaming down her cheeks, she bore witness that she literally felt she had been healed at that moment. The next day, her surgeon apologized for a mistaken diagnosis. The cancer was not present! Sue replied, "Four specialists didn't get it wrong; the Lord had mercy on me!" He agreed.[21] Praise God! Again, sacramental healing is not so much another model as it is an appropriation in faith of Christ's atonement provision. Should it be thought odd that when believers are celebrating a physical act with spiritual meaning and power that a powerful physical healing should occur?

This brief sketch of healing in the Christian churches from ancient times until the present prepares us for a closer look at a Pentecostal theology of healing in relation to the doctrine of salvation. The confrontational model resonates well with *Christus Victor* atonement theology (recall chapter 3), and the revelational model assumes the active and ongoing manifestation of the *charismata* (spiritual gifts), especially a message of knowledge. Gifts of healing and sacramental healing are deeply appreciated by Pentecostals. Yet, the soteriological model will be the focus of the following as it provides the standard theological justification of divine healing within the Pentecostal movement.

A PENTECOSTAL DOCTRINE OF DIVINE HEALING

Psalm 103:3 is one of the key texts often quoted by Pentecostals regarding the soteriological aspect of divine healing. The language of the strophe in Psalm 103:1–5 stresses divine benefits (v. 2, *gemûl*, works or actions, accomplishments; recompense or rewards) as extended to the whole person.[22] The idea is that the following list—forgiveness, healing, redemption from destruction, a life crowned with lovingkindness and tender mercies, satisfaction with good things, and renewed youth—enumerates that which is gained in salvation. In Pentecostal nomenclature, each is a *provision* of redemption.

20. Tomberlin, *Pentecostal Sacraments*, 119–222.

21. We had a wonderful surgeon who was respectful of our faith and our reliance on prayer. He has become a good friend as well as a brother in Christ. University of Tennessee Medical Center was a great partner in this process also. For more on Sue's healing, see *Frontiers*, https://spark.adobe.com/page/xT89lSbEodRUE/.

22. Keil and Delitzsch, *Commentary on the OT*, 5:646–47. Bloesch, *Last Things*, 123, observes that in Jesus' ministry forgiveness of sins and physical healing often occurred together.

Inclusion of the physical element of human existence and nature with the soulish/spiritual may arise out of an intention to highlight the psalmist's returning health after having been seriously ill, but who now in his recovery, resolves never to forget the goodness of God in granting the gift of divine healing.[23] Nevertheless, the psalmist's language can well indicate ongoing healing and deliverance with a connection between forgiveness and healing, although not necessarily inevitable (automatic).[24]

Isaiah 53:5, in conjunction with 1 Peter 2:24, is also a key divine healing text for Pentecostals. Although the passage context clearly indicates that healing Israel's (and humanity's) spiritual infirmities is in focus, that by no means excludes the totality of Christ's mediatorial work regarding physical suffering. Indeed, Matthew's Gospel explicitly connects Isaiah 53:5 with the Messiah's healing ministry and pointers toward Christ's atoning suffering and death (8:17).[25] Again, salvation of body and soul are connected; or to put it another way, salvation includes healing for both body and soul.[26] Divine healing is soteriological.

Various commentators confirm the inclusiveness of divine healing with salvation (at the least) implicit in these scriptural texts. Hints of the significant association between forgiveness and healing in Psalm 103:3 appear among many non-Pentecostal theologians, ancient and recent. For example, Augustine interprets this verse with emphasis on spiritual healing, that is, on salvation; but even so, he argues that the Creator of body and soul is the "Almighty Physician" who restores both body and soul well beyond the limitations of earthly physicians who do not treat that which is their own creation.[27] Commenting on Matthew 8:17, Chrysostom did not think it odd that salvation and healing are connected in Christ's atoning work, since sin and sickness, and even death itself—"the sum of all diseases"—are connected as well.[28]

23. White, "Psalms," 391–92.
24. Broyles, *Psalms*, 395.
25. Oswalt, *Isaiah*, 387–88.
26. Connection between body and soul in arguing for physical healing as part of salvation includes healing in God's purpose. Because healing is part of God's purpose, we view it in light of theodicy (the problem of evil, suffering). Thus, the question of why everyone does not receive healing is bound up in the general question of why suffering exists, and this itself is bound up in the way the divine purpose unfolds in each individual life.
27. Augustin, *Expositions on the Psalms*, 8:504–505.
28. Oden and Simonetti, eds., *Matthew 1–13*, 164. Really the various ways divine power/grace comes to humanity connects everything, and tends to be grounded in Christ overcoming sin, death, and the devil. Even the *Christus Victor* model is not reducible to spiritual warfare against the demonic. It is grounded in the triumph of Christ

Nevertheless, Matthew's application of the Isaiah redemption text to "the healing activity of Jesus in the physical realm" may appear unusually "striking" to some—unless relating healing to salvation.[29] While ancient writers such as Basil the Great, Severus of Antioch, Eusebius of Emesa, and Theodoret of Cyr interpret 1 Peter 2:24 with emphasis on the sacrifice for sins, Bede agrees but adds that Christ bore our sins on the tree "in order to give us eternal life as well as blessings in this world."[30] Bede's "blessings in this world" allusion appears to include material benefits in salvation. As such, they likely describe present physical healing redemption alongside "eternal life." Similarly, modern scholarship, again in light of Matthew 8:17, argues that 1 Peter 2:24 primarily refers to "the healing of sin-affected souls," but that it does not exclude physical healing.[31] "Not excluding" effectively implies "including." Again, a soteriological view of divine healing resolves apparent tensions as interpreters struggle to understand the appropriation of Isaiah 53:5 by Peter and Matthew. Arguably, biblically speaking, the question is not whether divine healing is soteriological.

Theologically speaking, it appears that a more appropriate question may be "What does it mean that divine healing is in some sense soteriological?" For the present work, the question is, more specifically, "In what sense does Pentecostal theology claim that divine healing is soteriological?" Vernon Purdy ably explicates Pentecostal belief in healing as a provision of the atonement or healing as part of salvation.[32] He argues: "If humankind was created by God intentionally for wholeness" then it is reasonable that "healing is, at least in a limited sense, part of God's salvific work in Christ."[33] Accordingly, a holistic anthropology (view of humanity) indicates that salvation as provided by the atoning death of Jesus Christ affects the whole human being—including not only the spiritual but also the physical nature—for good and for wholeness. A holistic anthropology runs counter to ancient Hellenistic (Greek) philosophical views, and especially gnostic

---

over death itself and from that it springs outward to all that works death.

29. Mounce, *Matthew*, 76.

30. Oden and Bray, eds., *James, 1–2 Peter, 1–3 John, Jude*, 96.

31. E.g., Hillyer, *1 and 2 Peter, Jude*, 87. Although a Pentecostal commentator, Roger Stronstad, "1 and 2 Peter," disagrees with recruiting 1 Peter 2:24 to defend divine healing, insisting on the basis of context that it speaks only to spiritual healing, 1447. This is somewhat ironic since arguably Peter's interpretative context includes the healing of his mother-in-law when Matthew applies Isaiah 53:5 to divine (physical) healing (Matt 8:17)!

32. Purdy, "Divine Healing," 489, 500–509.

33. Purdy, "Divine Healing," 500. Note that when expanding healing to the whole of salvation, he acknowledges a close alliance between healing and holiness or sanctity and sanity (in the Latin sense of *sanitas* as "health"). Note the shalom section below.

syncretistic heresies, and their contemporary counterparts, which deny the value of the material world and of physical existence (contending against not only divine healing but bodily resurrection).[34]

However, human beings exist as a duality (material and immaterial/physical and spiritual) but are nonetheless unitary in nature (existing and acting as a whole).[35] Accordingly, a biblical definition of salvation conjoined with a biblical definition of human nature establishes the unity of the physical and spiritual dimensions of human identity and existence, inclusive of the saving benefits of Christ for the whole person. Not surprisingly, the very word *salvation* itself (*sōtēria*) refers both to salvation and to healing according to context and has a great deal of overlap.

Although there is a correlation between sin and sickness and forgiveness and healing (Mark 2:5), there is not a necessary correlation on the individual level (John 9:1–3). Rather, sin entered the world and brought sickness and suffering. Accordingly, the atoning work of Christ provides redemption for the whole person, including the body. Significantly, although divine healing occurs as a present reality of accomplished salvation, "the full realization of this salvation" will occur at the resurrection.[36] In a sense, present healings of the bodies of believers are signifiers of the reality of the coming resurrection of the body. Divine healing, therefore, serves as an eschatological sign, as well as a present blessing (Heb 2:3–4; 6:5).

Nevertheless, the doctrine of divine healing as articulated by Pentecostal theology acknowledges the temporary and limited nature of the experience of healing this side of the eschaton.[37] Not everyone is healed. Those who are healed eventually may encounter some illness again; and everyone eventually dies. Yet, the reality of divine healing testifies for itself. God is faithful. "Thus, the healings we experience today are a first installment of the future redemption of our bodies."[38] In this case, that which is limited or incomplete naturally looks ahead to that which is finally perfected.

Note several observations concerning divine healing in relation to salvation. First, the doctrine of divine healing arises out of God's purpose for humanity in creation. Second, it arises out of a holistic understanding of created human nature as both spiritual and physical. Third, it contends that

---

34. Christian theologians battled mightily against gnosticism, most notably, Irenaeus in *Against Heresies*. See Behr, "Irenaeus of Lyons," 41, 46.

35. Purdy, "Divine Healing," 502.

36. Purdy, "Divine Healing," 505.

37. Purdy, "Divine Healing," 509. Bloesch, *Last Things*, 123, thinks it important to note that the renewal of the body in divine healing is "provisional and temporal," but the renewal of the inner person is "permanent."

38. Purdy, "Divine Healing," 509.

salvation addresses the damaging effects of sin—both spiritual and physical. Fourth, healing is anticipatory, bearing witness to the resurrection and appropriated through believing prayer, but is not automatic or mechanical. Fifth, complete and permanent healing is eschatological in nature, fully realized only at the resurrection. Arguably, implications of associating divine healing with the doctrine of salvation have great potential for fertile development.

Let us close this section with an important caveat. The doctrine of divine healing as provided in the atonement, the teaching on healing as part of salvation, does not mean that those who are not yet healed are not saved (not forgiven, not converted). In other words, not everyone who is saved will be immediately healed. We will address the "whys and wherefores" of this statement more fully below. For the present, suffice it to say that although Pentecostal theology argues that salvation/forgiveness and healing are related, even intricately associated, it does *not* affirm that they are received as synonymous, inseparable experiences. Yet, it is a great encouragement to suffering believers to know that the same salvation that provides forgiveness provides healing as well. The same Jesus who is Savior is also healer.

A CONTROVERSIAL COMMITMENT

Perhaps no other Pentecostal practice has generated quite the controversy with the general public (both religious and secular) as the commitment to divine healing. Sadly, much of the onus for that negative publicity falls squarely on the shoulders of Pentecostals themselves.[39] In misguided zeal to affirm the biblical doctrine of healing, some have gone far beyond the Scriptures.[40] They made serious errors as they wrongly reasoned that if a sufferer was not healed, then there must be a lack of faith or possibly hidden sin in their life. Some radicals further insisted that resorting to medical care—going to a physician or taking medicine—was a sign of a lack of faith and so attached a stigma to professional healthcare. As a result, many suffered needlessly; some died. The public outcry was loud—and legitimate. There are far too many stories of adults and even children suffering and dying who almost surely could have lived longer, healthier lives with proper healthcare.

According to Henry Knight, much of the confusion and misunderstanding concerning divine healing arises from failure to properly place the doctrine of divine healing in the context of the theological poles of God's

---

39. Sims, *Our Pentecostal Heritage*, 83.

40. Roberts, *Divine Healing*, 9–19, insisted that closer attention to Scripture would have avoided many painful mistakes.

faithfulness and God's freedom.[41] I think Knight is right; his observation certainly addresses erroneous views expressed when healing sometimes simply does not happen—views that seek to deny medical benefit, to blame individuals, or to dismiss normal human struggles. Ideally, believers can approach circumstances of sickness with the certainty of faith even while acknowledging the sovereignty of God in and over all situations. As Kydd well says, "The healings flow from God, and God keeps his own good counsel. It is enough that we know that God looks with mercy on human pain."[42] Pentecostals believe, and know, that God still heals. Faith and wisdom are sustained together without injury to either. The blessings of healing are lifted high and made available without resorting to excessive claims.[43]

With the preceding in mind, let's press on. As shown above, Pentecostals stand squarely in the anti-gnostic tradition in affirming that creation and redemption are inclusive of materiality and physicality (which the ancient heresy of Gnosticism denies). Again, many Christians throughout the ages have believed generally in divine healing, and there are important precedents for Pentecostal approaches to healing in the broader evangelical movement. However, more specifically, Pentecostals are direct heirs to the Holiness movement's distinctive emphasis on healing.[44] As stated, Pentecostals believe that physical healing is a gracious provision of the atonement of Jesus Christ, which may be confidently claimed by faith. Theologically, the radicalization of the Wesleyan-Holiness movement and its doctrine doubtless contributed to the origins and development of Pentecostal healing theology.[45] Consequently, Kimberly Alexander's detailed historical study of the formative years of Pentecostal healing thought in *Pentecostal Healing* shows abundantly how many early Pentecostals were grappling with questions of great importance for the Christian understanding of healing and its relationship to soteriology. While both "finished work" (Baptistic) Pentecostals and Holiness (Wesleyan) Pentecostals believe in divine healing, Alexander argues that Wesleyanism's therapeutic soteriology (salvation as healing from

---

41. Knight, "God's Faithfulness and God's Freedom." Cp. Sims, *Our Pentecostal Heritage*, 83.

42. Kydd, "Healing in the Christian Church."

43. Roberts, *Divine Healing*, labors to give a balanced discussion, listing many traditional considerations for receiving healing, such as prayer and faith; but also lifting up the recognition of medicine as a way that God heals along with the observance of natural laws for good health, 149–52 and 156.

44. Arrington, *Christian Doctrine*, 2:79–80.

45. Dayton, "Rise of the Evangelical Healing Movement in America."

sin and its effects) is especially well-suited for integration with the doctrine of divine healing.[46]

Pentecostals do differ somewhat from their Holiness forebears on bodily healing. In addition to affirming that bodily healing is a provision of Christ's atonement, Pentecostals further view healing as a manifestation of power—bearing witness, along with other signs and wonders, to Christ's glorious gospel (Acts 4:30).[47] As is often the case, Pentecostals draw heavily on their historical roots but add their own distinctive theological twists. Two implications are noteworthy. First, the view that divine healing is a provision of the atonement calls attention to the soteriological foundation of God's compassion toward human sufferers. Second, the view that divine healing is a miraculous sign confirming the truth and validity of the gospel calls attention to the missiological aspect with implicative responsibilities.

As indicated above, a primary consideration is whether salvation is for the whole person and what its implications may be. Pentecostals believe that salvation addresses the entire condition of the complete person in every area of life (Matt 9:22; Heb 7:25).[48] Just as sin has impacted the whole human person negatively and destructively, so salvation impacts the whole human person positively and therapeutically. We must go further. Amos Yong persuasively argues for an expansive soteriological multidimensionality. In this view full gospel salvation is extensive in scope, including the personal, familial, ecclesial, material, social, cosmic, and eschatological realms of human existence.[49] Therefore, salvation in Christ is far-reaching. It certainly is not limited to the spiritual only but includes the physical. Accordingly, physical/material suggests social implications regarding the transforming power of holiness and righteousness as the "healing" of a sin-sick society. Thereby, salvation-as-healing implicates a trifold application: healing of sin-sick souls, healing of sin-sick bodies, and healing of sin-sick communities/societies—not to mention that its ultimate objective is cosmological. Daniel Tomberlin says it well, "The healing of humanity, as well as of the cosmos, is the goal of the Incarnation and Pentecost."[50]

Furthermore, it is critical to understand divine healing in the context of the church's ministry to hurting people and its overall gospel mission. Therefore, Pentecostal ecclesiology envisions the church as, among other

46. Alexander, *Pentecostal Healing*, 23–42.

47. Arrington, *Christian Doctrine*, 2:83–84. Pentecostals' differences on healing as a manifestation of divine power in signs and wonders from that of the Holiness movement may be more a matter of emphasis than anything.

48. Arrington, *Christian Doctrine*, 2:160–61.

49. Yong, *Spirit Poured Out on All Flesh*, 91–98.

50. Tomberlin, *Pentecostal Sacraments*, 37.

things, a healing community.⁵¹ The church proclaims the gospel message of salvation as forgiveness; but as an intrinsic part of that very proclamation, the church's demonstration of the gospel shows compassion for the sick. Care for the sick can include prayer for healing as well as medical care. Local Pentecostal congregations exist as diverse healing communities.⁵² Wholeness (*shalom*) entails a holistic anthropology and soteriology with salvation/healing for spirit, soul, and body. Human affliction and suffering call for congregations to engage sincerely in believing prayer for healing and deliverance. Pentecostals believe that the church should offer help in the Lord for the whole person here and now as well as happiness with the Lord for all eternity.⁵³ Accordingly, not only forgiveness of sins and future blessedness but present healing and deliverance are intrinsic to the gospel and integral to the mission of the church.

Having looked briefly at the basic contours of Pentecostal healing theology, it seems appropriate to draw out a few feasible theological applications. First and foremost, divine healing is significant in relation to our doctrine of God (theology proper). The God of Pentecostals is not far removed from or unfeeling toward human affliction and suffering. Rather, God is compassionate and close at hand to call upon for help. Second, divine healing is significant in relation to the human person and other creatures, to all creation (anthropology and cosmology). God is not so otherworldly that material reality is outside the scope of divine concern. Rather, God cares for the overall well-being of human beings and, by implication, the entire created order.

Third, divine healing is significant in relation to salvation (soteriology). The God of Pentecostals is not simply a judge seeking to pass sentence on sin. God is the Great Physician, and the salvation of the Lord is therapeutic by definition and in application. Fourth, divine healing is significant in relation to eternity (eschatology). God is not inconsistent or irregular. Each specific instance of bodily healing is effectively an anticipatory witness to the bodily resurrection and to eternal enjoyment of wholeness in God's presence. And finally, divine healing is significant in relation to our theology of nature (healthcare, medical science). God is not contradictory. Scriptural truth and scientific truth, rightly understood and applied, mutually

---

51. Alexander, "Pentecostal Healing Community."

52. Onyinah, "Pentecostal Healing Communities."

53. This is all christologically centered, according to Robert P. Pope, "Why the Church Needs a Full Gospel." Pope remarks, "the Church is the *Church* only because Jesus redeems, sanctifies, empowers, heals, and instills in us the hope for his return," 283 (italics are original).

flow from the fount of the God of truth, offering strength and wisdom in life for all who truly love truth.

Before closing this topic, I would take note of a prevalent blind spot in Pentecostal healing faith and practice as it is sometimes implemented, or perhaps, I should say as it is all too often *not* implemented. Pentecostals typically enjoy testimonies extolling the blessings of divine healing. For example, I enjoy testifying about my son Joshua's instantaneous healing from crippled feet. As a toddler, he was diagnosed by his physician as having severe angle deformity. It would require surgery and braces. Running and playing or walking normally would be impossible. Yet, God instantly and totally healed him after an evangelist friend in a little country church revival prayed over him. An orthopedic specialist subsequently confirmed that his ankle bones were now normal. Josh never had surgery, never wore braces; but he did play elementary school soccer and high school football. God (still) can and (still) does miraculously heal.

Yes, we love those kinds of testimonies. However, not everyone is instantly healed. Admittedly, there are those who are not healed in this life at all. Authentic Pentecostal theology will be inclusive of the full range of actual life experiences. It must account for, include, and embrace those who are not yet healed.[54] It must reassure that in such cases God's sustaining grace and love are present and sufficient (2 Cor 12:9). The enduring, steady faith of those who are not healed immediately or completely, nonetheless, bears fruitful witness in remarkable manner.

Jerry Lynn, a youth at New Harvest church, grew into a tall and exceptionally strong man. Beginning when he was only thirty-eight years of age (in 1988), he had a series of debilitating strokes interspersed with critical heart attacks. Specialists eventually concluded that he suffered from a rare genetically transmitted blood disorder. For over two decades, he wrestled almost daily with life and death. He was hospitalized frequently. The physicians repeatedly "gave up" on him, telling his wife there was nothing else that could be done, that she should prepare for the worst. Faithfully she never gave up. Somehow, believing prayer pulled him through time and time again. His caregivers were always amazed. During all of this, Brother Jerry was a zealous witness of Jesus everywhere to everyone (literally). His unquestioning faith touched countless lives. He specifically instructed his wife and two daughters never to blame God for what had happened to him. Rather, he wanted everyone to know that he knew and loved God. Before losing the power of speech and eventually becoming unable to attend services, he loved to testify. He always said, "God is good!" His Lord finally

---

54. Clifton, "Dark Side of Prayer for Healing," 205–9.

(2010) took him home to glory. As his pastor, I preached on Jerry's favorite Bible verse at his funeral: "This *is* the day *which* the Lord hath made; We will rejoice and be glad in it" (Ps 118:24 KJV). It was a special blessing to catch just a glimpse of how his incredible faith had planted seeds of life in so many hearts. God does, indeed, work amazing miracles, but we should never limit God. God often works in ways beyond us.

The doctrine of divine healing as a provision of the atonement is an important and positive feature of Pentecostal theology. It is a biblically, historically, and theologically sound teaching and practice. Admittedly, it can be controversial and prone to misunderstanding or even abuse. However, it is well worth whatever effort required to understand it correctly and to practice it with integrity. Most importantly, affirming the soteriological nature of divine healing promotes a fuller view of what Christian salvation is and of the kind of Savior who has such great compassion and mercy on the suffering and afflicted.

8

Pneumatic Soteriology

(Spirit Baptism in Salvation)

Pentecostals argue that the biblical book of Acts provides a model for Christian life and service today, that Spirit baptism is a gracious empowerment subsequent to (following) conversion promised to every believer, and that speaking in tongues (glossolalia) is associated with reception of the experience of Spirit baptism (initial evidence).[1] This rather straightforward assertion has often put Pentecostalism at odds with the broader Christian tradition. Sifting through the back-and-forth debates over the years suggests a key issue is appropriately relating the doctrine of Spirit baptism to the doctrine of salvation. This chapter revisits the debates (really disputes!) with fresh engagement and recognizes some significant currents in contemporary Pentecostal theology. It concludes with a constructive proposal drawing on the best theological instincts of the classical Pentecostal movement.

CONFRONTING A CONUNDRUM

A conundrum confronts Christianity's various theological traditions. Its basis arises out of the conjunction of two belated realizations. The first

---

1. For a sympathetic summary of this perspective, see Williams, "Baptism in the Holy Spirit." Williams maintains that the theology of Spirit baptism "occupies a place of critical importance" for Pentecostals, 354.

realization is that it is no longer credible to discount the beneficial contributions of Pentecostal and charismatic renewal movements to the health and growth of global Christianity. The second realization is that non-Pentecostal or non-charismatic churches need to develop theologies that explain and affirm the experience of Holy Spirit baptism, which so powerfully fuels contemporary renewal. That is where the dispute begins. There are several possible approaches to solving this breach. The following engages a few of the most relevant ones.

When I was growing up Pentecostal, it was common to describe Christians in other traditions as "those people who do not believe in the Holy Ghost." Of course, they did not actually deny the third person of the holy Trinity.[2] Rather, they did not believe in the baptism in the Holy Spirit in the same sense as Pentecostals. To an extent, that has changed. There are many, many Christians today in non-Pentecostal churches who do believe in—and experience—Spirit baptism, including spiritual gifts such as speaking in tongues, prophecy, and divine healing. On the other hand, it has not changed. Most people in non-Pentecostal churches who believe in and experience Spirit baptism and spiritual gifts, nevertheless, tend to understand these experiences in terms of the existing theological categories of their own ecclesial traditions. In short, they still do not interpret Spirit baptism the same way Pentecostals do. However, bear in mind that much of the discussion below concerns those believers who *share* a priceless experience, but nevertheless *understand* it differently.[3] It is not because "those people do not believe in the Holy Ghost." Thank God!

The truly thorny theological problem for all Christian traditions is how to relate Spirit baptism to salvation. Charismatic renewal theologian Rodman Williams accurately explains that a Pentecostal theology of Spirit baptism presupposes conversion. Yet, based on biblical exegesis, Pentecostals view Spirit baptism as distinct from and subsequent to conversion.[4] Here, I might point out that when speaking of Spirit baptism and salvation, it is important to bear in mind distinctions within salvation itself regarding conversion and post-conversion experiences. Williams's statement that

---

2. Hunter, *Spirit Baptism*, notes that Pentecostals have often misunderstood the usual Protestant "one stage theology" as limiting the work of the Holy Spirit to Christian beginnings, 228.

3. Wesleyan scholar Don Thorsen, *Exploration of Christian Theology*, 224, celebrates Pentecostalism's leading role in reviving Christian emphasis on the person and work of the Holy Spirit and, although there is not complete agreement regarding the nature and extent of the Holy Spirit's work, affirms "that all agree about the centrality of the Holy Spirit in every aspect of Christian beliefs, values, and practices."

4. Williams, "Baptism in the Holy Spirit," 356–57.

the perennial Pentecostal question about receiving Spirit baptism "has essentially nothing to do with salvation" must be understood in this post-conversion light.[5] In other words, Pentecostals are not questioning one's conversion, one's personal salvation; emphatically, the question of Spirit baptism is appropriate only in the context of one's conversion, one's personal salvation. These, and other, pneumatological-soteriological issues call for clarification from Pentecostals.

For theologian Chad Owen Brand the first question to consider on Spirit baptism is how it relates to salvation (specifically, conversion). Only then does he ask how it relates to spirituality in general and to relationships among believers as well.[6] In congruence, classical Pentecostal historian Harold Hunter argues that failure to discuss Spirit baptism and *charismata* with attention to soteriology has resulted in "inferior formulations" regarding "the basic concept of soteriology."[7] Nevertheless, he thinks that "the essential pneumatological issue raised by Spirit baptism has not been called into question" but "must now be scrutinized in light of traditional dogmatic formulation of the ordo salutis."[8] I agree.

The assessment of Finnish theologian Veli-Matti Kärkkäinen, who is affiliated with both Pentecostal and Lutheran communions, goes even further than Brand or Hunter. After denouncing the almost across-the-board omission of Spirit baptism from the *ordo salutis* (order of salvation), he suggests that today's discussion of Spirit baptism may be comparable to the discussion raised in Luther's day regarding justification by faith.[9] If Kärkkäinen is correct, and historical comparisons between the enormity of the impact of the sixteenth-century Protestant Reformation and the twentieth-century Pentecostal revival seem to sustain his bold claim, then it would be nothing short of theological irresponsibility to neglect development of a robust theology of Spirit baptism that explicates soteriological elements.

A SACRAMENTAL INTERPRETATION

Not surprisingly, a sacramental interpretation of Spirit baptism is evident among Roman Catholic and Eastern Orthodox Christians. To elucidate this

5. Williams, "Baptism in the Holy Spirit," 357.
6. Brand, ed., *Perspectives on Spirit Baptism*, 1.
7. Hunter, *Spirit Baptism*, 202, 222.
8. Hunter, *Spirit Baptism*, 204. Hunter's own systematic appraisal in relation to soteriology favors "understanding Spirit baptism as part of the outworking of God's grace in the believer's life," 227.
9. Kärkkäinen, *Spirit and Salvation*, 393–94.

position, we will draw on the classic work of two highly respected Catholic scholars: Kilian McDonnell and George Montague. McDonnell and Montague base their conclusions on a study of the NT and of the first eight centuries of Christian history. They are convinced that the imparting of charisms (*charismata*/spiritual gifts) belongs to the celebration of the sacraments (particularly baptism, confirmation, and Eucharist).[10] The experience of Spirit baptism is therefore integral to Christian initiation, aligned with public liturgy rather than private piety, and identified as normative for the church. Later, they acknowledge that the experience itself of Spirit baptism often does not occur at "first conversion" but comes as a "new departure" with openness to the charisms. Thus, Spirit baptism, within these orthodoxies, is admittedly unique among conversion experiences. They also admit that not all Catholic charismatics inevitably interpret Spirit baptism in sacramental categories.[11]

As a NT scholar, Montague acknowledges that there is uncertainty regarding details of the initiation rite in the NT; but he, nevertheless, employs a sacramental hermeneutic interpreting the data in favor of Spirit baptism as Christian initiation via water baptism.[12] However, Montague insists that charisms continue to operate in the church, that the Pentecostal reality of experiencing Spirit baptism is undeniable and desirable, and that the Holy Spirit cannot be confined to any theological construct.[13] Accordingly, he refreshingly suggests that in following the NT pattern we should at least "create the *expectation* not only of an *experience* but of some *charismatic* manifestation as evidence of the reception of the Holy Spirit."[14]

McDonnell's analysis of historical theology draws on an "actualizing theology" that he attributes to Augustine but also finds in many ancient writers, including Tertullian, Cyril, and others.[15] This view interprets Spirit

---

10. Sacramental traditions consider confirmation (Western Christianity) or chrismation (Eastern Christianity) a sacrament that follows baptism and is associated with reception of the Holy Spirit. The Eucharist is another term for Holy Communion or the Lord's Supper.

11. McDonnell and Montague, *Christian Initiation and Baptism in the Holy Spirit*, xii–xiii. E.g., Francis Sullivan, "Baptism in the Spirit," represents a major exception.

12. McDonnell and Montague, *Christian Initiation and Baptism in the Holy Spirit*, 76–80. Meaning no disrespect, but Montague's sacramental assumptions reappear in his sacramental conclusions (cp. 77, 78).

13. McDonnell and Montague, *Christian Initiation and Baptism in the Holy Spirit*, 79–80.

14. McDonnell and Montague, *Christian Initiation and Baptism in the Holy Spirit*, 80 (italics are original).

15. McDonnell and Montague, *Christian Initiation and Baptism in the Holy Spirit*, 84–85, 332. However, drawing on Tertullian forces McDonnell to struggle a bit because

PNEUMATIC SOTERIOLOGY   167

baptism as part of an earlier rite of water baptism, which is later made actual or developed in personal experience. Employing a sacramental hermeneutic, he proposes that a communal ecclesiology with a primary sacramental identity is the context for participating in this experience.[16] Consequently, McDonnell bemoans a historical diminishment of the role of Jesus' baptism in water for understanding Spirit baptism through a shift to Calvary and Pentecost, calling for integration of these models with a corresponding emphasis on the sacramental nature of water baptism and, therefore, of Spirit baptism.[17]

In their final chapter, McDonnell and Montague argue that the water baptism of Jesus is the pattern for Spirit baptism but admit that certain historical traditions, especially Syrian Christianity, have thought of Spirit baptism as a kind of "second baptism"—but they consider this something of an anomaly or a departure from apostolic precedent.[18] They admit that "Baptism in the Spirit, as the awakening of the full life of the Spirit with the charisms (including the prophetic), does not belong to the essence of Christian initiation."[19] Yet for them, these charisms nevertheless represent "the full flowering of sacramental grace" so that the whole of Spirit baptism inevitably belongs to Christian initiation, that is, to the sacrament of water baptism.[20] McDonnell and Montague further explain that their tradition's acceptance of infant baptism establishes the momentum for a sacramental theology of Spirit baptism, although they mourn that the Spirit's charisms, when not evident as actualized, have been internalized and spiritualized in order to maintain their presence without actual evidence.[21] In other words, in a revisionist theology internalizing the work of the Holy Spirit, especially spiritual gifts, results in functional cessationism. Although this unfortunate trend may be evident in nonsacramental systems, it may be that viewing the sacraments as the tangible, visible sign of the Spirit makes sacramentalism

---

of Tertullian's later involvement with Montanism, an early Spirit movement ostracized by Roman Catholics, 106–121.

16. McDonnell and Montague, *Christian Initiation and Baptism in the Holy Spirit*, 91–92.

17. McDonnell and Montague, *Christian Initiation and Baptism in the Holy Spirit*, 306–8, 318–19.

18. McDonnell and Montague, *Christian Initiation and Baptism in the Holy Spirit*, 312–13, 326. McDonnell also dismisses, or at least downplays, the significance of the postbiblical theology of Eastern Christianity that "distinguishes between two moments" of water baptism and the gift of the Spirit but sees them as in some sense "inseparable," 316.

19. McDonnell and Montague, *Christian Initiation and Baptism in the Holy Spirit*, 314.

20. McDonnell and Montague, *Christian Initiation and Baptism in the Holy Spirit*, 315.

21. McDonnell and Montague, *Christian Initiation and Baptism in the Holy Spirit*, 328–29 (cp. 339–40).

particularly vulnerable. In any case, McDonnell and Montague are to be highly commended for insisting on actual charismatic evidence of the charisms in association with baptism in the Holy Spirit.

McDonnell and Montague desire to establish that their reading of the biblical texts and of ancient Christian writings links Spirit baptism to the sacrament of water baptism and thus makes it an integral and normative experience for Catholic believers.[22] This, I believe, is an admirable effort to open up theological space for Spirit baptism and spiritual gifts within their own faith tradition, although I do not agree with the sacramental approach to Spirit baptism. I do agree, however, with Daniel Tomberlin both regarding the importance of the sacraments in Pentecostalism's embodied spirituality and that salvation is "a crisis of conversion that transforms the repentant sinner."[23] Accordingly, I conceptualize neither Christian conversion nor Spirit baptism primarily in sacramental categories. Obviously, McDonnell and Montague appreciate the Pentecostal and charismatic renewal movements for the "admirable fruits" of Spirit baptism they have helped to foster.[24] Another laudable matter is their affirmation that "[the] Spirit is not, however, imprisoned in the divinely willed sacraments. The Spirit is free to bestow graces and charisms as the Spirit wills."[25] This significant concession appears to imply that a sacramental actualization theology may be a helpful way for those in sacramental traditions to approach and to appropriate Spirit baptism, without insisting that it is the only framework for viewing the experience or that others must accept it as such. What Pentecostal would not agree, that regardless of the framework through which Spirit baptism is viewed, "the important thing is that it *happened*"?[26]

---

22. McDonnell and Montague, *Christian Initiation and Baptism in the Holy Spirit*, 333.

23. Tomberlin, *Pentecostal Sacraments*, 59–88, 24. By the way, my decision to tackle this topic in this text at this time owes a great deal to several "coffee conversations" with Dan, characterized by his persistent insistence that it *must* be addressed. (By the way, Dan thinks the soteriological nature of Spirit baptism needs to be further unpacked. Now it is my turn to encourage him to take up that task.)

24. McDonnell and Montague, *Christian Initiation and Baptism in the Holy Spirit*, 336.

25. McDonnell and Montague, *Christian Initiation and Baptism in the Holy Spirit*, 339 (cp. 342).

26. McDonnell and Montague, *Christian Initiation and Baptism in the Holy Spirit*, 339 (italics are original).

A DIMENSIONAL APPROACH

Larry Hart, a charismatic evangelical Protestant theologian, addresses the soteriological nature of Spirit baptism.[27] He notes a traditional interpretation drawing on 1 Corinthians 12:13 to interpret Spirit baptism "in the initiatory sense" of the new birth with the indwelling of the Holy Spirit.[28] He acknowledges the Pentecostal view of Spirit baptism as subsequent to conversion, along with the organic or sacramental view. The "organic" view is both comparable and contrasting with the sacramental view in that it is rooted in Christian initiation via the new birth but not necessarily in the ordinance (sacrament) of water baptism. Accordingly, regeneration/new birth is one with Spirit baptism as a living whole. In this view, the experience of converts to Christ who later receive Spirit baptism is "an *appropriation* of a power and giftedness already present within the believer."[29] Hart also briefly describes Wesleyan and Holiness Christians' view that Spirit baptism is an experience subsequent to conversion essentially synonymous with sanctification.[30] Again, similarities with the sacramental view are obvious—excepting elimination of the sacramental emphasis itself (opting for an evangelical conversion theology).

Hart's creative solution to the confusion over how to interpret Spirit baptism is the *dimensional* approach. He argues that Spirit baptism is a broad metaphor with multiple applications, including: (1) Jesus' total eschatological redemptive work, (2) Christian initiation, (3) the Christian life, and (4) empowerment for Christian mission and ministry.[31] This multidimensional approach to Spirit baptism enables affirmation of key elements of the various traditions while still staunchly maintaining that the experiential charismatic element is a valid dimension. The dimensional approach may be thought of as an integrative understanding of Spirit baptism with amazing openness to synthesizing previously contesting elements.

The "everyone wins" solution of the dimensional approach cannot help but be attractive. It also has the advantage of affirming a broad range of the Spirit's work in believers. Nevertheless, a nagging concern is that the dimensional approach may contribute to Spirit baptism losing much of its distinctive value. If *everything* is Spirit baptism, then what is Spirit baptism *actually*? This is not about mere semantics. Rather, if Spirit baptism is just

---

27. Hart goes into much more depth on this topic in "Dimensional Charismatic Perspective."
28. Hart, *Truth Aflame*, 403–4.
29. Hart, *Truth Aflame*, 404.
30. Hart, *Truth Aflame*, 404.
31. Hart, *Truth Aflame*, 404.

another name for Christian initiation (whether sacramentally or conversionary) or just another term for sanctification, then why is there another term at all? What is the need for it? Of course, this is where Pentecostal empowerment comes in and where charismatic gifts must be considered. And if that is the case—no one was theologizing much at all about Spirit baptism until Pentecostals raised these bothersome issues—then does not that say something about what is distinctive about baptism in the Holy Spirit? I think it does.

Hart is certainly correct that Spirit baptism is not the monopoly of any single theological tradition.[32] In this regard, Pentecostals can and should rejoice that sisters and brothers in other faith traditions are stretching to find ways to theologize, and thereby to legitimize, the experience of the baptism in the Holy Spirit. There need be no rivalry in the Holy Spirit. Rather with Moses let us exclaim, "Oh, that all the Lord's people were prophets and that the Lord would put His Spirit upon them!" (Num 11:29).

AN ECUMENICAL PROBLEM

For Veli-Matti Kärkkäinen, Spirit baptism poses an "ecumenical problem." Accordingly, he offers "a constructive ecumenical proposal" for a theology of Spirit baptism.[33] He unflinchingly evaluates the traditional soteriological approach as a failure, because the essential element of empowerment is missing.[34] Additionally, although he praises Pentecostals for a robust approach, he sees the separation of Spirit baptism from water baptism as both a strength and a weakness that ultimately leads to a lack of coherence. To him, both the sacramental and nonsacramental charismatic views are more coherent than the classical Pentecostal theology of Spirit baptism.[35] Thus, Kärkkäinen places himself more in the charismatic camp than in the Pentecostal tradition, although affirming the tradition's emphases on experiential empowerment and gifting for service.

However, within Kärkkäinen's conviction, which of the two views, sacramental or nonsacramental, does he prefer? Kärkkäinen's solution rests on the word *ecumenically* (promoting unity among Christian churches). Kärkkäinen contends: "Personally, I find the nonsacramental-charismatic view stronger for the simple reason that it can be embraced by both (deeply)

---

32. Hart, *Truth Aflame*, 565.
33. Kärkkäinen, *Spirit and Salvation*, 397–401.
34. Kärkkäinen, *Spirit and Salvation*, 399.
35. Kärkkäinen, *Spirit and Salvation*, 399.

sacramental theologies and those that are not sacramental."³⁶ He explains this apparently arbitrary choice on the basis of his assessment that "the way the Pentecostal view and the two sacramental interpretations negotiate the relation of Spirit baptism to water baptism has little to do with pneumatology and everything to do with the divide between sacramental and nonsacramental traditions."³⁷ In my reading of his words, he is saying that neither the existing difference nor the decision about how to resolve it is primarily theological in nature (except perhaps in ecclesiology). It is more about reconciling different ecclesial traditions.

Compactly, Kärkkäinen's constructive proposal looks something like the following.³⁸ A holistic soteriology includes empowerment and charismatic gifting. Spirit baptism is a normal expectation and normative for Christian life. Spirit baptism may or may not occur in connection with the sacrament of water baptism. Spirit baptism will usually, but not necessarily, be accompanied by charismatic manifestations that will usually, but not necessarily, include speaking in tongues and/or prophecy. The purpose of Spirit baptism is to empower and to equip Christians for service. The initial experience of Spirit baptism is unique but may be/should be followed by continuing fillings with the Holy Spirit.

In my opinion, Kärkkäinen offers a laudable effort to explicate Spirit baptism, including (and this is extremely important and not to be taken lightly due to my subsequent questionings) a soteriology of empowerment for service and charismatic gifts, for broad Christian assimilation. Ironically, that seems to be both its strength and its liability. While I am also ecumenically inclined, I suspect few theologians would choose an option simply because it is more acceptable to more people.³⁹ In any case, it is not enough for me. If we dig down under the suggestion that the difference between Pentecostal and sacramental and nonsacramental interpretations of Spirit baptism is not about pneumatology so much as about ecclesial tradition, we discover that pneumatology *is* behind more of *that* difference than first assumed. One might ask, can believers experience the Holy Spirit directly? Must the experience of the Holy Spirit be mediated by church and priest? Or is the sovereign Holy Spirit free to move in fresh ways? Does the initial conversion encounter exhaust the possibilities for engagement with the Holy Spirit? The answers to these questions matter a great deal.

36. Kärkkäinen, *Spirit and Salvation*, 399.
37. Kärkkäinen, *Spirit and Salvation*, 399.
38. Kärkkäinen, *Spirit and Salvation*, 401.

39. Or would they? Perhaps some would but they probably would not admit it. Accordingly, we can applaud not only Kärkkäinen's theological skill but also his transparency.

Of course, baptism in the Holy Spirit is rooted in the reality of Christian conversion. There is continuity. Also, there is a subsequence to it. Spirit baptism really is something genuinely new in Christian experience. There is development of existing spiritual reality, yes; but there is also addition of something extra, that is, something *additional*.[40] There are two equal and opposite errors we should avoid. First, we must not *separate* Spirit baptism from Christian conversion-initiation. Second, we must not *assimilate* Spirit baptism into Christian conversion-initiation. Therefore, I argue for the *unity* of all redemptive experiences and, within that context, for the *uniqueness* of Spirit baptism.

Let me illustrate. Recently, I purchased a new cell phone. However, I was pleased that my original contact list could simply be transferred to my new one. Further, the foundational data and technology of my old phone still forms the basis of my new phone. In a sense, it seems like I do not have a new phone at all. The old one just keeps getting better. However, genuinely new technology continues to develop and to be added into subsequent models. Of course, even after acquiring my new phone, there are occasional updates to download. There is this dynamic between continuity and development that just never ends. So it is with Christian initiation and reception of Spirit baptism.

A WESLEYAN-HOLINESS HERMENEUTIC

The Wesleyan and Holiness traditions accentuate a distinction between "initial" and "entire" sanctification.[41] Regeneration is regarded as initial sanctification, because it involves impartation of new life with its implanting of a new nature with holy affections or dispositions (Titus 3:5).[42] Entire sanctification is regarded as an experience subsequent to new birth of becoming completely or fully consecrated to God in all one's being (1 Thess 5:23). Wesleyan theologian Melvin Dieter traces the place of the doctrine

---

40. Somewhat oddly, Benny C. Aker, "John," commenting on John 7:37–39, criticizes Pentecostals for interpreting Spirit baptism as an additional gift that "'finishes off' salvation," but then describes it as "essentially part of salvation" and "an empowerment for evangelism in the world and ministry in the church," 48–49. His reasoning is convoluted, but he appears to be subsuming Spirit baptism under conversion while still arguing for its distinctive function (cp. 45). In any case, Aker has grossly caricatured Pentecostals' affirmation of Spirit baptism as a subsequent, distinct work.

41. Cp. chapter 2 of the present volume.

42. John Wesley spoke of regeneration as "the threshold of sanctification, the first entrance upon it"; "On God's Vineyard," 7:202–13, in *Wesley's Works*, 7:205.

of Spirit baptism in a different context than either of the preceding: in its relation to sanctification, specifically, entire sanctification.[43]

The eighteenth-century English revivalist and theologian John Wesley did not himself employ the category of Spirit baptism for entire sanctification. However, his friend and faithful interpreter John Fletcher systematized Wesleyan holiness and sanctification themes around a Trinitarian-dispensationalist interpretation of Pentecost that accented Spirit baptism. In other words, the apex of redemptive experience in this life became Spirit baptism and was understood as entire sanctification. Dieter notes that Wesley warned Fletcher of possible dangers latent in this line of thought, and therefore a need for caution, but did not reject it outright.[44] Nevertheless, in later American Holiness revivalism theology, entire sanctification and Spirit baptism became virtually synonymous. Arguably, Mr. Wesley would have been quite uncomfortable with this virtual assimilation. However, the rise of the Pentecostal movement has seriously challenged the credibility of this narrow interpretation, as admitted by some Wesleyan and Holiness theologians, although still common among many others.[45]

Dieter suggests, and I concur, that Methodist, Holiness, and Pentecostal traditions, nevertheless, still share to a large extent the essence of Wesley's theological vision of Christian sanctification and spirituality.[46] In fact, historian William Faupel indicates that it was precisely a synthesis of Wesleyan-Holiness spirituality with apocalyptic millenarian eschatology that paved the way for Pentecostalism's rise as a distinctive force.[47] It is perhaps not surprising that Pentecostal theologian Steve Land essentially synthesizes and revises traditional Wesleyan-Holiness and Pentecostal language of purity and power—that is, of sanctification and Spirit baptism—via apocalyptic affections.[48] However, some dispute the Wesleyan-Holiness perspective presented by Dieter. From a Reformed perspective, Anthony

43. Dieter, "Wesleyan Perspective," 42–45.

44. Dieter, "Wesleyan Perspective," 43–44.

45. Dieter, "Wesleyan Perspective," 44–45.

46. Dieter, "Wesleyan Perspective," 45.

47. Faupel, *Everlasting Gospel*, 79. Faupel further indicates that this synthesis precipitated a radical paradigm shift, 80, 90. Acceptance of the developing Keswickian theology of Spirit baptism of the twentieth century as an enduement of power for service is also critical, 85. According to Faupel, combining these elements eventually led to the three-stage blessing theology of early Pentecostals of conversion, sanctification, and Spirit baptism, 87.

48. Land, *Pentecostal Spirituality*, 181–220. The view of Land and others along this line is often called the Wesleyan-Holiness-Pentecostal or simply Wesleyan-Pentecostal for brevity's sake. Historically, a basic version of this viewpoint was often called the Holiness-Pentecostal perspective.

Hoekema is dismissive of Dieter's presentation of both entire sanctification itself and any distinctive understanding of Spirit baptism apart from conversion.[49] Pentecostal Stanley Horton affirms the value of a Wesleyan-Holiness view but points out the distinctive nature of Spirit baptism in contrasting fashion as "the key difference between Wesleyans and Pentecostals."[50] J. Robertson McQuilkin's Keswickian interpretation, in agreement with Dieter, reminds that the book of Acts does report experiences of the Holy Spirit subsequent to regeneration but, in disagreement, that these are not presented in terms of experiential sanctification.[51] Finally, John Walvoord, an Augustinian-Dispensationalist, admits that Wesley was right about the need for and reality of an act of surrender or consecration subsequent to conversion, but then terribly confuses Spirit baptism, regeneration, and the infilling of the Spirit, essentially failing to distinguish them.[52]

McQuilkin's Keswickian response to Dieter is interesting. The Keswick "higher life" movement arose out of a series of alternating holiness conventions in the late nineteenth century between America and England. It emphasizes the Spirit-filled life in terms of ethical and relational holiness in a non-Wesleyan (more Reformed) way.[53] Although Keswickian theology influenced Pentecostal perspectives on Spirit baptism, its leadership had mixed reactions to the rise of Pentecostalism. For the present purpose it is enough to note McQuilkin's correct observation, contra the American Holiness movement, that the book of Acts does not present Spirit baptism in terms of experiential sanctification.

The great attraction of the Wesleyan and Holiness traditions is their recognition of the primary importance of the Holy Spirit's activity in making holy those who are in Christ Jesus (clearly the thrust of Romans 8:1–17). Accordingly, Land's integration of holiness and power, that is, of sanctification and Spirit baptism, is appealing for holiness-minded Pentecostals. Holiness and Holy Spirit baptism should never be severed from each other. Moreover, character and charisma must be kept inseparable in theology and in spirituality lest supposed proponents lose all credibility. However, integration is not assimilation. The baptism in the Holy Spirit must not be melted into oblivion by becoming just another synonym for something else, not even sanctification.

---

49. Hoekema, "Response to Dieter."
50. Horton, "Response to Dieter."
51. McQuilkin, "Response to Dieter," 55.
52. Walvoord, "Response to Dieter," 56–57.
53. McQuilkin, "Keswick," 174–78.

Significantly, there is one NT book, and only one, Acts, which actually portrays what Spirit baptism looks like, rather than as an additional gospel prophecy or an epistolary reflection. How does Acts portray Spirit baptism? Spirit baptism "is an intense spiritual experience through which the lives of believers are immersed into the Spirit of God" as a "supernatural, charismatic empowerment that equips the Church to fulfill its mission to the world" (Acts 1:5, 8; 2:4, 17–19; 9:31; 10:38, 44–45; 11:15–16; 13:2, 4).[54] Arrington makes a telling point that in his Pentecost Day sermon, Peter easily could have drawn on OT prophecies (Isa 61:6–7; Ezek 37:1–14) that emphasize the renewal of the heart (sanctification). Instead, Peter draws on Joel (2:28–32) "who promises charismatic and prophetic manifestations for the last days."[55] If the day of Pentecost is paradigmatic (and it is), then Spirit baptism is not synonymous with sanctification.

Holy Spirit baptism is, of course in a sense, inseparable from holiness of heart and life; but Spirit baptism is not synonymous with the experience of sanctification. Accordingly, not even the Wesleyan-Holiness tradition, to which Pentecostals are deeply indebted and for which they should be forever grateful, ought ever to be allowed to muffle the full-throated voices of true Pentecost. Over and over again, we see that Spirit baptism should be neither separated from overall redemptive experience nor assimilated into any other particular redemptive experience.

AN ANTICIPATORY RELATIONSHIP

At the crux of the conversation (conundrum!) are tendencies either to overidentify or underappreciate water baptism relative to Spirit baptism. Conversion-initiation and subsequence disputes are tied into these mistakes. For the most part, this is probably due to an ambiguity in the shared "baptism" terminology. Daniel Tomberlin notes that a majority of Pentecostals accept water baptism as a rite of initiation, but reject sacramental causality; and they view water baptism as unrelated to Spirit baptism.[56] Oneness Pentecostals are a major exception, viewing water baptism as essential to salvation and, at least ideally, closely related to Spirit baptism—although still denying traditional sacramental language and the concept of baptismal regeneration.[57] Tomberlin himself argues for the redemptive metanarrative context

---

54. Arrington, "Acts," 537.
55. Arrington, "Acts," 537.
56. Tomberlin, "Believers' Baptism in the Pentecostal Tradition," 424.
57. Tomberlin, "Believers' Baptism in the Pentecostal Tradition," 427. See Oneness theologian David Bernard, *New Birth, Pentecostal Theology*, 96–97, 122–54, 235–36.

of water baptism, including pneumatological, soteriological, and ecclesiological concerns in terms of Pentecostalism's embodied spirituality which he views as "essentially sacramental."[58] Especially relevant for the present work is Tomberlin's assertion that water baptism *anticipates and affirms* Spirit baptism.[59]

What might it mean, theologically, that water baptism anticipates Spirit baptism? Does water baptism have within it an expectation that Spirit baptism will follow, at some point at least, sooner or later? Does it have a predictive element, pointing ahead to what will eventually occur? As such, does water baptism serve as a forerunner of Spirit baptism? Might it act as a precursor? A precedent? An antecedent? Would an affirmative response to these interrogatives suggest close association but significant distinction between water baptism and Spirit baptism? If so, then I suggest that it is important to maintain their *unity* but not their *synonymity*. Arguably, Spirit baptism is not synonymous with anything, because it has its own distinctive meaning and purpose. Yet, Spirit baptism does not exist on its own, that is, alone or in isolation, but in intimate relation to all of redemption.

Here we might think of the movement between water baptism and Spirit baptism as analogous to that of John the Baptist as the forerunner to the Messiah. How appropriate that John was descriptively named for baptizing in water, but the Messiah is identified as the one who baptizes in the Spirit. Again, how telling that some mistook John for the coming Messiah; yet, John would have none of it. We should never mistake the forerunner for the Messiah, nor the water for the Spirit. The role of the forerunner is to prepare the way for the Messiah. Ideally, water baptism should prepare the way for Spirit baptism. But not everyone received John's witness.

An anticipatory character in water baptism's relation to Spirit baptism is just what Matthew's Gospel communicates. John the Baptist's explanatory prophecy comparing his own ministry of baptism in water with the Messiah's ministry of baptizing in the Holy Spirit includes the correlative conjunction *de*, translated "but," which both links and contrasts the two ministers and their distinctive ministries (3:11).[60] Shelton describes John's statement as an "antithetical parallelism" which serves to highlight the "superior baptism" of Jesus as Messiah on the basis that he is himself John's acknowledged

---

58. Tomberlin, "Believers' Baptism in the Pentecostal Tradition," 427, 429. British theologian-scientist Alister McGrath, *Born to Wonder*, 76, 94, argues that postmodernism's rejection of "big picture" or metanarrative understandings of reality are unconvincing and inconsistent, and actually an effort to invent (fabricate) alternative meaning, 108–14.

59. Tomberlin, "Believers' Baptism in the Pentecostal Tradition," 432.

60. Cp. Lukaszewski, notes on Matthew 3:11, *Syntactic Greek New Testament*.

superior.[61] If anything, Mark's Gospel depicts the contrast in even stronger terms. Mark includes *de* or "but" as well; however, it is in the form of an adversative conjunction used to express contrast between the immediate clause and the one preceding it (1:8).[62] Perhaps even more telling, NT commentator Jerry Camery-Hoggatt notes that Mark sets John's prophecy of the Messiah as the Spirit Baptizer in a context where "everything focuses on the contrast" and then "carries the contrast one degree farther."[63] Luke's Gospel (3:16) also employs *de* or "but," as does Jesus in Acts 1:5 when reminding of John's prophecy (Peter does also when quoting Jesus in Acts 11:16), in both cases as alternating particle, a combination of particles used to present or contrast multiple considerations.[64] Hence in the Synoptic Gospels and in Acts, one observes the clear contrast between John and Jesus and between water baptism and Spirit baptism with Jesus and Spirit baptism described as distinct from and superior to John and water baptism.

Like the Synoptics, John's Gospel also uses *de* or "but" with adversative force (1:26). However, John's Gospel, unlike the Synoptics which place John's prophecy prior to Jesus' baptism in water, separates the Baptist's statement into two parts, so that the former occurs before Jesus' baptism while the latter occurs at his baptism (1:26–27, 29–34). The force of this move is to impress upon the reader that while John's baptism served to reveal the Messiah to Israel, it was the Spirit's manifestation at Jesus' baptism which served to identify the Messiah to John himself in such a manner as to underscore Jesus' identity as the Spirit Baptizer, thus leading to his further, clearer revelation to Israel and to the churches as such. Peripherally, this strategy strengthens an association between water baptism and Spirit baptism, yet without weakening the distinction.[65]

---

61. Shelton, "Matthew," 142.

62. Lukaszewski, notes on Mark 1:8, *Syntactic Greek New Testament*.

63. Camery-Hoggatt, "Mark," 273. Interestingly, Camery-Hoggatt observes that while the Baptist may not have had in mind Spirit baptism as it later occurred, the community of Mark's readers would have experienced it in that way and thought of it accordingly, 273.

64. Lukaszewski, notes on Luke 3:16 and Acts 1:5, *Syntactic Greek New Testament*. Not surprisingly, Arrington, in commenting on the Lukan parallel passages, sees John's prophecy as completely consistent with the distinct work of the Holy Spirit in conversion and in subsequent Spirit baptism, Arrington, "Luke," 408. Cp. Arrington, "Acts," 537.

65. Contra Aker, "John," who oddly comments here that Spirit baptism refers "comprehensively to all of the Spirit's activities to and in the church" but then closely identifies it with regeneration, 15.

AN AFFIRMATIVE RELATIONSHIP

I have been building on terminology borrowed from Tomberlin that water baptism *anticipates* Spirit baptism (without claiming that he necessarily said what I am saying). But Tomberlin also said that in some cases, such as with Cornelius and his household (Acts 10:44–48), where there are those who are baptized in the Holy Spirit prior to being baptized in water, that water baptism *affirms* Spirit baptism. Pastors understand that this scenario occurs more often than some might think. For example, my youngest sister Andrea was baptized in the Holy Spirit at nine years of age. Because of her youth and other circumstances, however, I later had the privilege of baptizing her in water along with her fiancée Jeff as young adults. More than forty years later, they are still serving the Lord and active in the ministry of the gospel.[66]

What might it mean, theologically, that water baptism affirms Spirit baptism? Does it mean that water baptism encourages and supports the prior reception of Spirit baptism? Might water baptism validate or confirm Spirit baptism? If so—that is, if "affirm" in some sense signifies "confirm"— does subsequent water baptism ratify or uphold, as authentic and legitimate, the prior experience of Spirit baptism by the unbaptized? Whatever could it mean to suggest that the direct act of Christ the Spirit Baptizer would even need to be affirmed by a sacramental act of a church? To those who suppose that water baptism is little more than a public witness, would not the public witness of Cornelius and his household in receiving Spirit baptism have been sufficient? In fact, when called to account for preaching to Gentiles, Peter called on the witness of their Spirit baptism in just this fashion (Acts 11:15–17).[67] So then, why still insist on water baptism? Among other things, I would suggest that the sacrament of water baptism is much more important than we Pentecostals have supposed. Even baptism in the Holy Spirit does not supplant—does not supersede or replace—water baptism!

The experience of Cornelius and his household serve as a biblical paradigm, even an imperative, for water baptism after Spirit baptism. While Arrington acknowledges that water baptism normally precedes Spirit baptism, he explains that "The work of the Spirit is not tied to water baptism," but he does not elaborate on the affirmative role of water baptism in such cases.[68] Probably, most Pentecostals simply assume that new converts will follow Christ in believers' baptism as an act of discipleship (Matthew

---

66. Samuel, *Holy Spirit in Worship Music, Preaching, and the Altar,* 25, recounts an Azusa era conviction viewing a threefold stage of being "saved, sanctified, and baptized in the Holy Ghost" within a framework of spiritual growth.

67. Cp. Arrington, "Acts," 590–91.

68. Arrington, "Acts," 589.

28:19–20). However, the case of Cornelius and those with him is telling. Peter's challenge in Acts 10:47 appears to contain more than a hint for an affirmative aspect of water baptism following Spirit baptism: "Can anyone forbid water, that these should not be baptized who have received the Holy Spirit just as we *have?*" Water baptism signified the full acceptance of these Gentile believers by the Jewish church.[69] In this case, "affirm" indicates formal acceptance, genuine approval, and equal inclusion. Certainly, the same ideas are present in other such cases. Are those who receive their experience of the Spirit baptism in a different *order*, or even in a different *place* (not in a church!), accepted in and by the church? Yes!

What?! How could it be that God would need affirmation by the church? Does the act of God the Holy Spirit require corroboration or verification by anyone else? Can anyone add to God's act? It is not God who needs affirming. God's baptism in the Spirit is good and sound whether any church hierarchy accepts it as such or not—if truly it is of God. Yet, there is a delightful back-and-forth reciprocal movement. Water baptism affirms Spirit baptism's signal that the conversion has occurred to which water baptism bears witness. Recipients do, nonetheless, need the affirmation of the church, of the community of faith, for full inclusion and participation. Scripture commands testing or evaluation of spiritual encounters or charismatic experiences (1 John 4:1; 1 Cor 14:29). Further, I contend the church needs the benefit that the act of affirmation brings. What if the churches were to reject God's genuine work of the Spirit? Then, they would be found fighting against God (Acts 5:39). With no apologies for bluntness, Pentecostals know what it is to be told that their experience is neurotic or even demonic. It is important for both individual believers and for the churches that the work of God's Spirit be affirmed and accepted with integrity.

However, the efficacy of Spirit baptism is not established by water baptism. Is there an association? Yes. Is it a positive relationship? Yes. Should it be upheld? Yes. Yes, yes, yes. But it should never be implied that Spirit baptism is dependent upon water baptism in any way, shape, form, or fashion. It is not. Spirit baptism is dependent only on the Spirit Baptizer Jesus Christ, and on openness to his Spirit through faith in Jesus.

Once a causal relationship between water baptism and Spirit baptism is set aside, then the confusion/fusion of Spirit baptism with conversion-initiation is also set aside. As seen above, most of the arguments for Spirit baptism as conversion-initiation are nonsacramental versions of similar assumptions as in the sacramental perspective. Rejecting a causal relationship between water baptism and Spirit baptism in no way minimizes the

69. Polhill, *Acts*, 264.

unspeakable importance of conversion-initiation, or the sacraments in general, or water baptism specifically. It does defend and uphold the sovereignty, ability, and liberty of the Holy Spirit. And that is the critical point.

A PNEUMATIC SOTERIOLOGY

After having discussed background issues regarding Spirit baptism and soteriology with some important implications, it is now possible to move forward in a more informed manner. The question before us is: "How may a Pentecostal theology of Spirit baptism more ably articulate its relationship with soteriology while credibly retaining its original commitments to the distinctiveness of Spirit baptism?" Contemporary Pentecostal theologians such as Steven Studebaker have already begun addressing the relation of Pentecostal pneumatology and soteriology.[70] Unfortunately, although quite creative, the accent does not seem to fall on retaining the distinctive significance of Spirit baptism.[71] Furthermore, that departure appears to signal a trend.[72]

Recently, Studebaker's *The Spirit of Atonement* proposes a Pentecostal theology of the atonement moving from a primarily christological and crucicentric register to one that articulates the pneumatological and holistic nature of Pentecostal praxis. He suggests that classical Pentecostalism has relied on the Christocentric inclinations of Protestant evangelical atonement theology to its own detriment. He then develops a Pentecostal theology of atonement based on a biblical narrative of the Spirit of Pentecost, before offering an expanded vision of Pentecostal praxis based on the theological formation of the biblical narrative.

In an earlier article, Studebaker argued that classical Pentecostal theology has slavishly followed the Protestant/Western theological tradition of subordinating the Holy Spirit to Christ, especially in its soteriology.[73] He further argues that a concept of "redemptive justification" or "redemptive soteriology" that affirms the equal activity of the Holy Spirit in salvation,

---

70. Kärkkäinen, *One with God*, is doubtless correct that "The doctrine of salvation cannot be expressed in christological terms alone but requires pneumatological grounding as well," 129.

71. I am grateful to Steve for kindly commenting on an early draft of this chapter (12/15/2020). He responded to my statement with: "That represents my view when Spirit baptism is understood in the classical Pentecostal sense. But my argument is that CP actually depreciates the meaning of Spirit baptism by relegating it to post-conversion experience. My goal is to make Spirit baptism the central soteriological metaphor/image/paradigm."

72. See Macchia, "Justification and the Spirit."

73. Studebaker, "Pentecostal Soteriology and Pneumatology," 252–65.

rather than a bifurcated christological model, is preferable for Pentecostals.[74] Studebaker concludes:

> The most profound contribution of redemptive soteriology to Pentecostal theology is that it synthesizes pneumatology with Christology. This synthesis provides a way to transcend the implicit subordination of the Spirit in Pentecostal theology. Symptomatic of its historical origins, Pentecostal theology subordinates the chief work of the Holy Spirit by defining it in terms of Spirit baptism. Baptism in the Holy Spirit is subsequent to salvation and is not necessary for salvation. The problem is that this inadvertently renders the primary work of the Spirit optional for the Christian life. In redemptive soteriology, the primary work of the Holy Spirit is not annexed to a soteriological option. On the contrary, the work of Christ and the Spirit constitute the achievement and experience of redemption.[75]

Studebaker rightly identifies a dangerous trend in the broader Christian tradition of functionally subordinating the Holy Spirit to Christ and, consequently, undermining the role of the Holy Spirit in salvation.[76] Also, his intention of recovering the role of the Holy Spirit in salvation is viable. In fact, the first chapter of the present work on conversion experiences draws on a conviction shared with Studebaker that the Holy Spirit is active in all of redemption—and not merely in some peripheral fashion. However, I do not assume that distinct from and subsequent to *conversion* is synonymous with distinct from and subsequent to *salvation*. Conversion is an aspect of salvation but not its totality. Therefore, I prefer to describe Spirit baptism as

---

74. Studebaker, "Pentecostal Soteriology and Pneumatology," 266–69.

75. Studebaker, "Pentecostal Soteriology and Pneumatology," 270.

76. E.g., in what is in many other ways an excellent work, Christopher Wright, *Salvation Belongs to Our God*, manages to miss, or at least greatly minimize, the role of the Holy Spirit in salvation. When he sums up the main conclusions of his work in a series of bullet points, 194–95, there is not a single reference to the agency of the Holy Spirit. Oddly, every point begins with "Biblical salvation is . . ." but there is no mention of the biblical emphasis on the Holy Spirit. For another example, in chapter 5, on "Salvation and Our Experience," near the very end of the chapter, Wright tacks on a terse treatment of the role of the Holy Spirit in assurance with an almost apologetic comment that it "would be unfortunate" for readers to get the impression that assurance is some entirely objective matter bereft of the experience of the Holy Spirit, 135. However, he proceeds immediately to throw up qualifiers and disclaimers, lest experience become too pronounced; and then when he does get to it, he offers an anemic afterthought that quickly pivots to ethics, 135–37.

distinct from and subsequent to conversion but not as distinct from and subsequent to salvation.[77] That distinction and lack thereof makes a difference.

Nor am I convinced that recovering the role of the Holy Spirit in redemption alone is necessarily sufficient. It appears to me that the distinctive nature of Spirit baptism must be upheld as well.[78] If it is a mistake to reduce the role of the Holy Spirit to only applying Christ's work, and it is (Heb 9:14), then, arguably, it would also be a mistake to minimize the empowering purpose of Spirit baptism. Accordingly, I wish to look more closely at the purpose of Spirit baptism while addressing more directly the relationship of Spirit baptism and salvation, before offering a constructive proposal that is more consistent with Pentecostal theology's traditional values. Nevertheless, I appreciate Studebaker's assertion that Pentecostal theology needs to develop and explicate the relationship of Spirit baptism with soteriology. But I do not sense that Pentecostal pneumatology and soteriology are on a completely wrong track that requires an almost total redirection of classic emphases.

PRIMARY PURPOSE OF SPIRIT BAPTISM

Rodman Williams rightly notes that for Pentecostals "the primary purpose" of Spirit baptism is *power*, and that this *empowerment* has a specific purpose: bearing witness to Jesus Christ and the good news of the gospel (per Acts 1:8; Luke 24:49; cp. Luke 3:22 and 4:1).[79] Spirit baptism also includes power to do mighty works. However, even these miraculous deeds are no less in the context of bearing witness to the risen and ascended Christ.[80] Pentecostals note that Jesus was first conceived by the Holy Spirit (Luke 1:31–35) and then, thirty years later, anointed with the Holy Spirit to begin his ministry with power (Luke 3:21–22; 4:1). The parallel is obvious (for Pentecostals). Those born of the Spirit (John 3:1–8) may also be later anointed in Spirit baptism with power to witness of Christ (Acts 1:8). Thus, Spirit baptism

---

77. Here Steve Studebaker asked me, appropriately enough, "Okay, but does this distinction reflect CP or your nuance of the traditional doctrine of subsequence?" I think my distinction reflects the best instincts of classical Pentecostal theology, but I do not claim we have always made that as clear as we ought (hence this chapter).

78. Studebaker says, "I affirm the empowering nature of Spirit baptism, but unlike CP do not see empowerment as its primary purpose."

79. Williams, "Baptism in the Holy Spirit," 359. As Presiding Bishop of the Church of God, Timothy Hill says in *Living in the Spirit and Power of Pentecost*, the baptism in the Holy Spirit was not given for our *enjoyment* but for our *employment*, 14.

80. Williams, "Baptism in the Holy Spirit," 360.

equips for service by amplifying a believer's power in the Spirit for witness to Jesus Christ in word and in deed.[81]

In other words, in Pentecostal theology baptism in the Holy Spirit is largely, although not exclusively, missional or vocational in nature. It is an endowment of power by the Holy Spirit for accomplishing the mission of the church in fulfilling its calling in Christ. Accordingly, it is both ecclesial/communal and personal/individual in nature. This dual nature is consistent with the Acts 2 day of Pentecost setting in which each believer gathered with the community of faith was filled with the Holy Spirit. As a communal event, Pentecost/Spirit baptism is, nevertheless, a personal experience. As a personal experience, Pentecost/Spirit baptism is no less a communal event. Accordingly, Pentecost/Spirit baptism is not automatic. In other words, even though one receives Spirit baptism *as* a member of the church, one does not automatically receive Spirit baptism *by* being a member of the church. The Spirit-filled experience is not like taking a flight on autopilot. It involves awareness and intentionality. Receiving Spirit baptism occurs as a specific, definable moment.

How then does one receive Spirit baptism? How does receiving Spirit baptism relate to personal salvation? In a sense, these two questions represent two sides of one subject: the reception of the Holy Spirit. Williams points out that for Pentecostals the "basic requirement" for receiving the baptism of the Holy Spirit is faith (Acts 11:17; Eph 1:13; Gal 3:2). One accepts and personally appropriates the promise of the Spirit. However, "certain conditions" may become preparatory requisites, especially prayer, obedience, and yielding.[82] Receiving the Holy Spirit is often associated with prayer (Acts 1:14; 8:15; Luke 3:21–22; 11:13; 24:49). The importance of obedience is also made apparent (Acts 5:32; John 14:15–17). Yielding or surrender is implied in the baptismal terminology as well (Matt 28:18; Acts 1:5). Pentecostal belief in water baptism by immersion supplies the imagery for a Spirit baptismal candidate allowing him/herself to be plunged under the water of the Spirit without resisting. Baptism in the Holy Spirit by Jesus clearly suggests the same attitude of yieldedness as one who is immersed in water.

However, language such as "basic requirement" and, especially, "certain conditions," can be problematic. Do these terms imply that a believer somehow "helps accomplish" his/her baptism in the Spirit? If so, then does not that add an element of endeavor, that is, of human works? An affirmative answer to either question would unacceptably undermine the

---

81. Williams, "Baptism in the Holy Spirit," 360. Or as Keener, *Spirit in the Gospels and Acts*, contends, Pentecost marks the church "as a prophetic people, a people empowered to witness by God's Spirit," 200.

82. Williams, "Baptism in the Holy Spirit," 361–62.

gracious character of salvation. Williams advises that "[the] conditions just mentioned are best understood not as requirements but as expressions of faith."[83] Admittedly, some Pentecostals have, at times, gone too far in stressing conditions. Yet, the Pentecostal tradition as a whole fully affirms the gracious character of salvation and of Spirit baptism itself. Pentecostals are concerned with "active faith."[84] Praying, obeying, and yielding are active expressions of faith that appropriate God's gracious promise of the Holy Spirit. Rather than meeting meritorious conditions, they are more about setting a context for an unmerited experience. Accordingly, *baptism in the Holy Spirit is a gracious provision of redemption appropriated by faith*. Fleshing out that statement a bit is at the heart of my "constructive proposal" on Spirit baptism and salvation.

AS ASCENSION PROVISION

Pentecostal theology should endeavor to present Spirit baptism in its overall soteriological context with consideration of its distinctiveness. Christians realize that *salvation* is a broad term. For example, faith and repentance, justification and reconciliation, adoption and regeneration, assurance, sanctification, and so on are recognizably salvation-oriented in nature. Furthermore, this approach can be navigated without getting into a maze of detours about the *ordo salutis* (order of salvation) or, as preferred by many, the *via salutis* (way of salvation).[85] Really, the earlier chapters of this volume have already paved the way for this one. I will argue next for something of a constructive proposal placing Spirit baptism in Christian salvation along similar lines—although with some exciting differences.

Readers will be excused if they sometimes feel they are reading a theological version of an infomercial where the writer keeps shouting, "But wait, there's more!" This book previously asserted that after the collage of redemption experiences typically studied under the rubric of "conversion,"

---

83. Williams, "Baptism in the Holy Spirit," 362. When Pentecostals such as Niko Njotorahardjo, an Indonesian pastor and church leader, speak of being "willing to pay the price to receive the will of God," *Messenger of the Third Pentecost*, 249, they emphasize the sacrificial nature of ministry.

84. Williams, "Baptism in the Holy Spirit," 363.

85. Vondey, "Soteriology at the Altar," 7–8. Williams, "Patristic Theologies of Salvation," describes salvation in the early church as "more of a line than a point," 18–20. Although salvation has a definitive beginning in conversion, it is a lifelong process or journey—of knowing and loving God, of experiencing God's grace, of spiritual formation and growth, of discipleship and obedience, and so on—culminating in eternal fellowship and joy with God.

deliverance, healing, and spiritual warfare should be included in a Pentecostal doctrine of salvation as well. Now it extends the tally to include Spirit baptism, too.[86] To an extent, this "addition," if you will, is descriptive of how Pentecostals have long approached deliverance, healing, spiritual warfare, and yes, baptism in the Holy Spirit. However, here is an intentional effort to faithfully develop these trajectories further. Because the tradition addresses it more specifically in terms of atonement provision (see chapter 7), the Pentecostal doctrine of divine healing may well serve as a precedent and paradigm for relating Spirit baptism as redemption provision. This application is consistent with Vondey's observation that among Pentecostals worldwide "*all* elements of the full gospel are works of grace and thus possible entrance points to conversation and the way of salvation."[87]

However, divine healing and Spirit baptism draw on different, but of course, not disconnected, themes/streams of atonement/redemption provision. Bodily healing focuses on the *stripes/sufferings* of Christ, but Pentecost focuses on Christ's *ascension/exaltation* (Matt 8:17; Acts 2:33). The *suffering Savior* takes our sicknesses upon himself. The *victorious Savior* pours his Spirit upon us. Peter's Acts 2:33 interpretation of Pentecost places it squarely in the context of Christ's ascension and exaltation.[88] Pentecost serves as proof that Christ has defeated death and is now exalted by God's power to a place of honor at God's right hand.[89] Note that the Lukan explication of the ascension is Jesus' prophetic warning to the Sanhedrin that a pending change would result in his sharing God's rule and power (Luke 22:69), thus looking beyond his own death to his resurrection and, specifically, his ascension.[90] Pentecost vividly demonstrates the fulfillment of Jesus' prophecy.

Indeed, Luke not only gives the only actual description of Christ's ascension, he gives it twice—climaxing his Gospel (24:50–53) and introducing his Acts (1:9–11)—thus indicating the emphatic significance of the

---

86. After deciding to compare a soteriology of divine healing and a soteriology of Spirit baptism, I was delighted to discover that chapter 12, Kärkkäinen, *Spirit and Salvation*, although differently, effectively employs a similar approach.

87. Vondey, "Soteriology at the Altar," 7 (italics are original).

88. Keener, *Spirit in the Gospels and Acts*, notes that probably "the point in this case is less spatial than emphatic with regard to Christ's exaltation and reign," 192. In other words, Peter is not simply telling his audience where Jesus has gone so much as what the ascension means: enthronement.

89. Arrington, "Acts," 546.

90. Arrington, "Luke," 522. In a sense, "Jesus' enthronement takes place not at the *parousia* but immediately after his resurrection and ascension," Stein, *Luke*, 570–71. Pentecost is the first official act of the enthroned Messiah. As such, Pentecost occurs as a display of Christ's power in an impartation of the Holy Spirit's power. Thus, the NT church (then and now) is characterized by power.

ascension for Luke's theology.[91] The "link between the two volumes is Jesus' resurrection-ascension and the outpouring of the Holy Spirit."[92] The ascension gives theological *context*—and theological *content*—to both Christ's resurrection and Pentecost. Christ's entrance into glory and enthronement at God's side is the victorious culmination of his earthly ministry and the authoritative initiation of the Holy Spirit's earthly ministry in the church. Thus, it is a tragic mistake for theologians to "leapfrog" over Christ's death and resurrection to Pentecost. If we skip the ascension, we will have a minimized and, therefore, insufficient Pentecost.

Arrington puts the significance of Christ's ascension for Pentecost succinctly: "All that is seen and heard at Pentecost flows from the ascended Christ."[93] Not surprisingly, a pattern emerges. For instance, Paul, via Psalm 68:18, interprets the ministry gifts of the church in terms of Christ's ascension (Eph 4:8–11). Chrysostom insists that the outpouring of the Holy Spirit at Pentecost goes beyond demonstrating that Christ has defeated death; rather in his ascension, Christ is exalted to the extent that he is authorized by the Father to fulfill his grand promise of the Spirit, which in turn demonstrates the full scope of Christ's exaltation to power (fulfilling the prophecy of Psalm 110:1).[94]

According to the brilliant English theologian Bede (sixth/seventh century), the ascension provision for the outpouring of the Holy Spirit at Pentecost demonstrates that the one who received the Spirit as a human being could now pour out the Holy Spirit as God.[95] In this sense, Pentecost expresses continuity with Christ's incarnation while asserting its climax in Christ's exaltation. Therefore, those who are baptized in the Holy Spirit in human frailty become bearers of power in the Holy Spirit's divinity. Pentecostal emphasis on power is not carnal fascination with the supernatural. Rather, the power of Pentecost testifies to God's power at work in human

---

91. Keener, *Spirit in the Gospels and Acts*, refers to this twofold telling as a "recapitulation" serving to connect the two volumes around the theme of Jesus' "primary instructions" regarding the missional empowerment of the Spirit, 191.

92. Arrington, "Luke," 531.

93. Arrington, "Acts," 547.

94. Chrysostom, *Saint Chrysostom*, 11:40–41.

95. Oden and Martin, eds., *Acts*, 33–34. Marshall, *New Testament Theology*, describes "a natural development in Christology from the Gospels to Acts, once it is believed that God raised Jesus from the dead and exalted him," 192. Marshall recognizes that Christ is "the dispenser of the Spirit" as "the risen and exalted Lord," 357, and that it is "in connection with his ascent" that Christ bestowed the gifts of grace/gifts of the Spirit, 394. However, the significant point that Bede makes goes further: the Pentecost outpouring of the Holy Spirit by the ascended and exalted Christ is not merely a natural *development* from the incarnation but its climactic *fulfillment*.

beings for the glory of God in Christ.[96] Is it too bold to ask: "Would not a church bereft of Pentecost power fail to testify to this glorious truth of God's gracious operation?"

Conversely, Augustine interprets the distinctive gift of the Holy Spirit as primarily dependent on Christ's being "glorified" in his resurrection (via John 7:37–39). He admits, almost as an afterthought, that the actual outpouring of the Holy Spirit at Pentecost awaited Christ's ascension.[97] There is more to this matter than chronology. Carson's commentary on the same text describes Christ being "glorified" so that the Holy Spirit may be given "once he had died, risen and ascended to his Father."[98] In other words, the death, resurrection, and ascension of Christ is a unitary whole in Christ's experience of being glorified. We cannot eliminate the importance of the ascension in relation to the giving of the Holy Spirit at Pentecost without serious distortion of what Pentecost means. Thus, our understanding of Spirit baptism, set solidly in the context of Pentecost, would be drastically distorted also.

Here, I echo Studebaker's refrain that a Pentecostal vision of redemption must consciously incorporate the realities of Christ's death, resurrection, *and* ascension contra tendencies among many evangelicals to be almost exclusively crucicentric.[99] However, Studebaker interprets Christ's ascension primarily in terms of reconstituted or restored fellowship with the Triune God.[100] While restoration of divine fellowship, and its implications, are important for ascension theology (John 17:5), the theme of Christ's powerful victory, and its implications, are prominent in the Acts 2 account of Pentecost.[101] Therefore, a consistent Pentecostal theology of Christ's

96. Bird, *Evangelical Theology*, asserts, "The church, through its experience of the Holy Spirit, discovers its identity and receives power from on high because through the Spirit the church receives Christ," 419. I argue that the point of the ascension outpouring is not that through the Spirit the church receives Christ, though that is of course true, but that through Christ the church receives the Spirit. Therefore, the church's identity, power from on high, and the ascended Lord's gift of the Holy Spirit are woven from one fabric. The church of the ascended Lord is a church full of the power of the Holy Spirit.

97. Augustine, *Homilies on the Gospel of John, Homilies on the First Epistle of John, Soliloquies*, 7:195.

98. Carson, *Gospel According to John*, 328–29.

99. Studebaker, "Pentecostal Soteriology and Pneumatology," 266, 267, 268, 269.

100. Studebaker, "Pentecostal Soteriology and Pneumatology," 267, 269.

101. Acts 2:33 is conspicuous by its absence from Studebaker's article. Aulén, *Faith of the Christian Church*, 246, insists that any preaching of the passion of Christ that does not sound "the note of triumph" exemplified in Christ's exaltation "has lost its Christian character." Aulén goes so far as to say that *theologia crucis* (theology of the cross) is at the same time *theologia gloriae* (theology of glory), 245.

ascension highlights the nature of Pentecost, as both a demonstration of Christ's power and as an impartation of Christ's power through baptism in the Holy Spirit. This ascension theology neither subordinates the Holy Spirit to Christ nor subsumes the Spirit's work under Christ's work.[102] Rather, the Holy Spirit carries on the work of the Triune God in the power of Pentecost as Christ did in his incarnation, death, resurrection, *and* ascension. The crucified and risen Lord's ascension connects with the Holy Spirit through Pentecost. The soteriological missions of Jesus Christ and of the Holy Spirit do not *compete* with each other; they *complete* one another.[103]

In view of the preceding, Spirit baptism is best understood as the ascension provision of empowerment for the church and for the believer. This means that Spirit baptism is soteriological provision and empowerment, and it is praxis-oriented. As Vondey accurately observes, "From the viewpoint of Pentecostal theology, salvation in all its dimensions is in the fullest sense theological praxis."[104] Furthermore, Vondey asserts that "Pentecostal soteriology is always praxis."[105] Accordingly, I insist that the nature of Spirit baptism as an enduement of power for service is entirely consistent with the nature of Pentecostal soteriology's core concern for action, for practice, and for exercise. A Pentecostal doctrine of salvation is not directed only at theory but at the active practice of salvation with its missional implications and obligations. Spirit baptism is the ascension provision that meets that soteriological concern for ecclesial mission.

The Holy Spirit's agency is involved in Christ's atoning death (Heb 9:14) and in his bodily resurrection (Rom 1:4). The exalted Christ's ascension fulfillment of the promise of Pentecost provides the baptism in the Holy Spirit as empowerment for a life of service and victory in witness of Jesus Christ as Lord (Acts 2:33). There is perfect harmony and unity between Christ and the

---

102. To be clear, Studebaker's concern is not without merit. E.g., Bird, *Evangelical Theology*, rightly notes that "the Spirit is christologically endowed to the church," 685. However, his observation that some go so far as to describe the Spirit as "Christomorphed," 685, indicates that they go too far—and thus, Studebaker's concerns.

103. Thompson, "Eschatology as Soteriology," concludes, "[the] Christocentric flavor must be maintained, but with recognition of its patrocentric and pneumatocentric accents, and thus fully Trinitarian," 200. This is Thompson's way of addressing the "short shrift the Spirit has received in most eschatology in the West," 200. Cp. Aulén, *Faith of the Christian Church*, 249–54.

104. Vondey, "Soteriology at the Altar," 10 (cp. 11). Vondey's concern for praxis arises from his desire to establish a basis for a theological investigation of the Pentecostal altar call, 2–3. My objective here is to suggest that this "soteriology as praxis" manner of understanding Pentecostal theology also opens up a discussion about a theology of Spirit baptism that is both soteriological and missional/vocational.

105. Vondey, "Soteriology at the Altar," 12.

Holy Spirit. There is perfect unity and harmony between conversion experience and a distinct, subsequent experience of Spirit baptism. Assuredly and concretely, Spirit baptism occupies its appropriately distinctive place in the Pentecostal doctrine of salvation. Accordingly, I close this chapter, and thus this book, with Keener's exegetical/theological summation.

> For Luke, whatever the ways in which the Spirit's empowerment is manifested, the purpose of Spirit baptism is witness ([Acts] 1:8). The signs of [Acts] 2:1–12 are signs of the kingdom. The message of Peter stresses that God's people have been anointed as witnesses like the prophets, and the enthronement of Jesus as king at God's right hand has ushered in the time of salvation. While God's unchallenged rule over the world will be complete only at Jesus' return, Jesus' present rule in his Church by the Spirit is the dynamic manifestation of the Kingdom of God in this age, and this is divine empowerment for mission.[106]

---

106. Keener, *Spirit in the Gospels and Acts*, 201.

Bibliography

Aker, Benny C. "John." In *Full Life Bible Commentary to the New Testament: An International Commentary for Spirit-Filled Christians*, edited by French L. Arrington and Roger Stronstad, 1–118. Grand Rapids: Zondervan, 1999.
Alden, Robert L. *New American Commentary: Job.* Vol. 11. Nashville: Broadman & Holman, 1993.
Alexander, Donald L., ed. *Christian Spirituality: Five Views of Sanctification.* Downers Grove, IL: InterVarsity, 1988.
Alexander, Estrelda Y. *Black Fire: One Hundred Years of African American Pentecostalism.* Downers Grove, IL: IVP Academic, 2011.
Alexander, Kimberly Erwin. "The Pentecostal Healing Community." In *Towards a Pentecostal Ecclesiology: The Church and the Fivefold Gospel*, edited by John Christopher Thomas, 183–206. Cleveland, TN: CPT, 2010.
———. *Pentecostal Healing: Models in Theology.* Journal of Pentecostal Theology Supplement Series. Dorset, UK: Deo, 2006.
Althouse, Peter. *The Spirit of the Last Days: Pentecostal Eschatology in Conversation with Jürgen Moltmann.* New York: T. & T. Clark, 2003.
Althouse, Peter, and Robby Waddell, eds. *Perspectives in Pentecostal Eschatologies: World without End.* Eugene, OR: Pickwick, 2010.
Arminius, James. *Works of James Arminius.* Vols. I–III. Grand Rapids: Baker, 1991 reprint.
Arrington, French L. "Acts." In *Full Life Bible Commentary to the New Testament: An International Commentary for Spirit-Filled Christians*, edited by French L. Arrington and Roger Stronstad, 535–692. Grand Rapids: Zondervan, 1999.
———. *Christian Doctrine: A Pentecostal Perspective: Volume One, Two, Three.* Cleveland, TN: Pathway, 1993.
———. "Ecclesiology and the Great Commission." In *The Great Commission Connection*, edited by Raymond Culpepper, 105–26. Cleveland, TN: Pathway, 2011.
———. "Luke." In *Full Life Bible Commentary to the New Testament: An International Commentary for Spirit-Filled Christians*, edited by French L. Arrington and Roger Stronstad, 375–534. Grand Rapids: Zondervan, 1999.

———. *Maintaining the Foundations: A Study of 1 Timothy*. Cleveland, TN: Pathway, 1998.

———. "Once Saved, Always Saved?" *Church of God Evangel*, 104:4 (April 2014) 24–25.

———. *The Spirit-Anointed Jesus: A Study of the Gospel of Luke*. Cleveland, TN: Pathway, 2008.

Arrington, French L., and Roger Stronstad, eds. *Full Life Bible Commentary to the New Testament: An International Commentary for Spirit-Filled Christians*. Grand Rapids: Zondervan, 1999.

———. *Homilies on the Gospel of John, Homilies on the First Epistle of John, Soliloquies*. Edited by Philip Schaff et al. New York: Christian Literature Company, 1888.

Augustin. *Saint Augustin's Expositions on the Book of Psalms*. Edited by Philip Schaff. New York: Christian Literature Company, 1888.

Aulén, Gustaf. *Christus Victor: An Historical Study of the Three Main Types of the Idea of the Atonement*. Eugene, OR: Wipf and Stock, 2003, reprint.

———. *The Faith of the Christian Church*. Philadelphia: Muhlenberg, 1948.

Barry, John D., et al., eds. *The Lexham Bible Dictionary*. Bellingham, WA: Lexham, Logos Systems Research, 2016.

Barth, Karl. *Evangelical Theology: An Introduction*. Grand Rapids: Eerdmans, 1963.

Behr, John. "Irenaeus of Lyons." In *Theologies of Salvation: A Comparative Introduction*, edited by Justin S. Holcomb, 41–58. New York: NYU Press, 2017.

Bercot, David W. "Angels." In *A Dictionary of Early Christian Beliefs*, edited by David W. Bercot, 14–20. Peabody, MA: Hendrickson, 1998.

———. "Satan." In *A Dictionary of Early Christian Beliefs*, edited by David W. Bercot, 592–95. Peabody, MA: Hendrickson, 1998.

Bercot, David W., ed. *A Dictionary of Early Christian Beliefs*. Peabody, MA: Hendrickson, 1998.

Berg, Robert. "1–3 John." In *Full Life Bible Commentary to the New Testament: An International Commentary for Spirit-Filled Christians*, edited by French L. Arrington and Roger Stronstad, 1479–1525. Grand Rapids: Zondervan, 1999.

Bergen, R. D. *1, 2 Samuel*. Nashville: Broadman and Holman, 1996.

Bernard, David. *The New Birth, Pentecostal Theology*. Vol 2. Hazelwood, MO: Word Aflame, 1984.

Bernard, David K. *Justification and the Holy Spirit: A Scholarly Investigation of a Classical Christian Doctrine from a Pentecostal Perspective*. Hazelwood, MO: Word Aflame, 2007.

Bird, Michael F. *Evangelical Theology: A Biblical and Systematic Introduction*. 2nd ed. Grand Rapids: Zondervan Academic, 2013.

Black, Jonathan. *Apostolic Theology: A Trinitarian Evangelical Pentecostal Introduction to Christian Doctrine*. Foreword by Warren Jones. Luton, UK: The Apostolic Church, 2016.

Blair, Elizabeth. "In U2's 'I Still Haven't Found What I'm Looking For,' A Restless Search for Meaning." https://www.npr.org/2019/07/26/743620996/u2-i-still-havent-found-what-im-looking-for-american-anthem.

Bloesch, Donald G. *Essentials of Evangelical Theology: Volume 1: God, Authority, and Salvation*. Peabody, MA: Prince, 2001.

———. *The Last Things: Resurrection, Judgment, Glory*. Downers Grove, IL: InterVarsity, 2004.

Blomberg, Craig. *New American Commentary: Matthew.* Vol. 22. Nashville: Broadman & Holman, 1992.
Blumhofer, Edith L. *Her Heart Can See: The Life and Hymns of Fanny J. Crosby.* Grand Rapids: Eerdmans, 2005.
Boa, Ken. *Augustine to Freud: What Theologians and Psychologists Tell Us About Human Nature (And Why It Matters).* Nashville: Broadman & Holman, 2004.
Bradnick, David. *Evil, Spirits, and Possession: An Emergentist Theology of the Demonic: Global Pentecostal and Charismatic Studies.* London: Brill, 2017.
Bradshaw, Paul. "The Most Disturbing Movie Visions of Hell." November 22, 2018. https://www.denofgeek.com/movies/the-most-disturbing-movie-visions-of-hell/
Brand, Chad Owen, ed. *Perspectives on Spirit Baptism: Five Views.* Nashville: Broadman, 2004.
Breneman, Mervin. *New American Commentary: Ezra, Nehemiah, Esther.* Nashville: Broadman & Holman, 1993.
Brian, Rusty. "Arminianism, Calvinism, and Their Influence on John Wesley." *Holiness Today,* September/October 2017. https://www.holinesstoday.org/arminianism-calvinism-and-their-influence-upon-john-wesley.
Brown, Candy Gunther, ed. *Global Pentecostal and Charismatic Healing.* Oxford: Oxford University Press, 2011.
Brown, Robert McAfee. *The Spirit of Protestantism.* New York: Oxford University Press, 1961.
Broyles, Craig C. *New International Biblical Commentary: Psalms.* Peabody, MA: Hendrickson, 1999.
Büchsel, Friedrich. *Dorea.* In *Theological Dictionary of the New Testament,* edited by Gerhard Kittel, G. W. Bromiley, and G. Friedrich, 2:167. Grand Rapids: Eerdmans, 1964.
Bultmann, Rudolf Karl. *Jesus Christ and Mythology.* New York: Scribner, 1958.
Burgess, Stanley M., and Eduard M. Van Der Maas, eds. *New International Dictionary of Pentecostal and Charismatic Movements.* Grand Rapids: Zondervan, 2002.
Burke, Trevor J., and Keith Warrington, eds. *A Biblical Theology of the Holy Spirit.* Eugene, OR: Cascade, 2014.
Burpo, Todd, and Lynn Vincent. *Heaven Is for Real: A Little Boy's Astounding Story of His Trip to Heaven and Back.* Nashville: Thomas Nelson, 2010.
Cairns, Alan, ed. *Dictionary of Theological Terms.* Belfast: Ambassador Emerald International, 2002.
———. "Worship." In *Dictionary of Theological Terms,* edited by Alan Cairns, 265. Belfast: Ambassador Emerald International, 2002.
Camery-Hoggatt, Jerry. "Mark." In *Full Life Bible Commentary to the New Testament: An International Commentary for Spirit-Filled Christians,* edited by French L. Arrington and Roger Stronstad, 255–374. Grand Rapids: Zondervan, 1999.
Carpenter, Chris. "Zach Williams: the 'Rescue Story' that Changed His Life." https://www.l.cbn.com/music/zach-williams-rescue-story-changed-his-life.
Carson, D. A. *Pillar New Testament Commentary: The Gospel According to John.* Leicester, England/Grand Rapids: Inter-Varsity/Eerdmans, 1991.
Chrysostom, John. *Saint Chrysostom: Homilies on the Acts of the Apostles and the Epistle to the Romans.* Edited by Philip Schaff et al. New York: Christian Literature Company, 1889.
Church Hymnal. Cleveland, TN: Tennessee Music and Printing Company, 1979.

Clancy, Tom. *Clear and Present Danger*. New York: Putnam, 1989.
Clark, John. "Which Book Did C. S. Lewis Least Enjoy Writing?" *National Catholic Register*, May 1, 2017. https://www.ncregister.com/blog/which-book-did-c-s-lewis-least-enjoy-writing.
Clark, Kelly James, Richard Lints, and James K. A. Smith. *101 Key Terms in Philosophy and Their Importance for Theology*. Louisville, KY: Westminster John Knox, 2004.
Clifton, Shane. "The Dark Side of Prayer for Healing: Toward a Theology of Well-Being." *Pneuma* 36:2 (2014) 204–25.
Constantineanu, Corneliu, and Christopher J. Scobie, eds. *Pentecostals in the 21st Century: Identity, Beliefs, Praxis*. Eugene, OR: Cascade, 2018.
Conn, Charles W. "The Crisis of the Cross: The Turning Point for Lost People." *Church of God Evangel* 104:4 (April 2014) 10–12.
———. *Like a Mighty Army: A History of the Church of God*. Cleveland, TN: Church of God Publishing House, 1955.
———. "They Waited, But . . ." *Church of God Evangel* 110:8 (reprinted November/December 2020) 27.
Cooper, Lamar Eugene. *New American Commentary: Ezekiel*. Vol. 17. Nashville: Broadman & Holman, 1994.
Copan, Paul. "Following a Unique Christ in a Pluralist Society." *Enrichment Journal*, Fall 2008. http://enrichmentjournal.ag.org/200804/_040_Pluralistic.cfm.
Crisp, Oliver D. *Jonathan Edwards among the Theologians*. Grand Rapids: Eerdmans, 2015.
Cross, Terry L. *Answering the Call in the Spirit: Pentecostal Reflections on a Theology of Vocation, Work and Life*. Cleveland, TN: Lee University Press, 2007.
Culpepper, Raymond, ed. *The Great Commission Connection*. Cleveland, TN: Pathway, 2011.
Dayton, Donald W. "The Rise of the Evangelical Healing Movement in America." Paper read at the Society for Pentecostal Studies meeting in Tulsa, OK, 1980.
Dieter, Melvin E. "The Wesleyan Perspective." In *Christian Spirituality: Five Views of Sanctification*, edited by Donald L. Alexander, 11–46. Downers Grove, IL: InterVarsity, 1988.
Drewery, Benjamin. *Origen and the Doctrine of Grace*. Eugene, OR: Wipf and Stock, 2009.
Duffield, Guy P., and Nathan M. Van Cleave. *Foundations of Pentecostal Theology*. Los Angeles: L.I.F.E. Bible College, 1987.
Dupré, Louis, and Don E. Saliers with John Meyendorff, eds. *Christian Spirituality: Post-Reformation and Modern: Volume 18, World Spirituality: An Encyclopedic History of the Religious Quest*. New York: Crossroad, 1989.
Dyrness, William A., and Veli-Matti Kärkkäinen, eds. *Global Dictionary of Theology*. Downers Grove, IL: IVP Academic, 2008.
Ellingworth, Paul. *The Epistle to the Hebrews: A Commentary on the Greek Text*. Grand Rapids/Carlisle, UK: Eerdmans/Paternoster, 1993.
Elwell, Walter A., ed. *Evangelical Commentary on the Bible*. Grand Rapids: Baker, 1995.
Enns, Peter. "Yahweh, Creation, and the Cosmic Battle." February 2, 2010. https://biologos.org/articles/yahweh-creation-and-the-cosmic-battle/.
Faupel, D. William. *The Everlasting Gospel: The Significance of Eschatology in the Development of Pentecostal Thought*. JPTSup 10. Sheffield: Sheffield Academic, 1996.

Fields, Bruce L. *Introducing Black Theology*. Eugene, OR: Wipf and Stock, 2019.
Fitzgerald, F. Scott. "Babylon Revisited." In *A Treasury of Short Stories*, edited by Bernadine Kielty, 640–53. New York: Simon and Schuster, 1947.
Fogerty, John. *Fortunate Son: My Life, My Music*. New York: Little, Brown and Company, 2015.
Garland, David E. *New American Commentary: 2 Corinthians*. Vol. 29. Nashville: Broadman & Holman, 1999.
Gasper, Giles E. M. "Anselm of Canterbury." In *Theologies of Salvation: A Comparative Introduction*, edited by Justin S. Holcomb, 124–42. New York: NYU Press, 2017.
Gause, R. Hollis. *Living in the Spirit: The Way of Salvation*. Cleveland, TN: Pathway, 1980.
———. *Revelation: God's Stamp of Sovereignty on History*. Cleveland, TN: Pathway, 1998.
Gerleman, Gillis. "Realm of the Dead." In *Theological Lexicon of the Old Testament*, edited by Ernst Jenni and Claus Westermann, 1279–82. Peabody, MA: Hendrickson, 1997.
Gerig, Wesley L. "Reward." In *Evangelical Dictionary of Biblical Theology*, edited by Walter A. Elwell, 685–87. Grand Rapids: Baker, 1996.
Gilbert, Pierre J. "Spiritual Warfare." In *Global Dictionary of Theology*, edited by William A. Dyrness and Veli-Matti Kärkkäinen, 847–51. Downers Grove, IL: IVP Academic, 2008.
Gjelton, Tom. "Faith Leaders Nearly Unanimous in Condemning Assault on the Capitol." NPR, January 7, 2021. https://www.npr.org/2021/01/07/954581163/faith-leaders-nearly-unanimous-in-condemning-assault-on-capitol.
Greggs, Tom. "Karl Barth." In *Theologies of Salvation: A Comparative Introduction*, edited by Justin S. Holcomb, 300–317. New York: NYU Press, 2017.
Hahn, Heather. "Did Jesus descend into hell or to the dead?" April 22, 2011. http://www.pas.rochester.edu/~tim/study/Did%20Jesus%20descend%20into%20hell%20or%20to%20the%20dead%20%20-%20UMC.org.pdf.
Hardesty, Nancy A. *Faith Cure: Divine Healing in the Holiness and Pentecostal Movements*. Peabody, MA: Hendrickson, 2003.
Harris, Murray J. *The Second Epistle to the Corinthians: A Commentary on the Greek Text*. Grand Rapids/Milton Keynes, UK: Eerdmans/Paternoster, 2005.
Hart, Larry D. "A Dimensional Charismatic Perspective," In *Perspectives on Spirit Baptism: Five Views*, edited by Chad Owen Brand, 105–80. Nashville: Broadman, 2004.
———.*Truth Aflame: Theology for the Church in Renewal*. Grand Rapids: Zondervan, 2005.
Harvey, Van A. *A Handbook of Theological Terms*. New York: Collier MacMillan, 1964.
Hemingway, Ernest. "The Snows of Kilimanjaro." In *The Complete Short Stories of Ernest Hemingway: The Finca Vigia Edition*, 39–56. Foreword by John Patrick and George Hemingway. New York: Scribner, 1987.
Hill, Timothy M. *Living in the Spirit and Power of Pentecost: Experiencing Life Empowered by the Holy Spirit*. Cleveland, TN: Pathway 2018.
Hillyer, Norman. *New International Biblical Commentary: 1 and 2 Peter, Jude*. Peabody, MA: Hendrickson, 1992.

Hoekema, Anthony A. "Response to Dieter." In *Christian Spirituality: Five Views of Sanctification,* edited by Donald L. Alexander, 47–49. Downers Grove, IL: InterVarsity, 1988.

Hogg, David. "Theologies of Salvation in the Middle Ages: An Introduction." In *Theologies of Salvation: A Comparative Introduction,* edited by Justin S. Holcomb, 115–23. New York: NYU Press, 2017.

Holcomb, Justin S., ed. *Theologies of Salvation: A Comparative Introduction.* New York: NYU Press, 2017.

Horton, Stanley M. "The Last Things." In *Systematic Theology,* edited by Stanley M. Horton, 597–638. Rev. ed. Springfield, MO: Logion, 1995.

———. "Response to Dieter." In *Christian Spirituality: Five Views of Sanctification,* edited by Donald L. Alexander, 50–52. Downers Grove, IL: InterVarsity, 1988.

Horton, Stanley M., ed. *Systematic Theology.* Rev. ed. Springfield, MO: Logion, 1995.

Huey, F. B. *Jeremiah, Lamentations.* Nashville: Broadman & Holman, 1993.

Hunter, Harold D. *Spirit Baptism: A Pentecostal Alternative.* Eugene, OR: Wipf & Stock, 2009.

Isaacson, Walter. *Benjamin Franklin: An American Life.* New York: Simon & Schuster, 2004.

Jackson, Griffin Paul. "Half of Americans Say Evangelicals Are Discriminated Against." *Christianity Today,* April 25, 2019. https://www.christianitytoday.com/news/2019/april/evangelicals-face-discrimination-pew-research-antisemitism.html.

James, Frank A., III. "Theologies of Salvation in the Reformation and Counter-Reformation: An Introduction." In *Theologies of Salvation: A Comparative Introduction,* edited by Justin S. Holcomb, 181–90. New York: NYU Press, 2017.

Jamieson, Robert, A. R. Fausset, and David Brown. *Commentary Critical and Explanatory on the Whole Bible.* Vol. 1. Oak Harbor, WA: Logos Research Systems, 1997.

Jeremias, Joachim. *Paradeisos* (transliteration). In *Theological Dictionary of the New Testament,* edited by Gerhard Kittel, G. W. Bromiley, and G. Friedrich, 5:769. Grand Rapids: Eerdmans, 1964.

Johnson, Van. "Romans." In *Full Life Bible Commentary to the New Testament: An International Commentary for Spirit-Filled Christians,* edited by French L. Arrington and Roger Stronstad, 693–797. Grand Rapids: Zondervan, 1999.

Kärkkäinen, Veli-Matti. *One with God: Salvation as Deification and Justification.* Collegeville, MI: Liturgical, 2004.

———. *Pneumatology: The Holy Spirit in Ecumenical, International, and Contextual Perspective.* Grand Rapids: Baker, 2002.

———. *Spirit and Salvation: A Constructive Christian Theology for the Pluralistic World.* Grand Rapids: Eerdmans, 2016.

Keener, Craig S. *The Spirit in the Gospels and Acts: Divine Purity and Power.* Peabody, MA: Hendrickson, 1997.

Keil, C. F., and F. Delitzsch. *Commentary on the Old Testament.* Peabody, MA: Hendrickson, 1996.

Kelly, J. N. D. *Early Christian Doctrines.* Rev. ed. New York: HarperCollins, 1978.

Kendall, R. T. *More of God.* Lake Mary, FL: Charisma House, 2019.

Kennedy, Earl W. "Heaven and Hell." In *Dictionary of Christianity in America,* edited by Daniel G. Reid et al., 368–72. Downers Grove, IL: InterVarsity, 1990.

Kerrigan, William. *Johnny Appleseed and the American Orchard: A Cultural History.* Baltimore: Johns Hopkins University Press, 2012.
Knight, Henry H., III. "God's Faithfulness and God's Freedom: A Comparison of Contemporary Theologies of Healing." *Journal of Pentecostal Theology* 1:2 (1993) 65-89.
Kraft, C. H. "Spiritual Warfare." In *New International Dictionary of Pentecostal Movements,* edited by Stanley M. Burgess and Eduard M. Van Der Maas, 1091-96. Grand Rapids: Zondervan, 2002.
Kydd, Ronald A. N. "Healing in the Christian Church." In *New International Dictionary of Pentecostal and Charismatic Movements,* edited by Stanley M. Burgess and Eduard M. Van Der Maas, 698-711. Grand Rapids: Zondervan, 2002.
———. *Healing through the Centuries: Models for Understanding.* Peabody, MA: Hendrickson, 1998.
Ladd, George Eldon. *A Theology of the New Testament.* Grand Rapids: Eerdmans, 1974.
Land, Steven Jack. *Pentecostal Spirituality: A Passion for the Kingdom.* Cleveland, TN: CPT, 2010.
———. "Pentecostal Spirituality." In *Christian Spirituality: Post-Reformation and Modern: Volume 18, World Spirituality: An Encyclopedic History of the Religious Quest,* edited by Louis Dupré and Don E. Salier with John Meyendorff, 479-99. New York: Crossroad, 1989.
Lange, Johann Peter, et al. *A Commentary on the Holy Scriptures: Psalms.* Bellingham, WA: Logos Bible Software, 2008.
Lenski, R. C. H. *The Interpretation of the Acts of the Apostles.* Minneapolis: Augsburg, 1961.
Lewis, C. S. *The Collected Works of C. S. Lewis: The Pilgrim's Regress, Christian Reflections, and God in the Dock.* New York: Inspirational, 1996.
———. *The Great Divorce.* New York: HarperOne, 1945.
———. *Mere Christianity.* New York: Macmillan, 1952.
———. *The Screwtape Letters.* New York: MacMillan, 1976.
Leulseged, Philemon. *Pneumatic Hermeneutics: The Role of the Holy Spirit in the Theological Interpretation of Scripture.* Cleveland, TN: CPT, 2019.
Lovett, Leonard. "Positive Confession Theology." In *New International Dictionary of Pentecostal and Charismatic Movements,* edited by Stanley M. Burgess and Eduard M. Van Der Maas, 992-94. Grand Rapids: Zondervan, 2002.
Lukaszewski, Albert L., ed. *The Lexham Syntactic Greek New Testament: SBL Edition.* Bellingham, WA: Logos Systems Research, 2011.
Ma, Julie C., and Wonsuk Ma. *Mission in the Spirit: Towards a Pentecostal/Charismatic Missiology.* Regnum Studies in Mission. Eugene, OR: Wipf & Stock, 2010.
Macchia, Frank D. "Justification and the Spirit: A Pentecostal Reflection on the Doctrine by which the Church Stands or Falls." *Pneuma* 22 (2000) 3-21.
———. *Justified in the Spirit: Creation, Redemption, and the Triune God.* Grand Rapids: Eerdmans, 2010.
Mangum, Douglas, et al. *Lexham Theological Wordbook.* Bellingham, WA: Lexham, Logos Systems Research, 2014.
Marsden, George M. "Challenging the Presumptions of the Age: The Two Dissertations." In *Legacy of Jonathan Edwards,* edited by D. G. Hurst et al., 99-113. Grand Rapids: Baker Academic, 2003.

Marshall, I. Howard. *New Testament Theology: Many Witnesses, One Gospel*. Downers Grove, IL: InterVarsity, 2004.
Martin, Francis. "Healing, Gift of." In *New International Dictionary of Pentecostal and Charismatic Movements*, edited by Stanley M. Burgess and Eduard M. Van Der Maas, 694–98. Grand Rapids: Zondervan, 2002.
Martin, Lee Roy. *A Praying People: A Pentecostal Study of the Vital Prayer Life*. Discipling Pentecostals. Cleveland, TN: Church of God Adult Discipleship, 2020.
———. *Spirit-Filled Worship*. Miami, FL: Senda de Vida, 2017.
———. *Unheard Voice of God: A Pentecostal Hearing of the Book of Judges*. Dorset, UK: Deo, 2008.
Martin, William C. "Atonement." In *The Layman's Bible Encyclopedia*, 69–72. Nashville: Southwestern, 1964.
———. *The Layman's Bible Encyclopedia*. Nashville: Southwestern, 1964.
Mathews, Joshua G. "Blessing." In *Lexham Theological Wordbook*, edited by Douglas Mangum et al. Bellingham, WA: Lexham, Logos Systems Research, 2014.
Mathews, Kenneth A. *Genesis 11:27–50:26*. Vol. 1B. Nashville: Broadman & Holman, 2005.
McCall, Thomas H. "John Wesley." In *Theologies of Salvation: A Comparative Introduction*, edited by Justin S. Holcomb, 261–80. New York: NYU Press, 2017.
McDonnell, Kilian, and George T. Montague. *Christian Initiation and Baptism in the Holy Spirit: Evidence from the First Eight Centuries*. Collegeville, MN: Liturgical, 1991.
McGrath, Alister E. *Born to Wonder: Exploring Our Deepest Questions—Why We Are Here and Why Does It Matter?* Carol Stream, IL: Tyndale Momentum, 2020.
———. *Christian Theology: An Introduction*. 4th ed. Malden, MA: Blackwell, 2007.
McGuckin, John A. "The Book of Revelation and Orthodox Eschatology: The Theodrama of Judgment." In *The Last Things: Biblical and Theological Perspectives on Eschatology*, edited by Carl E. Braaten and Robert W. Jenson, 113–34. Grand Rapids: Eerdmans, 2002.
McQuilkin, J. Robertson. "The Keswick." In *Christian Spirituality: Five Views of Sanctification*, edited by Donald L. Alexander, 151–83. Downers Grove, IL: InterVarsity, 1988.
———. "Response to Dieter." In *Christian Spirituality: Five Views of Sanctification*, edited by Donald L. Alexander, 53–55. Downers Grove, IL: InterVarsity, 1988.
Melanchthon, Philip. *Melanchthon on Christian Doctrine: Loci communes 1555*. Translated and edited by Clyde L. Manschreck. Introduction by Hans Engelland. Grand Rapids: Baker, 1982.
Melick, Richard R. *New American Commentary: Philippians, Colossians, Philemon*. Vol. 32. Nashville: Broadman & Holman, 1991.
Menzies, William W., and Stanley M. Horton. *Bible Doctrines: A Pentecostal Perspective*. Springfield, MO: Gospel, 1994.
Merriam-Webster's Collegiate Dictionary. 11th ed. Springfield, MA: Merriam-Webster, 2003.
Millard, Bart, with Robert Nolland. *I Can Only Imagine: A Memoir*. Nashville: Thomas Nelson, 2018.
Moltmann, Jürgen. *The Coming of God: Christian Eschatology*. Minneapolis: Fortress, 2004.
Morris, Leon. *The Epistle to the Romans*. Grand Rapids: Eerdmans, 1988.

Mounce, Robert H. *Matthew. New International Biblical Commentary.* Peabody, MA: Hendrickson, 1991.
———. *New American Commentary: Romans.* Vol. 27. Nashville: Broadman & Holman, 1995.
Murray, Andrew. *The Inner Life.* Springdale, PA: Whittaker House, 1984, reprint.
Muzorewa, Gwinyai H. *The Origins and Development of African Theology.* Ossining, NY: Orbis, 1985.
Njotorahardjo, Niko. *Messenger of the Third Pentecost.* Translated by Andrew Chandra. Jakarta, Indonesia: WFC Production, 2019.
Novak, David. "Law and Eschatology: A Jewish-Christian Intersection." In *The Last Things: Biblical and Theological Perspectives on Eschatology,* edited by Carl E. Braaten and Robert W. Jenson, 90–112. Grand Rapids: Eerdmans, 2002.
O'Brien, Peter T. *The Letter to the Ephesians.* Grand Rapids: Eerdmans, 1999.
Oden, Thomas C. *John Wesley's Scriptural Christianity: A Plain Exposition of His Teaching on Christian Doctrine.* Grand Rapids: Zondervan, 1994.
———. *Life in the Spirit: Systematic Theology: Volume Three.* Peabody, MA: Hendrickson, 2001.
Oden, Thomas C., and Gerald Bray, eds. *Ancient Christian Commentary on Scripture: New Testament XI: James, 1–2 Peter, 1–3 John, Jude.* Downers Grove, IL: InterVarsity, 2000.
Oden, Thomas C., and Gerald Bray, eds. *Ancient Christian Commentary on Scripture: New Testament VI: Romans.* Downers Grove, IL: InterVarsity, 2005.
Oden, Thomas C., and Mark J. Edwards, eds. *Ancient Christian Commentary on Scripture: New Testament VIII: Galatians, Ephesians, Philippians.* Downers Grove, IL: InterVarsity, 1999.
Oden, Thomas C., and Andrew Louth, eds. *Ancient Christian Commentary on Scripture: Old Testament I: Genesis 1–11.* Downers Grove, IL: InterVarsity, 2001.
Oden, Thomas C., and Francis Martin, eds. *Ancient Christian Commentary on Scripture: New Testament V: Acts.* Downers Grove, IL: InterVarsity, 2006.
Oden, Thomas C., and Manlio Simonetti, eds. *Ancient Christian Commentary on Scripture: New Testament Ia: Matthew 1–13.* Downers Grove, IL: InterVarsity, 2002.
Olson, Roger E. "The Dialectic of 'Nature and Grace' in Christian Theology." April 13, 2015. https://www.patheos.com/blogs/rogereolson/2015/04/the-dialectic-of-nature-and-grace-in-christian-theology/.
Online Etymology Dictionary. "Recompense." https://www.etymonline.com/word/recompense.
Onyinah, Opoku. "Pentecostal Healing Communities." In *Towards a Pentecostal Ecclesiology: The Church and the Fivefold Gospel,* edited by John Christopher Thomas, 207–24. Cleveland, TN: CPT, 2010.
Oswalt, John N. *The Book of Isaiah: Chapters 1–39: The New International Commentary on the Old Testament.* Grand Rapids: Eerdmans, 1986.
Pannenberg, Wolfhart. "The Task of Christian Eschatology." In *The Last Things: Biblical and Theological Perspectives on Eschatology,* edited by Carl E. Braaten and Robert W. Jenson, 1–13. Grand Rapids: Eerdmans, 2002.
Parker, Christian. "Popular Religion." In *Global Dictionary of Theology,* edited by William A. Dryness and Veli-Matti Kärkkäinen, 679–83. Downers Grove, IL: IVP Academic 2008.

Patzia, Arthur G. *New International Biblical Commentary: Ephesians, Colossians, Philemon*. Peabody, MA: Hendrickson, 1990.

Peach, Michael E. "Heaven." In *Lexham Theological Wordbook*, edited by Douglas Mangum et al. Bellingham, WA: Lexham, Logos Systems Research, 2014.

Pecota, Daniel B. "Saving Work of Christ." In *Systematic Theology: Revised Edition*, edited by Stanley M. Horton, 325–74. Springfield, MO: Logion, 1995.

Plavcan, Sarah. "Mortal Reason and Divine Infinity: Justifying the Ways of God to Men in Book VI of *Paradise Lost*." *Inquiry: University of Arkansas Undergraduate Research Journal* 19:7 (Fall 2015). https://scholarworks.uark.edu/cgi/viewcontent.cgi?referer=https://www.google.com/&httpsredir=1&article=1014&context=inquiry#:~:text=In%20the%20opening%20of%20Paradise,and%20omniscient%20(Fallon%2033).

Polhill, John B. *Acts: The New American Commentary*. Vol. 26. Nashville: Broadman & Holman, 1992.

Pope, Robert P. "Why the Church Needs a Full Gospel." In *Towards a Pentecostal Ecclesiology: The Church and the Fivefold Gospel*, edited by John Christopher Thomas, 272–84. Cleveland, TN: CPT, 2010.

Pseudo-Macarius. *Pseudo-Macarius: Fifty Spiritual Homilies*. Edited by George Maloney. Mahwah, NJ: Paulist, 1992.

Purdy, Vernon L. "Divine Healing." In *Systematic Theology: Revised Edition*, edited by Stanley M. Horton, 489–523. Springfield, MO: Logion, 1995.

Reed, David A. *"In Jesus' Name": The History and Beliefs of Oneness Pentecostals*. JSup 31. Dorset, UK: Deo, 2008.

Reeves, Ryan M. "Theologies of Salvation from the Eighteenth to the Twenty-First Centuries." In *Theologies of Salvation: A Comparative Introduction*, edited by Justin S. Holcomb, 252–60. New York: NYU Press, 2017.

Reid, Daniel G. "Heaven." In *Global Dictionary of Theology*, edited by William A. Dyrness and Veli-Matti Kärkkäinen, 368–72. Downers Grove, IL: IVP Academic, 2008.

Reid, Daniel G., et al., eds. *Dictionary of Christianity in America*. Downers Grove, IL: InterVarsity, 1990.

Richie, Tony. *Essentials of Pentecostal Theology: An Eternal and Unchanging Lord Powerfully Present and Active by the Holy Spirit*. Eugene, OR: Resource, 2020.

———. "'The Grand Design of God in All Divine Operations': Pentecostal Retrieval of Jonathan Edwards' Distinctive Contribution to the Positive Significance of Non-Christian Religions." In *Pentecostal Theology and Jonathan Edwards: T & T Clark Systematic Pentecostal and Charismatic Theology*, edited by Steven M. Studebaker and Amos Yong, 210–26. Edinburgh: T. & T. Clark, 2021.

———. "Is Pentecostalism Just Another American Success Story? A Response to Jürgen Moltmann on the Place of Optimism in the Pentecostal Tradition." *Refleks* 5:2 (2006) 77–93.

———. "Pragmatism, Power, and Politics: A Pentecostal Conversation with President Obama's Favorite Theologian, Reinhold Niebuhr." *Pneuma* 32:2 (Summer 2010) 241–60.

———. *Toward a Pentecostal Theology of Religions: Encountering Cornelius Today*. Cleveland, TN: CPT, 2013.

———. "Transposition and Tongues: Pentecostalizing an Important Insight of C. S. Lewis." *Journal of Pentecostal Theology* 13:1 (October 2004) 117–37.

———. "The Value of Creeds." *PTS Thrive*, June 25, 2020. https://youtu.be/aZIpdfvC_QE.

Riggs, Ralph M. *The Spirit Himself*. Springfield, MO: Gospel, 1977.

Roberts, Philemon. *Divine Healing*. Orlando, FL: Daniels, 1982.

Rodrigues, Adriani Milli. "Atonement." In *Lexham Theological Wordbook*, edited by Douglas Mangum et al. Bellingham, WA: Lexham, Logos Systems Research, 2014.

Rybarczyk, Edmund J. "Pentecostal Perspective on Salvation." In *Pentecostals in the 21st Century: Identity, Beliefs, Praxis*, edited by Corneliu Constantineanu and Christopher J. Scobie, 76–93. Eugene, OR: Cascade, 2018.

Sailhamer, John H. *The Pentateuch as Narrative: A Biblical-Theological Commentary*. Grand Rapids: Zondervan, 1992.

Samuel, Josh P. S. *The Holy Spirit in Worship Music, Preaching, and the Altar: Renewing Pentecostal Corporate Worship*. Cleveland, TN: CPT, 2018.

Schleiermacher, Friedrich. *The Christian Faith*. New York: T. & T. Clark, 2004, reprint.

Schreiner, Thomas. "The Miraculous Gifts and the Question of Cessationism." The Gospel Coalition, 2021. https://www.thegospelcoalition.org/essay/miraculous-gifts-question-cessationism/.

———. *New American Commentary: 1, 2 Peter, Jude*. Vol. 37 Nashville: Broadman & Holman, 2003.

Scheck, Thomas P. "Origen of Alexandria." In *Christian Theologies of Salvation: A Comparative Introduction*, edited by Justin S. Holcomb, 22–40. New York: NYU Press, 2017.

Shelton, James. "Matthew." In *Full Life Bible Commentary to the New Testament: An International Commentary for Spirit-Filled Christians*, edited by French Arrington and Roger Stronstad, 119–253. Grand Rapids: Zondervan, 1999.

Simmons, William A. "Regeneration." In *Lexham Theological Wordbook*, edited by Douglas Mangum et al. Bellingham, WA: Lexham, Logos Systems Research, 2014.

Sims, John A. *Our Pentecostal Heritage: Reclaiming the Priority of the Holy Spirit*. Cleveland, TN: Pathway, 1995.

Smith, James K. A. "Teaching a Calvinist to Dance." *Christianity Today*, May 16, 2008. https://calvin.edu/news/archive/q-a-with-jamie-smith-on-pentecostalism.

———. *Thinking in Tongues: Pentecostal Contributions to Christian Philosophy*. Grand Rapids: Eerdmans, 2010.

Snyder, Howard A. "Wesleyanism, Wesleyan Theology." In *Global Dictionary of Theology*, edited by William A. Dyrness and Veli-Matti Kärkkäinen, 929–36. Downers Grove, IL: IVP Academic, 2008.

Snyder, Howard A., and Joel Scandrett. *Salvation Means Creation Healed: The Ecology of Sin and Grace: Overcoming the Divorce Between Earth and Heaven*. Eugene, OR: Cascade, 2011.

Southern, R. W. *Western Society and the Church in the Middle Ages: The Pelican History of the Church: 2*. Middlesex, UK: Penguin, 1972.

Spittler, Russell P. "Spirituality, Pentecostal and Charismatic." In *New International Dictionary of Pentecostal and Charismatic Movements*, edited by Stanley M. Burgess and Eduard M. Van Der Maas, 1096–1102. Grand Rapids: Zondervan, 2002.

Spurgeon, C. H. *All of Grace*. New Kensington, PA: Whittaker House, 1983.

Stamps, J. Wesley. "Ephesians." In *Full Life Bible Commentary to the New Testament: An International Commentary for Spirit-Filled Christians*, edited by French L. Arrington and Roger Stronstad, 1019–86. Grand Rapids: Zondervan, 1999.

Stein, R. H. *New American Commentary: Luke.* Vol. 24. Nashville: Broadman & Holman, 1992.
Stephenson, Christopher A. *Types of Pentecostal Theology: Method, System, Spirit.* New York: Oxford University Press, 2013.
Sterling, Larry, Jr. "Our Only Hope in a Pluralistic World." *Church of God Evangel* 97:12 (December 2007) 8–9.
Stronstad, Roger. "1 and 2 Peter." In *Full Life Bible Commentary to the New Testament: An International Commentary for Spirit-Filled Christians,* edited by French L. Arrington and Roger Stronstad, 1431–78. Grand Rapids: Zondervan, 1999.
———. *The Charismatic Theology of St. Luke.* Foreword by Clark Pinnock. Peabody, MA: Hendrickson, 1984.
Studebaker, Steven M. "Pentecostal Soteriology and Pneumatology." *Journal of Pentecostal Theology* 11:2 (2003) 248–70.
———. *The Spirit of Atonement: Pentecostal Contributions and Challenges to Christian Traditions.* Systematic and Pentecostal Theology. London: T. & T. Clark, 2021.
Studebaker, Steven M., and Amos Yong, eds. *Pentecostal Theology and Jonathan Edwards: T & T Clark Systematic Pentecostal and Charismatic Theology.* Edinburgh, Scotland: T. & T. Clark, 2021.
Sullivan, Francis. "Baptism in the Spirit." In *Charisms and Charismatic Renewal,* 59–75. Eugene, OR: Wipf & Stock, 1982.
Tertullian. *Apology.* In *Ante-Nicene Fathers,* vol. 3, edited by Alexander Roberts and James Donaldson, 17–60. Peabody, MA: Hendrickson, 1999, reprint.
Thomas, John Christopher. *The Apocalypse: A Literary and Theological Commentary.* Cleveland, TN: CPT, 2012.
———. *The Devil, Disease and Deliverance: Origins of Illness in New Testament Thought.* Cleveland, TN: CPT, 2010.
———. *The Pentecostal Commentary on 1 John, 2 John, 3 John.* The Pentecostal Commentary: New Testament. Cleveland, TN: Pilgrim, 2004.
Thomas, John Christopher, ed. *Towards a Pentecostal Ecclesiology: The Church and the Fivefold Gospel.* Cleveland, TN: CPT, 2010.
Thompson, Matthew. "Eschatology as Soteriology." In *Perspectives in Pentecostal Eschatologies: World without End,* edited by Peter Althouse and Robby Waddell, 189–204. Eugene, OR: Pickwick, 2010.
Thorsen, Don. *An Exploration of Christian Theology.* Peabody, MA: Hendrickson, 2008.
Tillich, Paul. *Systematic Theology: Volume Two.* Chicago: University of Chicago Press, 1957.
Tomberlin, Daniel. "Believers' Baptism in the Pentecostal Tradition." *The Ecumenical Review: A Dialogue on Believers' Baptism* (October 2015) 423–35.
———. *Pentecostal Sacraments: Encountering God at the Altar.* Cleveland, TN: Center for Pentecostal Leadership and Care, Pentecostal Theological Seminary, 2010.
Tozer, A. W. *The Knowledge of the Holy.* New York: Harper & Row, 1961.
Trueman, Carl R. "Martin Luther." In *Theologies of Salvation: A Comparative Introduction,* edited by Justin S. Holcomb, 191–207. New York: NYU Press, 2017.
Turner, Max. "The Spirit as the Spirit of Prophecy in Ephesians." In *A Biblical Theology of the Holy Spirit,* edited by Keith Warrington and Trevor J. Burke, 187–97. Eugene, OR: Cascade, 2014.
In *Christian Spirituality: Five Views of Sanctification,* edited by Donald L. Alexander, 53–55. Downers Grove, IL: InterVarsity, 1988.

Van Buskirk, George P. "John Wesley's Practical Eschatology." Boston University School of Theology, Doctoral Conference, March 24, 2012.

Van der Laan, Paul N. "Catching a Butterfly—The Identity of Pentecostal Theology." Presented at the Annual Meeting of the European Pentecostal Theological Association, Scenic, Slovakia, June 24–27, 2008.

Vest, Lamar. *Reflections on the Journey: Memoirs of Lamar Vest*. Cleveland, TN: Pathway, 2018.

Vincent, Marvin R. *Word Studies in the New Testament*. Vol. 2. New York: Charles Scribner's Sons, 1887.

Vondey, Wolfgang. "Soteriology at the Altar: Pentecostal Contributions to Salvation as Praxis." *Transformation* 34:3 (November 16, 2016) 1–16.

Walvoord, John F. "Response to Dieter." In *Christian Spirituality: Five Views of Sanctification*, edited by Donald L. Alexander, 56–57. Downers Grove, IL: InterVarsity, 1988.

Warrington, Keith. *Pentecostal Theology: A Theology of Encounter*. New York: T. & T. Clark, 2008.

Warrington, Keith. "The Synoptic Gospels." In *A Biblical Theology of the Holy Spirit*, by Keith Warrington and Trevor J. Burke, 84–103. Eugene, OR: Cascade, 2014.

Warrington, Keith, and Trevor J. Burke, eds. *A Biblical Theology of the Holy Spirit*. Eugene, OR: Cascade, 2014.

Wesley, John. "Upon Our Lord's Sermon on the Mount: Discourse 4" (Matthew 5:13–16), 1872 edition. http://www.wordsofwesley.com/libtext.cfm?srm=24&hl=26080.

———. *Wesley's Works*, Vol. I–XIV. Peabody, MA: Hendrickson, 1991, reprint.

White, R. E. O. "Psalms." In *Evangelical Commentary on the Bible*, edited by Walter A. Elwell, 367–98. Grand Rapids: Baker, 1995.

Williams, D. H. "Patristic Theologies of Salvation: An Introduction." In *Theologies of Salvation: A Comparative Introduction*, edited by Justin S. Holcomb, 11–21. New York: NYU Press, 2017.

Williams, J. Rodman. "Baptism in the Holy Spirit." In *New International Dictionary of Pentecostal and Charismatic Movements*, edited by Stanley M. Burgess and Eduard M. Van Der Maas, 354–63. Grand Rapids: Zondervan, 2002.

Wolcott, Carrie Sinclair. "Writings, The." In *The Lexham Bible Dictionary*, edited by John D. Barry et al. Bellingham, WA: Lexham, Logos Systems Research, 2016.

Wright, Christopher J. H. *Salvation Belongs to Our God: Celebrating the Bible's Central Story*. Christian Doctrine in Global Perspective. Downers Grove, IL: InterVarsity, 2007.

Wright, N. T. *Justification: God's Plan & Paul's Vision*. Downers Grove, IL: IVP Academic, 2009.

Yong, Amos. *The Hermeneutical Spirit: Theological Interpretation and Scriptural Imagination for the 21st Century*. Eugene, OR: Cascade, 2017.

———. *The Spirit Poured Out on All Flesh: Pentecostalism and the Possibility of Global Theology*. Grand Rapids: Baker Academic, 2005.

———. *Spirit, Word, Community: Theological Hermeneutics in Trinitarian Perspective*. Eugene, OR: Cascade, 2002.

Name and Subject Index

Alexander, Estrelda Y., 62, 191
Alexander, Kimberly Erwin, 158–59, 160, 191
Althouse, Peter, 68, 133, 191, 202
American Holiness Movement, 12, 19, 20, 44, 158–59, 169, 172–73, 174
Angelology, 84, 111
Anselm of Canterbury, 74, 89, 90, 195
Anthropocentrism, 32
Anthropology, 9, 22, 155–56, 160
Arminianism, 14, 16, 18–20, 38, 44, 73
Arminius, James, 18, 27, 191
Arrington, French L., 1, 17, 41, 42, 43, 44, 45, 62, 70, 121, 143, 175, 177, 178, 186, 191
Augustine of Hippo, 14, 18, 45, 49, 79, 154, 166, 187, 192
Aulén, Gustaf, 32, 70, 73, 82, 106, 113, 120, 187, 192
Authority, moral, 75, 93; scriptural, ix, 8, 15, 19, 44, 70, 105, 108, 120, 151; spiritual, 29, 64, 85, 88, 90, 102, 122, 132, 190
Azusa Revival, 16, 19, 36, 178

Barth, Karl, 10, 85, 87, 107, 129, 192
Bede, The Venerable, 155, 186
Bernard, David, 175, 192
Bird, Michael F., 144, 145, 187, 188, 192
Black, Jonathan, 14, 17, 192

Bloesch, Donald G., 32, 43, 45, 57, 58, 99, 102, 105, 107, 108, 109, 112, 153, 156, 192
Boa, Ken, 141, 193
Brand, Chad Owen, 165, 193
Brown, Candy Gunther, 147, 193
Brown, Robert McAfee, 2, 35, 126, 133, 134, 193
Bultmann, Rudolf, 108, 193

Calvin, John, 16–17, 18, 45, 120, 121
Calvinist/Reformed Theology, 14–17, 18, 19, 20, 35, 73, 173–74, 202
Cessationism v. Continuationism, 16, 41, 167, 201
Charisms/Charismata (Spiritual Gifts), 16, 29, 41, 51, 55, 120, 127, 152–53, 164, 165–68, 202
Christocentricism, 180, 188
Christology, 3, 9, 41, 181, 186
Chrysostom, John, 124, 154, 186, 193
Conn, Charles W., 15, 145, 184
Constantineanu, Corneliu and Christopher J. Scobie, 55, 194, 201
Cosmocentrism, 32
Cosmology, 32, 85, 88, 127, 160
Crisp, Oliver, 137, 194
Crucicentrism, 180, 187
Cruciform, 15
Cyprian, 125, 148

NAME AND SUBJECT INDEX

Dayton, Donald W., 158, 194
Demonology, 106–07
Dieter, Melvin E., 172–74, 194
Doxological, 37, 65–66, 88
Duffield, Guy P. and Nathan M. Van
    Cleave, 42, 138, 194

Ecclesiology, 42, 88, 90, 159–60, 167,
    171, 202
Edwards, Jonathan, 15, 45, 91, 101,
    137, 202
Empowerment (Pneumatic), x, 80, 104,
    106, 119, 123, 128, 144, 160,
    163, 169–72, 175, 182–83, 186,
    188–89
Enlightenment, 70, 99, 108
Eschatology, 22, 32, 33, 43, 56, 129–30,
    134, 135–36, 142–46, 149, 160,
    173, 188, 191, 194, 198
Ethics, 33, 144, 181
Evangelicalism, 15–16, 18–20

Faupel, D. William, 43, 173, 194
Fletcher, John, 173,
Fundamentalism, 17, 68, 135

Gause, R. Hollis, 116, 143, 195
Gnosticism, 131, 155–56, 158

Hamartiology, 9, 21, 99
Hardesty, Nancy A., 151, 195
Hart, Larry D., 70, 169–70, 195
Hoekema, Anthony A., 174, 196
Hermeneutics, 8–9, 44, 92, 138, 166–
    67, 172, 197, 203
Holcomb, Justin S., 3, 192
Homiletics, 24, 40, 47, 81, 91, 121, 127,
    149, 150, 162, 176, 178, 187,
Horton, Stanley M., 129, 174, 196
Hunter, Harold D., 164–65, 196

Inspiration of Scripture, 8, 11, 19, 26,
    44, 70, 85, 108, 126, 143
Irenaeus of Lyons, 73, 148, 156, 192

Kärkkäinen, Veli-Matti, 52, 165, 170–
    72, 180, 185, 196

Keener, Craig S., 183, 185, 186, 189,
    196
Kelly, J. N. D., 73, 130, 196
Kendall, R. T., 35, 57, 196
Knight, Henry H. III, 157–58, 197
Kydd, Ronald A. N., 148–51, 158, 197

Ladd, George Eldon, 85, 197
Land, Steven, 5, 41, 131–32, 173, 197
Lewis, C. S., 83, 102, 107, 113–14, 197
Liberalism, 74, 76, 85, 105, 138–39
Liturgy, 35, 51, 65, 111, 166
Lovett, Leonard, 151, 152, 197
Luther, Martin, 14–15, 120, 121, 202

Ma, Julie and Wonsuk Ma, 42, 197
Macchia, Frank D., 52, 197
Marshall, I. Howard, 186, 198
Martin, Lee Roy, 96, 198
McDonnell, Kilian and George T.
    Montague, 166–68, 198
McGrath, Alister E., 3, 44, 61, 62–63,
    70, 92, 136, 176, 198
McQuilkin, J. Robertson, 174, 198
Means of Grace, 50–51, 52
Melanchthon, Philip, 100, 198
Missiology, 42, 43, 143, 159, 197
Moltmann, Jürgen, 33, 57, 62, 85, 129,
    136, 198
Monergism, 19

Oden, Thomas C., 137, 199
Olson, Roger E., 50, 199
Oneness Pentecostals, 13, 175, 200
Origen of Alexandria, 45, 85, 87, 105,
    109, 130, 148, 194

Pannenberg, Wolfhart, 135, 144, 199
Patristics, 70, 73, 121, 130, 137, 184,
    203
Pecota, Daniel, 62, 70, 200
Pentecostals, Classical, 10, 12, 18, 113,
    163, 165, 170, 180, 182
Philosophy, 3, 43, 108, 109, 131, 151–
    52, 155–56,
Pneumatology, 41, 52, 142–45, 171,
    180–82, 196, 202

Prayer, Theology and Praxis, x, xi, 10, 35, 51, 54, 60, 80, 81, 88, 110, 112, 113–14, 115, 125–27, 147, 149, 150–51, 153, 157, 158, 160, 161, 183, 194, 198
Pseudo-Macarius, 83, 200
Purdy, Vernon L., 155, 200

Reed, David A., 13, 200
Religious/Spiritual Experience, 8, 20, 23, 35, 68–69, 127–28, 167, 175, 183,
Richie, Tony, 4, 7, 41, 78, 82, 101, 143, 200–201
Rybarczyk, Edmund J., 102, 201

Sacraments, 51, 52, 55, 148, 152–53, 165–71, 175–76, 178–80, 202
Samuel, Josh P. S., 36, 178, 201
Schleiermacher, Friedrich, 138–39, 201
Seymour, William J., 16, 19
Signs and Wonders, 70, 159, 189
Smith, James K. A., 17, 108, 201
Snyder, Howard A., 55–56, 201
Spirituality, Pentecostal, ix, 11, 19, 41, 51, 76, 106, 173, 197
Spurgeon, Charles H., 28, 40, 201
Stephenson, Christopher A., 41, 202
Stronstad, Roger, 6, 155, 202
Studebaker, Steven M., 180–81, 182, 187, 202
Sullivan, Francis, 166, 202
Synergism, 19, 50, 158

Testimony, 2, 13, 35, 45, 47, 51, 76, 80, 90, 92, 94, 114, 115, 152, 161,
Tertullian, 82, 125, 148, 166, 202
Theocentrism, 32, 151
Theodicy, 22, 106, 154
Theology, Pentecostal, ix, x, 3–4, 6, 9, 12, 13–20, 25, 41–45, 50–52, 55, 61, 68, 92, 95–96, 105, 106, 123, 126, 128, 130, 132, 133, 136, 138, 144, 146, 147, 152–53, 155–57, 161, 162, 163, 164, 170, 180–84, 187, 188, 194, 200, 202, 203
Thomas, John Christopher, 84, 115, 117, 118, 119, 202
Thompson, Matthew, 33, 188, 202
Thorsen, Don, 70, 80, 88, 107, 164, 202
Tillich, Paul, 109, 202
Tomberlin, Daniel, 152, 159, 168, 175–76, 178, 202
Tozer, A. W., 59–60, 202
Trinitarian Pentecostals, 13, 41, 173, 188, 192, 203
Trinity, 13, 21, 42, 70, 74, 90, 164, 187–88, 197

Van der Laan, Paul N., 203
Vondey, Wolfgang, 3–4, 185, 188, 203

Walvoord, John, 174, 203
Warrington, Keith, 41, 106, 203
Wesleyan/Holiness Movement, 18, 19–20, 34, 120–21, 158–59, 172–175
Wesley, John, 15, 18, 21, 25, 27, 31, 36, 44, 45, 68, 100, 109, 121, 172–73, 174, 203
Williams, J. Rodman, 163, 164–65, 182, 183–84, 203
Worship, Theology and Praxis, ix, 41, 51, 54, 62–63, 65–66, 81, 84, 87, 90, , 92–93, 102, 107, 111, 127, 131, 150, 152, 198, 201
Wright, Christopher J. H., 56, 132, 181, 203
Wright, N. T., 3, 19, 26–27, 52, 142, 203

Yong, Amos, 159, 203

Scripture Index

THE OLD TESTAMENT

Genesis
1:2	32
1:4, 10, 12, 18, 21, 25, 31	131
1:26	32
1:26–27	99
2:15–17	24
2:16	139
3:1–7	23
3:13	106
3:15	70
6:2, 4	84
11:1–9	131
15:6	26
18:1–15	110
28:10–22	111
43:14	94

Exodus
2:23	68
3:14	58
4:22	30
5:1	65
6:6	64
7:16	65
8:1, 20	65
9:1, 13	65
10:3	65
14:13	5
15	64
15:3	98
15:11, 14–15	66
15:1–21	71
18:10	64
22:18	111
33:12–17	48
34:9	48

Leviticus
2:24	66
19:31	111
20:6, 27	111

Numbers
11:29	170

Deuteronomy
5:15	68
14:1	30
18:1–11	111
32:6	30

Joshua

5:13–15	110
23:6	36

Judges

6:12	83
10:11	64

Ruth

Book of Ruth	92

1 Samuel

17:38–40	19
22:6	139
28:3–25	111

1 Kings

18:21	124
18:28	127
19:12	127
20:28–30	84
22:19	84
22:20–23	84

2 Kings

2:11	110
6:17	110

2 Chronicles

20:19	127

Esther

4:3, 16	92
9:31	92

Job

1:6	84
2:1	84
1:6–2:10	118
9:10	138
38:7	84
42:2	110

Psalms

6:6	139
8:4	99, 100
16:10–11	23, 140
18:2, 50	64
18:24	162
24:1	132
24:4	110
29:2	66
32:2	26
32:7	64
34:19	79
34:21	79
40:17	64
47:1	127
49:15	56
51:4	102
68:18	120, 186
70:5	64
89:5–7	84
96:9	66
98:1	95
101:3	36
103:1–5	153–54
106:20	58
110:1	102, 186
139:6	89
139:8	139
144:2	64
146:3–6	101
147:5	101
150:2	53

Proverbs

14:14	37

Ecclesiastes

3:20	140
11:3	139
12:7	140

Isaiah

13:11	132
14:9	139
14:12	107
19:16–25	96

19:20	96, 97
26:3	36
26:19	140
32:17	35
42:13	98
43:16–21	64
45:23	102
49:28	95
51:4	102
51:9–11	64
52:11	134
53:5	154–55
57:17	37
59:2	109
59:16	95
61:6–7	175
65:3	95
65:17	33
66:1	84
66:22	33

Jeremiah

2:11	58
2:19	37
3:6–25	37
6:16	76
14:7	37
14:13	36
17:9	99
17:9–10	96
17:14	5
20:11	96
23:18, 22	84
31:3	25
31:9	30
31:22	37
34:13	63
49:4	37

Ezekiel

11:19	33
18:31	33
36:26	33
37:1–4	175

Daniel

1–6	92–94
1:8	118
3:1–30	82
3:18	94
6:1–28	82
10:12–14	126
12:2	56

Hosea

1:10	30
4:7	58
11:1	30
11:7	36–37
14:4	36–37

Joel

2:28	58
2:32	64
2:28–32	175

Jonah

4	98

Habakkuk

2:4	28

Haggai

2:9	58

Zechariah

12:10	53

THE NEW TESTAMENT

Matthew

1:21	64
1:34	88
2:5	156
3:13–17	103
4:1–11	105, 115, 125
4:8–11	107

Matthew (continued)

4:24	150
5:1–11	137
5:5	66
5:8	110
5:12	136
5:22, 29, 30	87
5:45	49
5:46	137
6:1, 2, 4, 5, 6, 16, 18	137
6:33	31, 69
8:16	150
8:17	154, 155, 185
9:2, 32	150
9:20–22	149
9:22	159
10:22	117
10:28	87, 139
10:34	79
10:41–42	137
12:28	123
12:32	129
13:38	132
12:42–43	137
14:35	150
16:13–17	41
16:18	42, 82, 112
16:26	129, 134
16:27	137
17:1–8	110
17:16	150
18:8	139
18:9	87
18:21	27
18:21–38	27
19:28	31, 32
19:27–30	32
22:37–40	68
23:15, 33	87
23:23	69
24:13	38, 110
24:21	143
24:44	145
25:34	66
25:41, 46	139, 143
28:18	183
28:19	43
28:19–20	132, 178–79

Mark

1:9–11	103
1:14–15	24
3:29	139
7:21	99
7:37	95
8:27–33	23
8:36	129, 134
9:43	139
10:28–30	32
10:29–31	66
10:30	83
10:45	42, 70
16:15	132

Luke

1:26–33	110
1:31–35	182
1:37	95
3:16	177
3:21–22	182, 183
3:21–23	103
3:22	182
4:1	182
4:1–2	123
4:16–19	62
5:28–29	141
6:19	150
7:24–30	127
7:37–39	172
7:36–50	27
8:13	37
8:26–39	123
9:1–3	156
9:25	129, 134
11:13	54, 183
12:28–29	23
12:40	145
12:41–48	144
12:45	145
12:48	137
15:7, 10	87, 91
15:11–32	1, 6

16:22–23	139, 140	14:15–17	183
16:22–31	139	14:30	116
17:20–21	132	15:1–17	118
18:27	95	15:13	27, 122
18:28–30	32	16:8–11	24
18:30	129	17:5	58, 187
19:10	21, 62	17:22	56
21:36	43	18:36	132
22:28–30	79	20:19–23	42
22:40	115	20:28	9
22:42	94	20:31	2, 43
22:69	185		
23:43	140	**Acts**	
24:49	58, 144, 182, 183	1:4	58
24:50–53	185	1:5	177, 183
		1:5, 8	175
John		1:6–7	132
1:12	29	1:8	144, 182, 189
1:14	58	1:9–11	185
1:26	177	1:14	183
1:26–27, 29–34	177	2	16, 183, 187
3:1–8	73, 182	2:1–4	41, 142
3:3	32	2:1–4, 33	103
3:3–8	31	2:1–12	189
3:4	32	2:4	52
3:16	21, 43, 74, 97, 138	2:4, 17–19	175
3:16–17	132	2:1–21	43
3:17	138	2:14–36	142
3:18	43, 139	2:17	58, 106
3:18–21	138	2:21	64
3:38	6	2:33	xi, 185, 187, 188
4:42	82	2:33, 39	58
6:44, 65	25	2:36	120
6:67–71	23	2:37	24
7:37–39	60, 187	2:38	54, 55
7:39	58	2:38–39	24, 54
8:34–36	63	4:12	19, 41
8:44	31	4:30	159
10:1–18	115	4:33	120
10:10	115	5:32	183
10:28	38	5:33–39	98
11:23–24	56	5:39	179
12:16, 23	58	8:1	91
12:31	107	8:14–17	103
12:32	25	8:15	183
13:31–32	58	8:20	54, 55
14:6	19, 41	8:37	23

Acts (continued)

9:31	175
10:38, 44–45	175
10:44–48	103, 178
10:45	54, 55
10:47	179
11:15–16	175
11:15–17	178
11:16	177
11:17	54, 55, 183
12:5–11	110
13:1	91
13:2, 4	175
13:43	54
14:9	150
14:17	49
14:22	79
19:1–7	103
19:11–12	149
19:13–20	123
20:32	66
23:1	146
23:6	140
24:15	140
24:16	146

Romans

1:4	120, 188
1:5	24, 54
1:16	19
1:17	26, 28
2:4	49
2:6	137
3:1–20	26
3:4	102
3:22	26
3:25	72
3:26	27
3:31	28
4	26
4:1–25	26
4:11, 13	26
5:1	55
5:1–2	26, 28
5:1–11	140
5:3–5	28
5:5	28
5:6–21	28
5:12–21	9
5:15, 16, 18	47
6–8	27, 28
6:1–2	27
6:10	102
6:15–23	63
6:23	21, 28, 137
8:1	36
8:1–17	174
8:7	124
8:12–17	35
8:14–17	29
8:16	29
8:17–18	117
8:19	132
8:22	32, 132
8:23	30
8:24	146
8:25	146
8:26–27	126
8:30	56
9–11	18
9:4	30
9:1–3	86
9:30	26
10:9–10	23
10:9	45
11:33	89, 138
11:33–36	56
12:2	130
12:9	161
15:15–16	49
16:26	23

1 Corinthians

1:2	91
1:9	42
2:9–10	56
3:8	137
3:10	54
3:12–15	137
5:7	71
5:9–10	134
6:9–10	66
6:11	52
7:31	33, 132

9:24	74	11:3	106
9:27	37	12:1–7	111
10:6	97	12:9	49
10:26, 28	132	13:5–7	37
11:26	33	13:13	42
12:1–10	55		
12:1–11	16		
12:4	140		
12:8	150		
12:8–10	152		
12:9, 28, 30	152		
12:13	169		
14:1–5, 14–19	126		
14:29	179		
15:1–8	47		
15:10	47		
15:19	43		
15:20	56		
15:28	117		
15:42–44	56		
15:46	68		
15:48–49	140		
15:49	58		
15:50	66		
15:54–57	70		
15:55–56	139		
16:22	146		

Galatians

1:4	64, 107
2:20	23
2:8	47
3:2	183
3:11	28
3:14	58
3:21–22	26
4:1–5	29
4:5–6	29
5	27
5:4	37
5:6	28
5:16–26	131
5:21	66
5:22–26	28
5:24	116
6:1	37
6:15	33

2 Corinthians

1:22	29
3:7	132
3:17	19
3:18	57
4:4	107
4:13	23
5:7	109
5:8	140
5:12–21	134
5:17	32, 33, 55, 132
5:18	139
5:21	26
6:1	54
6:14–7:1	134
7:10	25
9:8	49, 54
10:3–6	112
10:4	123

Ephesians

1:5	29
1:7–10	60
1:10	84
1:11	66
1:13	58, 66, 183
1:13–14	29
1:18	66
1:19–23	120
1:21	88, 90
1:22	88
1:22–23	42
2:1	139
2:2	107
2:3	31
2:5, 7	45
2:8, 9	45
2:8–10	45
2:15–16	124
3:3	90

Ephesians (continued)

3:7–8	47
3:9	90
3:10	84, 88, 89, 90, 91
3:11	89
3:21	88
4:1–16	120
4:7–10	120
4:8–11	186
4:9	120, 121
4:15	51
4:27	116
5:5	66
5:7	57
6:10–18	112
6:10–20	123–26
6:12	84, 85, 88
6:17	125
6:18	125
6:17–18	x
6:20	134

Philippians

1:6	129
1:21	139
1:23	139, 140
2:5–11	102
2:10–11	102
2:12–13	51
2:13	19, 47
3:12	3
3:18	83
3:20	131
3:21	56

Colossians

1:5	30
1:12	66
1:13	64, 107
1:16	88, 90
1:16, 20	85
1:18	88
1:22	88
1:27	57
2:2	35
2:10	88
2:10, 15	85
2:15	70, 88, 120
2:22	35
3:21	88
3:24	66

1 Thessalonians

1:5	35
1:10	64
4:16–17	143
4:17	130
5:23	49

2 Thessalonians

1:7–9	139
1:9	139
2:1–12	107
2:3	37

1 Timothy

1:15	13
2:4–5	97
2:6	1, 70
2:18–20	37
3:1	13
3:16	52, 102
4:1–3	37
4:9	13
4:10	98
6:11–16	23
6:12	119

2 Timothy

1:12	38
2:1–3	118
2:10	57
2:11	13
2:13	118
3:1	106
3:12	79
4:7	38, 74, 119
4:7–8	137

Titus

1:6	37

2:11–13	50	4:4	124
2:11–14	45	4:7	116
2:13	146	5:20	139
3:4–7	49		
3:5	31, 33, 172	**1 Peter**	
3:8	13	1:3	140
		1:3–5	37
Hebrews		1:4	30, 66
1:6	87	1:5	37
1:14	66	1:7	115
2:3	34	1:10, 13	48
2:3–4	156	1:12	87
2:4	55	1:15	49
2:17	72	1:18	121
2:18–22	37	1:23	33
2:24	70	2:11	59
3:17	37	2:16	37
4:12	126	2:21	75
6:2	139	2:24	24
6:3	37	4:4	59
6:4	54, 55	4:10	48, 54
6:5	156	5:5, 10, 12	54
6:11	35	5:8	118
6:12	66	5:10, 12	48
7:25	159		
7:27	102	**2 Peter**	
9:14	182, 188	1:4	52
9:28	143	2:4	87
10:22	35	2:18–22	37
10:29	53	2:19	63
10:38	28	3:3–4	145
11:1	109	3:9	98
11:13–16	30, 59, 133	3:17	37
11:19	94	3:18	50, 51, 54
11:35–38	82		
12:14	28	**1 John**	
12:14–15	50	1:6	42
12:15	37	2:2	72
12:18–22	67	2:8, 17	33
		2:15–17	69, 130, 134
James		2:29	33
1:12	115	3:2	56
1:14–15	116	3:9	33
2:14–26	137	3:14	139
2:16	69	3:18–21	36
2:20–24	28	4:1	179

1 John (continued)

4:4	122
4:4–6	134
4:7	33
4:10	72
4:14	84
4:17–18	36, 146
5:1	33
5:4–5	83
5:4, 18	33

3 John

1:2	152

Jude

1:1	38
1:7	139
1:17–22	126

Revelation

1:5	132
1:9–20	58
1:18	70
2:1–7	117
2:7	140
5:5	70
10:6	141
12:1–17	84
12:1–14:20	84
12:9	106
12:11	115
12:17	117
14:4–5	117
17:1–19:3	131
19:10	149
20:1–3	116
20:1–6	143
20:9	118
20:11–15	129
20:13	139
20:13–15	139
21 & 22	109
21:1	119
21:1–5	33, 57
21:3	58, 109
21:4	67
21:7	66
22:4	110
22:4–5	32
22:8–9	149
22:17	19, 49, 142